BECOMING A PHYSICAL EDUCATION TEACHER

Teaching physical education is a challenging but rewarding occupation. Finding a way into the profession can be a daunting task, while regular changes in government policy can make it hard to stay up to date. This engaging new book explains the process of becoming and being a teacher of secondary school physical education, from the various routes of entry into the profession to the realities of being a qualified physical education teacher, to the ways in which experienced teachers can become teacher educators and nurture the next generation. It combines rich personal accounts of teaching in, and being taught, physical education, with practical advice for trainees, newly qualified teachers and established professionals, with an emphasis throughout on the importance of critical self-reflection.

The book begins by exploring the nature and purpose of physical education and examining the historical development of initial teacher training. It examines recent changes in training, policy and curriculum and offers an overview of the various ways of becoming a physical education teacher, including the Postgraduate Certificate in Education (PGCE) and school- and employment-based routes. The book offers advice on what to expect at interview, meeting the standards for qualifying to teach and how to survive the difficult first year as a newly qualified teacher. It also outlines the challenges and rewards of being a qualified teacher, mentor or curriculum leader, as well as a teacher educator within higher education.

Concise, helpful and filled with sensible insights based on real experiences of teaching physical education, *Becoming a Physical Education Teacher* is an essential read for anybody considering entering the profession or for students, trainees, newly qualified or experienced teachers wanting to understand better the process of becoming, and being, a successful physical education teacher.

Gary Stidder is the PGCE and School Direct route leader for physical education initial teacher training and coordinator of initial teacher education for physical education at the University of Brighton's School of Sport and Service Management.

Gary is an ex-secondary school physical education teacher and was awarded a Fulbright Scholarship to the USA during 1990–91. Gary is the co-founder of the University of Brighton's pioneering 'Football 4 Peace International (F4P) Project' in Israel, Palestine, Jordan, Northern Ireland and the Gambia, which has been operating since 2001. In July 2008, Gary was presented with a national award from the Association of Physical Education for his contribution to research and scholarship in the field of physical education. In 2013, Gary was awarded the University of Brighton's Award for Staff Excellence in Community Engagement in recognition of his contribution to widening participation.

Other publications

Hayes, S. and Stidder, G. (eds) (2003) *Equity and Inclusion in Physical Education: Contemporary Issues for Teachers, Trainees and Practitioners*, London, Routledge.

Stidder, G. and Hayes, S. (eds) (2010) *The Really Useful Physical Education Book: Learning and Teaching Across the 7–14 Age Range*, London, Routledge.

Stidder, G. and Hayes, S. (eds) (2012) *Equity and Inclusion in Physical Education and Sport* (Second Edition), London, Routledge.

BECOMING A PHYSICAL EDUCATION TEACHER

Gary Stidder

Routledge
Taylor & Francis Group

LONDON AND NEW YORK

First published 2015
by Routledge
2 Park Square, Milton Park, Abingdon, Oxon OX14 4RN

and by Routledge
711 Third Avenue, New York, NY 10017

Routledge is an imprint of the Taylor & Francis Group, an informa business

© 2015 G. Stidder

British Library Cataloguing-in-Publication Data
A catalogue record for this book is available from the British Library

Library of Congress Cataloging-in-Publication Data
Stidder, Gary, 1962-
Becoming a physical education teacher / Gary Stidder.
pages cm
Includes bibliographical references and index.
ISBN 978-1-138-77827-6 (Hardback) — ISBN (invalid) 978-1-138-77828-3
(Paperback) — ISBN 978-1-315-77208-0 (ebook) 1. Physical education
teachers—Training of—United States. 2. Physical education and
training—Study and teaching (Secondary) I. Title.
GV361.S77 2015
613.7'07—dc23
2014032936

ISBN: 978-1-138-77827-6 (hbk)
ISBN: 978-1-138-77828-3 (pbk)
ISBN: 978-1-315-77208-0 (ebk)

Typeset in Bembo
by FiSH Books, London

To Oliver and Lily
for
Megan

CONTENTS

SECTION THREE
Moving on   **129**

FOREWORD

'Becoming Mr Sugden'

I do not remember having any particular ambition to become a physical education (PE) teacher. My own school PE experiences had echoes of the PE classes experienced by the young outsider and kestrel-loving Billy Casper in Ken Loach's iconic film, *Kes*. The villain of this film is the stereotypical bullying PE teacher, memorably played by Brian Glover in the role of my namesake, Mr Sugden. Ironic, given the fact that I actually did become a PE teacher, at least for a short while. This happened by chance rather than through considered vocational planning. I qualified in the mid-1970s via a one-year Postgraduate Certificate of Education (PGCE) course that I undertook at the University of Liverpool in my home town, having spent my first postgraduate year in Africa, in the Sudan, as a volunteer English language teacher. After Africa, I had returned to London, where I worked on a number of casual labouring jobs on building sites throughout the city. I remember thinking that my labouring endeavours were not a particularly appropriate use of my undergraduate education, which had yielded a degree in politics and sociology undertaken at the University of Essex. In truth, I spent more time playing and organising football than studying or attending lectures and seminars. Because of my interest in and experience of university sport, a good friend who, at the time, was a school teacher in Merseyside, told me about a one-year physical education teacher training course that was being offered at the University of Liverpool, which was recruiting people with backgrounds like mine. It is hard to believe this today, with competition to get on PGCE courses so intense that having a highly graded sport-related undergraduate degree and some related teaching experience is the minimum threshold for recruitment, but back then possessing any undergraduate degree alongside a decent record of sports performance could be enough to get you in. So, fed up with life on the building sites of London, I decided to apply and much to my surprise I was accepted.

Thus, one morning in 1978, I turned up at Liverpool University's sports centre to meet the course leader and my fellow students. There were 12 of us, all male of course, as back then mixed-sex PE classes were unheard of and this was reflected in sex-segregated PE teacher training. That first morning is etched on my memory as we gathered in a relatively small, oblong, wooden-floored dance studio. We students were asked to line up along one wall. The opposite wall was covered with a mirror the length of the room. I remember looking at our collective reflections in the glass, feeling nervous but, judging by the fidgeting of my peers, I was obviously not alone in this apprehension. After the course leader, Mr Ian Ward, had introduced himself, we were asked to do likewise and in doing so to say what degrees we had studied and what sports we had played. There was a spectrum of degrees but, in terms of sports, almost to a man there was a narrow mixture of team ball players dominated by soccer players and rugby men, the exception being one chap, Malcolm, who bravely confessed to being a badminton player, drawing a muted gasp from the rest of the assembly. Once these formalities were over with, there were nervous mutterings as Mr Ward set up a full vaulting box, crash mat and spring board at one end of the studio. Dressed in black teaching slacks, white plimsolls and crisp white polo shirt, Mr Ward marched to the other end of the studio, stood and to attention, saying, 'Gentlemen I want you to watch me carefully because I want you to copy what I am about to do', before, gazelle-like, taking off and sprinting the length of the studio and executing a perfect headspring over the fully stacked vaulting box, followed by an exquisite perpendicular statuesque landing. I am certain that mine was not the only Adam's apple travelling in my throat as we witnessed this. I learned later that, like me, most of my new colleagues had not done any gymnastics for many years and the prospect of trying to emulate Mr Ward's feat was, to say the least, daunting. Demonstration complete, Mr Ward turned to face us and asked, 'okay who would like to go first?' Unsurprisingly there were no volunteers, so he picked out a lad a few feet down on my right hand side saying 'Mr Higham, I think we'll start with you'. Bob Higham, as I recall, was a footballer from Watford who could best be described using the uncharitable terminology of the football dressing room as 'a donkey centre half'. To his immense credit, Bob took up his starting position at the top end of the dance studio and, on command, took off thundering down the runway; he hit the springboard before head-butting the top layer of the vaulting box knocking it off before landing in a stunned heap at the side of the box. Unperturbed, Mr Ward stepped forward and dragged poor Bob to the side of the room to recover before turning to face the rest of us and clapping his hands crisply once before saying, 'Next!' And so it went on for the rest of the morning until eventually we had all undertaken our terrifying gymnastic initiation, which was to mark my formal entry into the PE fraternity. Fortunately, no one was seriously injured but it is a memoir that has lived with me ever since. In fact, that whole year was very memorable and for the most part enjoyable experience. The 12 of us became a veritable band of brothers as we battled our way together through the course attempting to cram in enough practical performance and teaching skills that would enable us to survive once we were put in front of real children in some of Liverpool's toughest secondary schools. Which is probably just as well for me as, when I actually did briefly become Mr Sugden, I taught for a few terms for the Inner London

Education Authority in Brixton and Kennington during turbulent times, important experiences which, if nothing else, convinced me that perhaps studying for a doctorate and pursuing a career in higher education was more suited to my skill sets than actually being a PE teacher!

My otherwise fond memories of my PGCE experiences are also tinged with tragedy and I would like to finish this foreword with one final but sad story. Along-side the main PE curriculum subjects, we had the option of taking some outdoor education electives. I was keen to do this, as were a number of others, particularly a young man called Bob Mooney, with whom I became very close, as we often teamed up together on various hiking and climbing expeditions in Wales and finally in Scotland, where we went hiking and climbing in the mountains of the Isle of Skye. One early spring morning with the rest of the group, we set off to scale Mount Gillean, one of the highest peaks in Skye's Cullin range. Although there was still some ice and snow in the gullies and valleys that we encountered on the trek up, it was otherwise quite a clear morning and conditions were set fair as we set off. But, as can so often happen at that time of year in the mountains, by the time we got close to the summit the weather began to close in. We encountered another group who were lost and ill-equipped to deal with the deteriorating conditions. Our party leader elected to stay with them to help them get safely off the mountain, so Bob and I were asked to turn around and lead the rest of the team back to base. In retracing our steps, we had to repeat a traverse across a snow-clad gully, reusing the steps we had cut in with our ice axes on the way up. I went over first cautiously and Bob followed. About half way across, Bob slipped and sat down on the snow. He turned to me and smiled before he suddenly began to slide down the slope, slowly at first but then accelerating rapidly downhill. Helplessly, I looked on in horror as Bob headed inexorably towards a pile of rocks at the bottom of the gully. When I got down to him, I found him unconscious and unresponsive so, in desperation, I proceeded to give him mouth-to-mouth resuscitation. This turned out to be a fruitless exercise. I was to discover later that, despite wearing a protective helmet, poor Bob had suffered a fractured skull on first impact with the rocks and had died instantly. Needless to say, I have never climbed since that fateful day and I would like to dedicate this short essay to the memory of Robert Mooney, whom I am sure, unlike me and the fictional Mr Sugden, would have made an excellent PE teacher.

The contents of this book will provide aspiring PE teachers with an insight into a world that is informed by theory and practice. It is a text that will inspire the next generation of PE teachers to make a difference to young people and to reflect upon the practices of the past. I have spent a great deal of time reflecting on my profes-sional journey. This book will help individuals to do the same just as the author has throughout.

Professor John Sugden
Professor of Sociology of Sport
University of Brighton

ACKNOWLEDGEMENTS

I never thought that I would ever get to write a book. I wish to thank Professor John Sugden for giving me the tools and the confidence to do so. I also wish to acknowledge the work of other British scholars in the field of physical education who have inspired me to write an entire text about becoming a physical education teacher: John Evans, Ken Green, David Kirk, Margaret Talbot, Anne Flintoff, Susan Capel, Margaret Whitehead, Kathleen Armour – to name but a few.

The chapters of this book contain autobiographical accounts of my own experiences of living inside the physical education world. Some chapters are intertwined with current 'real life' stories of practising and trainee physical education teachers. I would like to thank all of the individual physical education teachers and trainee teachers who willingly and enthusiastically agreed to bring me up to speed with what is actually going on in secondary schools today and allowing me to draw upon their own unique experiences of a world I once lived in.

I am told that every author needs a critical friend. I found one in Dr Marc Keech. I would like to express my sincere thanks to him for putting the initial manuscript through the wash and helping me to iron out the many creases caused by my own inadequacies.

I also wish to thank my wife, Karen, and our children, Megan, Oliver and Lily, who are the reasons why I continue with my academic pursuits.

ABBREVIATIONS

AfL	Assessment for Learning
AfPE	Association for Physical Education
AoL	Assessment of Learning
ASA	Amateur Swimming Association
BA QTS	Batchelor of Arts with Qualified Teacher Status
BBC	British Broadcasting Corporation
BERA	British Educational Research Association
BME	Black Minority Ethnic
BTEC	Business and Technology Education Council
CDP	Continued Professional Development
CDT	Craft Design and Technology
CRB	Criminal Records Bureau
CSE	Certificate of Secondary Education
CSLA	Community Sports Leader Award
DBS	Disclosure and Barring Service
DCFS	Department for Children Families and Schools
DCMS	Department for Culture Media and Sport
DES	Department of Education and Science
DfE	Department for Education
DfEE	Department for Education and Employment
DfES	Department for Education and Skills
DNH	Department of National Heritage
F4P	Football 4 Peace
FIFA	Federation Internationale de Football Association
GCSE	General Certificate of Secondary Education
GNVQ	General and National Vocational Qualification
GTP	Graduate Training Programme

HEI	Higher Education Institution
HSLA	Higher Sports Leader Award
ICT	Information Communications Technology
ISA	Independent Safeguarding Authority
ITT	Initial Teacher Training
JCGQ	Joint Council for General Qualifications
JSLA	Junior Sports Leader Award
KS	Key Stage
NCPE	National Curriculum for Physical Education
NCTL	National College of Teachers and Leaders
NDTA	National Dance Teachers' Association
NGB	National Governing Body
NPQH	National Professional Qualification for Headteachers
NSPCC	National Society for the Prevention of Cruelty to Children
OFSTED	Office for Standards in Education
PESS	Physical Education and School Sport
PESSCL	Physical Education School Sport Club Links
PESSYP	Physical Education and Sport Strategy for Young People
PGCE	Post Graduate Certificate in Eductaion
QCA	Qualifications and Curriculum Authority
QTS	Qualified Teacher Status
SCITT	School-Centred Initial Teacher Training
SIMS	School Information Management System
SLA	Sports Leader Award
SSCo	School Sport Coordinator
SSP	Schools Sport Partnership
TA	Teaching Agency
TDA	Teacher Development Agency
TES	Times Educational Supplement
UCAS	University and College Admissions System
VLE	Virtual Learning Environment

GLOSSARY OF TERMS

academy	A state-funded school independent of local authority control, which must meet the core requirements of the national curriculum for England and is subject to government inspection; some academies are run by government approved sponsors
BTEC	Business and Technology Education Council; a school-leaving qualification and further education qualification in England, Wales and Northern Ireland, equivalent to other qualifications such as the GCSE (levels 1–2), A level (level 3) and university degrees (levels 4–7). BTECs are undertaken in vocational subjects.
DBS	Disclosure and Barring Service – formed from a merger between the Criminal Records Bureau and the Independent Safeguarding Authority
Erasmus Exchange Programme	A European exchange programme for university students and lecturers.
free school	A non-profit independent state-funded school introduced after by the UK Coalition Government in 2011; free schools can be set up by parents, teachers, charities and businesses
GCSE	General Certificate of Secondary Education; taken by most UK pupils between the ages of 14 and 16 across a range of subjects, including physical education

independent school   A private, independently run school that receives no government funding and is fee-paying

induction year   The first year of teaching in schools

maintained school   A state-funded school accountable to the local authority

national curriculum   The subjects that must be taught and the standards pupils should reach in state-funded schools

NCTL   National College of Teachers and Leaders, previously the Teaching Agency

NQT   newly qualified teacher; the status afforded to those individuals who have just qualified to teach

Ofsted   Office for Standards in Education – the UK inspectorate for schools

pastoral system   The system used in schools for ensuring the holistic development and wellbeing of pupils

pedagogy   The art or science of teaching

PGCE   Postgraduate Certificate in Education – a certificate awarded to graduates following a 36-week teacher training programme.

primary school   A school for pupils aged 5–11 years

PSHCE   personal, social, health and citizenship education

School Direct   A school-led teacher training programme accredited by a university

School Games   The Sainsbury's School Games was introduced by the UK Coalition Government after the election in 2010 and is designed for young people across the country to take part in more competitive school sport; the games are made up of three levels of activity: competition in schools, between schools and at a county/area level

school sport   Competitive sport that takes place outside of the formal curriculum

secondary school   A school for pupils aged 11–16

SCITT   school-centred initial teacher training – a school-led teacher training programme where the training occurs predominantly in one school over the course of one year

specialist sports college   Sports colleges were introduced in 1997 as part of the specialist schools programme in the United Kingdom; the system enables secondary schools to specialise in certain subjects, such as physical education, sport and dance

Teachers' Standards   The standards that trainee teachers must meet to gain qualified teacher status (Department for Education 2013a)

Troops to Teachers   An employment-based teacher training programme for ex-servicemen and women sponsored by the Ministry of Defence and the Department for Education

INTRODUCTION

Why have I written this book? Who am I writing it for? What have I got to say? These are three fundamental questions that I have asked myself as I have pursued an undertaking such as this. I have spent many hours seeking the answers to these questions and have learned a great deal about myself in the process. The time invested in writing this book has certainly been worthwhile. It has allowed me to reflect as a practitioner of physical education and contemplate the future direction of the subject I trained to teach, so that the next generation of physical education teachers might be better informed and prepared for teaching in schools. Like the many physical education teachers I have met, got to know and become friends with, I have been driven by a desire to 'make a difference' – a difference to the way in which children experience physical education lessons at school and ultimately a difference to those in positions to make a difference, namely physical education teachers.

A text of this nature would be impossible to write without the vast body of research conducted around the world by other far more qualified and distinguished academics, who have provided testimonies to the construction of evidence-based bodies of knowledge about physical education (Penney and Evans 1999; Green 2003: Bailey and Kirk 2010, for example). Equally, I would not have been able to write a text of this length without being inspired by the many students that I have had the privilege to teach and train and who have been so keen to learn. You will hear more from them in subsequent chapters of this book. These are the individuals who have kept me on my toes and have got the very best out of me.

So, what have I got to say? Certainly more than I ever expected to say. Based on 30 years of professional experience of physical education as a teacher, academic and researcher I have decided to answer the 'call to arms' (Green 2003) and make my own modest contribution to the physical education profession and give something back. It is the very least I can do for the next generation of physical education teachers. From my perspective, I have been an 'insider', so to speak, and understand how the professional pressures and political developments in physical education impact on teachers' lives. One has to experience them in order to appreciate them. Because I have been both a practitioner and a researcher of physical education, I have recognised the impasse between the views of politicians, academics and physical education teachers with respect to teaching physical education in a pragmatic and practically orientated way (Green 2003: ix). Teachers, academics and politicians have historically begged to differ in their views about what it means to be 'physically educated' and today there remains a lack of consensus. The aim of this book is to shed some light on the matter and to establish exactly what physical education teachers are expected to do, what they are not expected to do and what they can realistically achieve in the time at their disposal.

Few would disagree that having outstanding physical education teachers teaching high-quality physical education lessons is an expectation that all parents have for their children. Well-trained and qualified physical education teachers can inspire young people while poorly trained and unqualified physical education teachers can put children off for life. Some, therefore, may be sceptics while others may be 'true believers' in the value of physical education as a curriculum subject (Green 2008: 1).

What is an outstanding physical education teacher? What does it take to become one? How and why did I become a physical education teacher? What are the aims and purpose of physical education? What are the right types of activities that make up the physical education curriculum? These are difficult questions to answer because there are no definitive answers to the unresolved question of what physical education teachers need to know and it is almost impossible to formulate a definitive knowledge base because the knowledge needed will be different depending on the context, course and each person's ideological position (Tindall and Enright 2013: 107). The aim of this book, however, is to attempt to answer these and other pragmatic questions and is the reason why the title given to this book is 'Becoming a physical education teacher'.

'Becoming a physical education teacher' is more than just a no-nonsense user guide or a manual for apprentices. In writing this book, my intention is to dispel the myth that secondary school physical education teachers are the poor relations in the world of academia and to challenge the public perception that physical education teachers just coach sport. I hope to show that physical education teachers are more than just games masters and mistresses, sports coaches, physical trainers or fitness instructors, which are often the stereotypes the media choose to portray on the television and in the cinema. My intention is to inspire those with ambitions of becoming a physical education teacher to aspire to be the very best teacher they can be and to develop a personal philosophy that will take them through to retirement. This book expands on existing literature in terms of what might be expected of individuals seeking a career as a physical education teacher and more importantly the means of getting there. It examines the influences that lead individuals to become physical education teachers in the first place and how these affect what, why and how they teach. You will read in subsequent chapters of this book that becoming a physical education teacher is certainly more than having subject expertise. Just because an individual is an outstanding athlete does not mean they will be an outstanding physical education teacher, in the same way that an outstanding musician will not necessarily be able to teach a musical instrument effectively or a multi-linguist may not be able teach modern foreign languages well. How young people are taught physical education is just as important as what they are taught, whether it is on the playing field, in the gymnasium, sports hall, swimming pool or dance studio. And yet, what constitutes an outstanding physical education teacher is not sufficiently clear to make any sense of what might be expected of them.

This book aims to show that simply having the subject knowledge is not enough. Readers will see in other chapters of this book that outstanding physical education teachers understand pedagogy and the interface between curriculum, teaching and learning. They are committed, enthusiastic individuals who provide positive role models, listen to their pupils and constantly aim to improve their subject expertise. They regularly reflect on their philosophies and practices but also have empathy, patience and compassion (Green 2008: 223). Having a commitment to pupils' learning, being critically reflective, adaptable and being prepared to take 'risks' with their teaching is an asset that all outstanding physical education teachers share. Outstanding physical education teachers are creative and are able to deal with the unexpected. They think outside the box. They are innovative and, as strange as it may sound in physical education, they set tasks without boundaries or rules. They approach teaching with original thought and imagination. Inventive thinking, within safe parameters, through pupil-led learning leads to creative teaching. Passion, drive and moral leadership for teaching and learning are all defining features of an outstanding physical education teacher. Ownership of learning and a commitment to process rather than task outcomes are what counts. Organisational skills, the ability to work with others and, above all else, resilience, are essential components of an outstanding teacher. Equally, one of the defining characteristics of an outstanding physical education teacher is a commitment to career-long professional development (Armour et al. 2010: 37). Capel (2010: 2) defines an 'effective' physical education teacher as someone who can help all pupils, including those who do not readily enjoy or who are not as able and successful in physical activities, to enjoy participating and to value their experiences and, hence, to be physically educated. Teaching physical education has been referred to as an art and science that requires basic skills and competences, professional judgement and broader knowledge and understanding of pupils' individual learning needs but there is no one right way to teach as teachers have their own unique teaching style (Capel and Whitehead 2010). Becoming a physical education teacher, therefore, is an individual, unique experience, with biography, course content and school context all playing a significant part (Tait 1996: 86).

As a physical education teacher, it is essential to recognise that what a child learns derives not only from the content of the physical education curriculum but also from the manner in which it is organised and taught. Schools and their respective physical education teachers have always had the autonomy to make important decisions on behalf of their pupils and a great deal of leverage related to the specific activities to be incorporated in the physical education curriculum, the time devoted to these activities, the way in which they are organised and the manner in which they will be taught. Physical education teachers play a pivotal role with respect to curriculum design, grouping arrangements, staffing and ultimately delivery. Critical decisions depend on their judgement. These decisions can 'make or break' a child's enjoyment of the subject and participation in future. As Lamb (2014: 121) eloquently states, 'what occurs in the physical education classroom in terms of organisation, content and delivery has an important bearing on the identities, attitudes and opportunities for pupils'. And yet, readers of this book will see that pupils are rarely consulted and often have radically different views about physical education compared to the perspectives of their teachers (Green 2008:20). You will also read in this book that establishing and developing fundamental movement skills in the primary years is the basis of all physical education and that physical activity in the early years and childhood are strong indicators of future behaviours including educational attainment, health and emotional wellbeing. But, readers will see that there are very few specialist teachers of physical education in primary schools and an overemphasis on discrete sports too early in the teaching of primary aged children often taught by teachers who have had as little as six hours of formal training to teach physical education. Almond and Ezzeldin (2013: 55) concluded that fundamental movement skills are more concerned with sport and developing a commitment to a sporting pathway from the early years through to adulthood. The consequences of a sport-focused physical education curriculum in the primary school can be the neglect of pedagogy and the omission of dance, adventurous activities and swimming leading to children learning in rows and taking part in a 'one size fits all' approach to physical education.

This book will appeal to those who wish to study or who are currently studying physical education initial teacher training courses at both undergraduate and postgraduate level. It will also have relevance as an academic text to those who are following sport science, sport coaching or sport studies degrees who intend to train as subject specialist teachers of physical education in future, as well as those engaged in school-led training routes such as the School Direct programme and the Troops to Teachers initiative. The book contains an eclectic mix of academic analyses blended with investigative, autobiographical and anecdotal experiences of school physical education lessons. It has been arranged into three distinctive sections that follow the professional journey an individual is likely to experience when pursuing a professional career teaching physical education. Her Majesty's Chief Inspector of Schools for England, Sir Michael Wilshaw, stated that if you were to ask our most successful sportsmen and sports women to list their greatest influences on the road to sporting glory, many of them would volunteer the name of a teacher (Ofsted 2014: 2). Each chapter of this book, therefore, begins with a testimony from a successful athlete regarding their own physical education teachers when they attended school.

Section One of this book contains all the essential information that an aspiring physical education teacher needs to know. It includes examples of my own chronological career pathway and the experiences I have had. Chapter 1 sets the scene by asking the reader to consider why they wish to become a physical education teacher. Chapter 2 discusses the various training pathways available to those who wish to train to become a physical education teacher. Chapter 3 provides context to the journey, emphasising a need to understand what it means to be a physical education teacher within the modern education system. This chapter covers issues such as the public and media perception of physical education teachers and poses the question of whether there is a need to be 'qualified' in the sense of undertaking formal training that leads to a form of certification. Chapter 4 discusses the aims and purpose of physical education, highlighting contemporary issues within the physical education profession such as the legacy of the London 2012 Olympic and Paralympic Games and their impact on physical education in schools. Chapter 5 highlights the policy process through which physical education has evolved and the implications for teachers introducing a revised national curriculum for physical education, which was implemented in schools in 2014. This chapter also discusses the question of whether adopting the independent fee-paying school approach to competitive school sport as suggested by Ofsted (2014) is in the best interests of all pupils who attend maintained secondary schools or academies and what might be the implications for physical education teachers teaching in these schools.

Section Two charts the journey ahead. It is broken into component parts describing the various chronological stages of becoming and being a physical education teacher. Chapter 6 discusses the experiences of trainee physical education teachers, highlighting particular landmarks and stages of professional career development. This chapter is slightly different to each of the other chapters of this book because of the use of primary data. It draws upon the gendered dimension of physical education initial teacher training using a particular case study of a male trainee teacher to illustrate the point. The first year in any profession can be a daunting time and presents many challenges. Chapter 7 offers some practical advice for secondary school physical education teachers embarking on their first year in teaching and meeting the requirements for newly qualified teachers through the induction programme. This chapter draws upon the first of a series of vignettes from newly qualified teachers and their reflections of their first year in the teaching profession and discusses the role and the type of experiences qualified teachers can expect to illustrate the challenges and rewards that come from being a physical education teacher. Chapter 8 covers the process of becoming a curriculum leader (head of department) for physical education in schools and how to get there. Advice is provided in terms of expectations, roles and responsibilities of middle managers such as managing staff, curriculum design and accountability. Other vignettes are included to highlight the experiences of current curriculum leaders of physical education and to illustrate the contemporary role of the curriculum leader for physical education.

Section Three is about moving on in the teaching profession. It focuses upon the multiple roles and career pathways open to physical education teachers. Chapter 9 highlights the need to be a critically reflective practitioner in order to understand and navigate the journey to be undertaken which for many will be the equivalent to entering unchartered waters. This chapter discusses the value of reflective practice for professional development. A series of autobiographical and anecdotal life stories is included, drawing upon critical self-reflection as the basis for understanding professional identity and what constitutes high-quality physical education and good professional practice. Chapter 10 explains the role of the mentor in school-based initial teacher training and the importance of supporting trainee teachers with their professional development through effective mentoring. Once again, a number of vignettes have been included to highlight the role of the physical education mentor. Chapter 11 discusses the wider role of being a physical education teacher and addresses issues such as the physical education teacher's extracurricular responsibilities, together with the development of health education, teaching accredited courses in physical education across the 14–18 years age range, being a form tutor and routes into senior management positions.

Chapter 12 brings all the central themes together and provides an overview of the journey that has been travelled. In light of the introduction of school-led training routes into teaching and the emphasis on providing more 'proper' team sports into the school day, this chapter discusses the merits of such a policy and the role of the twenty-first century physical education teacher within this structure. This chapter also includes examples of what I consider to be 'textbook' physical education lessons based on my own observations of lessons taught by trainee physical education teachers within secondary schools. It also seems fitting in this final chapter to include the last of a number of vignettes, in this case from graduating trainee teachers of physical education and their reflections of their initial teacher training as they enter the world of physical education teaching in 2014. What words of wisdom can they offer others as they come to the end of their four year journey? What will the teaching of physical education look like under their leadership in years to come?

In concluding this chapter and indeed this book, a number of critical questions regarding the role of the twenty-first century physical education teacher's role are posed. Are physical education teachers trained by schools or by universities better equipped to tackle the so-called obesity epidemic among young people? What type of physical education teacher will be teaching the primary school children of today in the secondary schools of tomorrow? Is it a naive aspiration to expect the poor eating habits and weight management of young people to be solved in the gymnasium or on the playing fields of our state-funded and independent secondary schools? Can we expect the twenty-first century physical education teacher to influence lifestyle changes and combat sedentariness among young people through providing more competitive school sport? The final chapter attempts to answer these questions and considers the role of the twenty-first century physical education teacher.

In writing this book, I have tried to explain that the building blocks of a very good physical education lesson are how the learning experiences are managed and organised. It is how the subject is presented to pupils. In this respect, the 'holy trinity' or staple ingredients of a 'textbook' physical education lesson should be based on providing pupils with opportunities for individual, cooperative and competitive learning experiences that develop confidence and raise self-esteem. I have always believed that physical education teachers should not blind pupils with science; that a picture paints a thousand words; that failure to prepare is preparation for failure; and finally, that if you tell a pupil, they will forget. If you show a pupil, they will remember and if you involve a pupil they will understand.

I acknowledge that my views about teaching physical education will not be universally accepted and I hope that I might be forgiven for any shortcomings or notable omissions from this text. It is merely an attempt to interpret the world I live in and to share some insights into the past, as well as some thoughts about becoming a physical education teacher in the future. I hope that on all counts that I will not be judged on any imperfections associated with this book but on its practical application to the career development of physical education teachers. If anything, I would like readers to assess my response for the need to have physical education teachers' daily, weekly and monthly lives at the forefront of research and to empathise with the demands that they face. This book, therefore, offers a perspective of physical education as well as the means of becoming a qualified physical education teacher. It outlines the processes that shape and facilitate the journey from novice-apprentice to expert-teacher, highlighting how policy and practice influences the success of this and what might be done in the future. It is an educational analysis rooted in the development of pedagogically informed practitioners based upon my own considered and, I hope, well-informed, views of scholarship. I hope that the amalgamation of each of these chapters will provide readers of this book with a greater understanding of what it means to be a physical education teacher within contemporary education. I do not know whether this book will make a difference to the future careers of aspiring physical education teachers but I feel comfortable with the knowledge that at least I have tried. Ultimately, readers of this book will be the best judges of that.

SECTION ONE

What you need to know

1

WHY BECOME A PHYSICAL EDUCATION TEACHER?

Did she help to form my character? Well, she had a gritty determination about her, a competitive nature. On a Friday afternoon, she'd always give us an hour of playing rounders. Once I was batting and I tapped the ball, then did the bare minimum to get to first base. 'Ferguson' she roared. 'You tap that ball again and I will have you'. So I batted the next ball out of sight and ran like hell. She was good like that. She got you performing, you know? Yes, I think there is a part of me that comes from her. That determination and that sense of drive. That 'never give in' attitude she had about all her students.
Sir Alex Ferguson, former manager of Manchester United Football Club[1]

If you have just read this sentence . . . then please thank a teacher.

It is often said that everyone has a good book inside them and an interesting story to tell. This publication is, therefore, my own modest attempt to do just that. At some point in their lives, most people in the developed world have been taught by a physical education teacher. After all, virtually every secondary school has at least one member of staff with a specialist physical education qualification and, in a 35-year career, a single physical education teacher might teach as many as 30,000 physical education lessons to over 100,000 pupils (Green 2008: 216). It is therefore, reasonable to assume that most people will have memories of physical education lessons during the time they had attended school. Every teacher remembers their very best pupils but also the ones they would choose to forget. Children are no different. A large proportion of them will have some direct experience of physical education lessons and will base their perceptions on these experiences. For most adults, their previous experiences of school physical education lessons conjure up and evoke common memories. They will remember their former physical education teachers either with deep nostalgia or with deep contempt. Even the public perceptions of physical education teachers are informed primarily by individual experiences gained throughout their school life (Ives and Kirk 2013). Indeed, as Lamb (2014: 120) has shown, the rich history, tradition and ritual associated with physical education can be the root cause of the condoning of pupils' self-exemption from physical education lessons by parents, who are influenced by their own values towards physical education, which are embedded by their own negative school experiences and dispositions. I often wonder how my former pupils remember their physical education lessons. More to the point, how do they remember me as their physical education teacher when they attended secondary school in the 1980s and 1990s? Alexander Miller's comedy sketch of a heart surgeon about to perform a second heart bypass operation on his former physical education teacher puts this into stark context.[2] This has led me to ask myself why I became a physical education teacher. Take a moment to reflect upon your own recollections of physical education lessons at secondary school. Who taught you? What activities were provided for you? How were your physical education lessons organised? Whether or not you attended a single-sex or mixed-sex school, the chances are that you were taught by a same-sex physical education teacher, competed in sex-appropriate team sports and participated with other same-sex pupils. That is exactly the way that I experienced physical education as a pupil in the 1970s. But why was I taught that way and why do some pupils continue to experience physical education this way?

So, who becomes a physical education teacher? What does it take to become a physical education teacher? How do they become a physical education teacher? And why do they become a physical education teacher? If you have picked up and turned the pages of this book then it is highly likely that you will want answers to these very questions and are intent on becoming a physical education teacher. Sociologists have analysed and sought to understand why physical education teachers do what they do and why they think what they think so that physical education teachers, academics and teacher trainers do not 'talk past' one another (Green 2003: 165). This book aims to build upon existing knowledge and attempts to explain the who, what, when, where, why and how of becoming a physical education teacher.

I was at the 'sharp end' of physical education for 13 years and performed the practice of physical education to many pupils in secondary schools. Based upon my own individual experiences and sharing the stories of others I believe that I am well qualified to close the gap between all interested parties involved in physical education. I was a 'first generation' university student within my family. For me, being a physical education teacher was a privileged position. I would always remind myself that being a teacher was one of the most trusted professions in society. Equally, I would often recall my father's words of advice that if you find something you enjoy doing for living then you will never have to do a day's work in your life. After nearly 30 years in the teaching profession, I do not think I have ever done a day's work and have continued to like what I do rather than do what I like. That is why I became a physical education teacher. I have also been fortunate enough to avoid becoming the type of teacher who believes that the only good things about the teaching profession are July and August.

When I was growing up in the 1970s, much of my involvement in competitive sport and physical activity relied on the encouragement and financial investment of my parents. My parents made sacrifices. My interest in sport and physical activity was also influenced by my own physical education teacher when I was a secondary school pupil. I cannot say that my experiences at primary school had much to do with it. Research shows that many physical education teachers become physical education teachers because of their physical education teacher (Armour and Jones 1998). My physical education teacher was a committed professional who was, and still is, a truly altruistic person. Looking back at my own schooldays, it was remarkable what he achieved, given the inadequate facilities at his disposal and the time constraints that he faced. There were no manicured playing fields, unlike at the grammar school for boys just down the road. There was no indoor space suitable for a class of 30, no swimming pool, athletic track or dance studio. Instead, we were taught physical education at local council facilities, which were off site, as well as in an on-site multi-use tarmac area that doubled-up for staff car parking. My background and experiences of physical education and sport have continued to influence my thinking as a professional and as I have matured I have realised that, in the right hands, physical education, sport and physical activity can be a very powerful tool as a means to educate young people about wider social issues.

I was born on Christmas Day 1962. During the 1960s, I was a junior school pupil. During the 1970s, I was a secondary school student and a sixth-former. During the 1980s, I was a trainee teacher and a newly qualified teacher. During the 1990s, I was a mentor and middle manager. For 15 years, I have been a university lecturer and researcher. These experiences have provided the foundations of this book and the scaffolding around which I have constructed the text. The bricks and mortar are what follows in the subsequent chapters of this book with regards to the development of my own career. At this point, it would be remiss of me not to inform the readers that this book is about becoming a secondary school physical education teacher. Other texts (Griggs 2010) have more than adequately discussed the processes of teaching physical education in the primary phase of education highlighting the fact that it is this stage of a child's development that is the most significant period for teaching gross motor movement competencies. That is not to ignore the processes involved in becoming a primary school teacher of physical education but to acknowledge that it is typically the secondary model of physical education that tends to influence, directly or indirectly, what happens in primary school physical education lessons (Green 2008: 207).

I used to be an educator of children. Today, I am an educator of teachers. Since 1986, I have taught physical education in secondary schools and high schools in England and North America. Many of my cross-cultural teaching experiences have helped me to identify the commonalities between different countries but also the distinct differences. The field of comparative physical education is a recent addition within social science research and has informed many of the chapters of this book.

Comparative physical education is the interactive study of two or more systems of physical education or elements of these systems, aimed at increasing understanding of their operational and policy processes (Penney 2002). Much of the impetus for its use in academia has been because the study of education has tended to focus on sets of problems unique for a single system. Consequently, there has been a growth in international cooperation and the comparison of different education systems, which has looked for diversity rather than universally valid rules. Penney (2002) points out that the potential value of adopting comparative perspectives in policy studies is particularly useful as it can reveal what could be different or what is missing from the policies with which teachers are most familiar. I hope to show in subsequent chapters of this book, therefore, how comparative physical education can help us all to consider what we do well and what we could do better.

Since 1998, I have taught in higher education, working primarily with students following undergraduate and postgraduate teacher training programmes in physical education. Some of my teaching within higher education has been in association with other European institutions through the Erasmus exchange programme, such as in Belgium, Germany and the Czech Republic. These experiences have provided me with an international dimension and understanding of the nature and purpose of physical education in different parts of the world. I have also attended and presented at a number of international conferences in Portugal, Spain, Scotland, France and Denmark and have engaged in academic debates with my European counterparts. Moreover, I have contributed to the development of initial teacher education in physical education in countries such as Mauritius. Experiences such as these have been invaluable in helping me to appreciate the common trends and issues in physical education and have, therefore, provided international relevance to much of the content of this book. I have also taught in troubled areas of the world where there are deep social divisions, such as in Israel, Palestine and Northern Ireland, using sport and physical activity as a means of building cultural bridges between children from divided societies, as well as a mechanism for capacity building, social development and the promotion of human rights. The impetus for writing this book has emanated from these experiences of physical education and is informed by professional experiences of teaching, training and lecturing in physical education.

The book is also based on stories shared with me by old and young over the years with respect to their childhood memories of school physical education lessons. It is not an over-exaggeration to say that it has been a conservation piece in many different environments. Some had been traumatised while others had been enthused. Some had loathed the experience; for others, it was the reason to go to school. Many of the recollections of school physical education lessons shared with me have been primarily based on experiences of sport at school rather than physical education lessons. This is hardly surprising, given that there has been a long-established tendency for the routine of physical education to be wedded to the practice of sport (Green 2010: 144). It has become very evident to me as a practitioner and researcher that physical education in secondary schools has been masquerading as sport for nearly half a century. Indeed, I think that I can confidently claim that this has been the worst-kept secret within the physical education profession since I qualified to teach. Kirk (2013: 222) maintains that today's physical education has remained stagnant for many years and has been scarcely relevant for the past 30 years of the twentieth century, let alone the first 15 years of the twenty-first century, revolving predominantly around sport-based, multi-activity forms of the subject, leading Kirk to ask whether the subject and the teachers of the subject are 'fit for purpose'. Just for these reasons alone, a book about becoming a physical education teacher would seem to be an essential text for aspiring teachers of physical education.

In some sections of this book I have deliberately written in the first person, in order to put theory into practice through critical self-reflection. I have drawn upon a reflective narrative of myself to understand my professional journey over 30 years and have taken on a dual role as both researcher and researched. This method of inquiry, if done well, is where the art of storytelling meets the science of research (Amour and Chen 2012: 247). For Green (2008: 225), critical self-reflection helps us to begin to understand why there is a tendency towards conservatism among physical education teachers, which manifests itself in the passing on of skills-orientated and sports-dominated curricula. I have therefore attempted to evaluate my rite of passage through critical self-reflection and to assess the various factors that have influenced my own professional development and how these factors have been responsible for my own perceptions and actions as a teacher of physical education. The process of self-reflection has allowed me to ask critical questions of myself and others, in terms of how I have arrived at where I am, assessing my own professional journey. In some chapters of this book, I have also included reflective accounts from 'real' physical education teachers operating at the 'chalk face' in England. These have been included to help others embarking on the same professional journey from trainee to newly qualified teacher to curriculum leader, to mentor and beyond. They are a 'warts and all' account of the reality of becoming and being a physical education teacher. These vignettes are not subject to critical analytical enquiry or academic scrutiny. I make no apologies for the factual and descriptive nature of these texts. Instead, they are straight from the horse's mouth. They tell it exactly how it is. It may deter some but I hope that it might encourage most readers to continue with their professional pursuit into the world of physical education teaching. I have also collected a number of prominent news stories that have appeared in the public domain over the past three years, to illustrate ways in which wider social issues might affect the values, beliefs and attitudes of would-be physical education teachers. They are stories that will shock but they are also stories that highlight the significant progress that has been made in the world of sport and education.

As with most young aspiring physical education teachers, my passion for and achievements in playing and coaching competitive team sport has led to a 30-year career in the world of physical education and sport. It has consumed my life to the extent that I teach it, talk about it, practise it and write about it on a daily basis.

This has been noted by researchers as a significant contributory factor for choosing a career in teaching physical education and the beliefs and values that future teachers of physical education bring with them (Armour and Jones 1998; Green 2008; Cale 2010). I am aware that, for the majority of readers, I will be preaching to the converted in respect of the importance of physical education in the lives of young people. I am equally aware and very conscious that I may run the risk of patronising the many committed practitioners in the profession and hope that my attempt to write this book is not perceived as teaching physical education teachers to 'suck eggs'. I realise, however, that, for some children, their experiences of physical education lessons and school sport may have been less than enjoyable. Anyone who has ever listened to the lyrics of the song 'The Headmaster Ritual'[3] by 1980's indie band, The Smiths, will know exactly what I mean.

This book is not about how physical education *should* be taught but inevitably it does reflect my own set of values and beliefs in relation to what the focus of attention in physical education should be or what Green (2003) refers to as 'philosophies' or ideologies. I realise that I may end up outside the head teacher's office in some secondary schools because of my views about the teaching of physical education. I would like to make it clear to readers from the outset, however, that I am not against competition, I am not anti-sport and I am not in favour of banishing all forms of traditional team games from the physical education curriculum. I have personally benefited from all three. As Ofsted (2014: 5) points out, there are wider benefits of competitive school sport in building a school's culture and identity ensuring academic achievement and well-rounded individuals. But competitive school sport and physical education are as different as chalk and cheese. Physical education and school sport are like two different pairs of shoes and we all know what happens when you wear the wrong pair of shoes – you get blisters! I do not question that, in the right hands, competitive school sport can build self-esteem and confidence. It can, as Sir Michael Wilshaw pointed out, shape a youngster's character and reinforce the drive to compete and excel academically (Ofsted 2014: 2). That said, many state-funded schools do not enjoy the financial advantages and facilities available to the independent schools and this may account for the fact that they are unable to offer competitive school sport in a meaningful way or, as Sir Michael Wilshaw put it, 'They get on the bus but fail to turn up on the pitch' (Ofsted 2014: 2). I recognise that modern-day life could be perceived as competitive but without human resources, facilities and a positive attitude towards school sport, poor teaching and management of sporting competitions can deprive young people of the lessons that can learned from winning and losing. I have run a marathon; I have made a century; I have scored a hat trick. I have coached a national winning youth football team. I know what it takes to perform at this level but I have come to realise that there are longer-term benefits to this that have stood me in good stead in other aspects of life, such as forging positive relationships with others and working collectively as a team. Sport, team games and carefully managed competition do have a place on the contemporary physical education curriculum but not at the expense of education and the exclusion of less-talented pupils. It is the way in which pupils experience physical education and the manner in which it is presented by teachers that is critical. This requires highly trained individuals who understand pedagogy and are committed to the holistic development of pupils. All too often, though, the content of physical education lessons is based upon staff interests, at the expense of the development of the child through physical education (Stidder and Griggs 2012). Learning in the affective and social domains will be familiar to most teachers. According to Bloom's taxonomy (Bloom and Krathwohl 1956), a classification of learning objectives within education and the way in which skills are learned in the affective domain typically relate to the emotions and feelings experienced. Social learning outcomes related to behaviours and responsibility are an integral part of the learning within which pupils acquire certain values and attitudes. These are the key principals that underpin my philosophy, irrespective of the context in which I have taught.

Armour *et al.* (2010: 49) argue that physical education researchers should support teachers' professional learning by working more explicitly within a physical education professional learning community leading to stronger career-long support for teachers. This book aims to address that very suggestion. Other credible and informative texts have been written to help and support aspiring teachers of physical education to understand the complexities and contradictions that sometimes exist when pursuing a career of this nature (Capel and Whitehead 2013; Capel 2010; Green 2008, for example). These texts have helped me to reflect on my own professional journey and view the art or science of teaching through a critical pedagogical lens. With the exception of Kirk (1992), Armour and Jones (1998), Tinning *et al.* (2001) and Green (2003) few texts have specifically covered the career paths of physical education teachers or explored the major issues that physical education teachers encounter in their daily professional lives. This book aims to fill that void and has provided the impetus for writing my own version of becoming a physical education teacher as an accompaniment to other scholarly texts, providing a perspective on current issues facing the culture of physical education and, I hope, making a contribution to a wider body of knowledge. The motive, therefore, is based on the fact that if I do not write it then perhaps no one else will. My intention is to engage with contemporary and established debates through my own critical self-reflection so that beginner and experienced teachers might gain insights into the physical education profession and develop their own thinking based on theoretical knowledge and understanding. I do not claim, however, to have all the correct answers, merely food for thought with an interpretation and possible ways forward.

My interest in teaching and learning physical education was and continues to be inspired by Loughborough University academic John Evans (1986, 1988, 1993). During my final year as an undergraduate student, I was particularly influenced by John Evans' 1986 edited text, *Physical Education, Sport and Schooling: Studies in the Sociology of Physical Education.* There were many questions that prompted me to ask why the physical education profession had clearly failed in its mission to equip pupils with the desire to participate in physical activity, both at school and once they had left. I am still seeking answers to these very questions. The seminal work of John Evans influenced me to pursue my own postgraduate studies (Stidder 1998, 2009a) and ultimately led to the publication, with my colleague and co-editor, Sid Hayes, of *Equity and Inclusion in Physical Education and Sport* (Hayes and Stidder 2003; Stidder and Hayes 2013). David Kirk's research into teacher socialisation, education and recruitment has been influential in steering me towards researching my own professional identity and career trajectory. More recently, Ken Green's erudite publications, *Physical Education Teachers on Physical Education* (2003), *Understanding Physical Education* (2008) and *Key Issues in Youth Sport* (2010), as well as Ken Hardman and Ken Green's (2011) edited text, *Contemporary Issues in Physical Education*, have provided the impetus for me to proceed with my scholarly pursuits and have prompted me to write this particular publication related to the process of becoming a physical education teacher.

You will read in subsequent chapters of this book that in order to understand the process of becoming a physical education teacher it is important that those who aspire to the profession have a clear understanding of the nature and purpose of the subject and the roles and responsibilities they can expect to undertake. You will also see in other chapters of this book that the role of the secondary school physical education teacher is, however, fraught with misconceptions, ambiguities and role conflict. It is a subject that has become increasingly difficult to 'pin down' (Green 2008: 2). Academics have claimed that physical education is camouflaged as sport, as many physical education teachers continue to view sport rather than physical activity as the most suitable vehicle of achieving other educational goals (Green 2003: 143). Even among the physical education teaching community, there is confusion and contradiction, with many holding very insular views that typically centre on enjoyment, health, skills, character building and, ironically, competitive sport – one of the things that appears most likely to alienate a good number of pupils from physical education (Green 2008: 17).

It may be that physical education teachers simply don't know what they don't know. In 2013, this was still a topic of lively debate, suggesting that we are no closer in defining physical education than we were in 1993. Hawman (2013: 13) concluded that if physical education and school sport are to cease being political footballs, there needs to be a consensus on where they are, what they can be, and what they can achieve, but even physical education professionals cannot agree on that and, until they can, the political footballs cannot be kicked into touch. Armour and Jones (1998: 137) concluded in their analysis of eight case studies of physical education teachers' lives and careers that physical educationalists are long on opinion but rather short on substantiated claims about the educational value of their subject, as sport remains central to the teaching of their subject. Capel and Whitehead (2013: xii) suggest that teachers who do not have a philosophy of teaching have not examined their views or cannot articulate them, with some regarding their role as transferring subject knowledge into empty vessels, while others view it as guiding pupils on a voyage of discovery. This chapter intends to help aspiring and emerging teachers of physical education to reflect on why they want to become a physical education teacher but also the processes they are likely to experience and the challenges they will probably encounter.

Green (2008: 1) suggests that physical education professionals tend to write and talk about the subject in a manner that not only takes certain beliefs for granted but also presents them as orthodox, even factual. One of those taken-for-granted assumptions is that physical education is about sport and this has led to a lack of coherence and continued concern about the relationship between physical education and participation in sport (Green 2008: 2). In effect, the waters between physical education and sport have been muddied. My own observations suggest that physical education teachers have not been speaking with one collective voice when defining the subject. Some physical education teachers appear to have severed all ties with the very subject to which they have purported allegiance and have defected to the coaching of sport, while others have divided loyalties. To some physical educationalists, the relentless pressure to convert their subject into sport has meant that many teachers of physical education have been led into the profession under false pretences. On one hand, their training has been pedagogically based and, on the other, their respective physical education departments have focused on the performance outcomes of competitive school sport. The extent to which physical education teachers practice what they preach, therefore, casts doubt over what the subject is actually about and who the main culprits are in terms of pupil dissatisfaction related to the content and delivery of physical education. Quite often, physical education teachers perceive a 'supply and demand' system in operation and therefore provide what they believe their pupils want in physical education lessons, in the form of competitive sport. Some physical education teachers have resisted the pressure to succumb to the coaching of sport despite feeling under duress, while some have resorted to more extreme forms of defence similar to wearing a bulletproof vest to protect them from the sports lobby. Certainly, the history of physical education suggests that there is overwhelming evidence that the efforts of pedagogues to restore the educational nature of physical education may have just been a pointless exercise. It may well have been a foregone conclusion in the race between the sports protagonists and their physical education counterparts. Traditionally, a 'belt and braces' approach to the teaching of physical education has been adopted, in order to raise activity levels among young people but, to educationalists, the teaching of sport has been nothing more than a blunt instrument in promoting the holistic education of young people.

Sport is often seen as the conduit between physical education and physical activity. In this respect, the physical education teaching profession has not been singing from the same hymn sheet. Rather than being a choir, they have tended to be more like a quartet. It has certainly not been a case of 'united we stand, divided we fall'. To the purists, teaching physical education in state-funded schools is not about washing kits, chasing fixtures, checking teams, driving minibuses, refereeing matches and running competitions. Instead, it is about high-quality teaching based on well-planned lessons across a broad and balanced range of physical activities that is fully inclusive and accessible to all pupils (Marchant 2013). What the research tells us about becoming a physical education teacher is that many physical education teachers rely on their own childhood recollections of physical education and replicate the way in which they were taught (Brown 2005). I have heard some physical education teachers justifying this by the fact that 'it never done them any harm', lending credence to Green's (2008) observations that 'beginning' teachers are intuitively orientated towards reproducing and preserving the physical education they have experienced and adopting a 'custodial' orientation which they themselves grew up with. Most physical education trainee teachers have been elite performers at school and therefore believe that the failed model is indeed successful (Marchant 2013), resulting in somewhat of a wedge being driven between physical education and sport. In effect, a self-perpetuating cycle, or what Green (2008: 17) refers to as 'an in-built constraint or inertia', is constantly in motion. Physical education teachers take for granted that their own physical education lessons as pupils themselves were models of good practice and frequently act as carriers of a de facto physical education curriculum that typically revolves around team games and sport (Green 2008: 209). They become not just physical education teachers but disciples of their subject, with all the ideological and associated vested interests that entails (Green 2008: 209). As a result, a preoccupation with the immediate present in physical education and an ignorance of the past has not bought about real substantial or desirable change in physical education (Kirk 2010).

I believe, more than ever, that actions need to speak louder than words. The physical education profession has to recruit well-trained individuals, to ensure that the development of the subject can prosper at both primary and secondary level. But the landscape of initial teacher training has changed. Universities are no longer trusted to equip and prepare the next generation of teachers for fear that the trendy, politically left-leaning lecturers may fill their heads full of untried and untested educational theories rather than pragmatic, back to basics, rote-type teaching and learning. It is also regrettable that very little research enters the thinking of policy makers in government or is fed into the practice of initial teacher training and schools (Evans and Davies 2002: 24). Indeed, there is a gulf between what academics have to say about the nature and purpose of physical education and what politicians want physical education teachers to do. But Green (2008: 120) alludes to the fact that it is far from easy to challenge established norms and expectations, as significant barriers exist both within and beyond the arena of physical education and school sport, such as in the views of parents, colleagues, senior teachers, pupils and policy makers, all of whom have a particular vision of what physical education is 'about', what a typical physical education lesson should 'look like' and what children should learn. I hope this book, however, encourages potential physical education teachers to take note of research; not to be afraid of change; to ask the 'why' questions and to learn from experience. For this to happen, fresh approaches to the induction and training of physical education teachers is critical, rather than leaving them to rely on experienced physical education teachers as their 'standard setters' (Keay 2005). As Evans and Davies (2002: 11) put it, ideas and innovation are our friends not our enemies.

Teaching physical education in secondary schools has certainly changed since I qualified to teach in 1986 and has evolved into a modern profession. The changes that I have witnessed have all been a result of short-, medium- and long-term changes, which Green (2008: 2) refers to as cyclical, episodic and cumulative related to policy, practice and professionalism. However, Green's assertion that the practices of physical education teachers have far more to do with the contexts in which they teach is a particular concern for school-led training routes and for trainee teachers of physical education. Constraints on practice mattering more than theory in determining what teachers do and how they do it is also a worrying trend and observation. What is of even greater concern is that there remains a paradox between physical education teachers in schools and academics in universities as to what physical education represents. This has led some experts (Kirk 2013) to comment that the physical education profession has failed to achieve the ubiquitous aspiration, common to physical education around the world, of long term physical activity. Kirk makes no bones about it: 'How long can this state of affairs continue before the truth about physical education in its current form is finally out?' (Kirk 2013: 229).

In the following chapters of this book, you will see that, for some physical education teachers, sport is synonymous with physical education, where competitive games occupy the vast majority of curriculum time, often at the expense of lifestyle or lifetime activities. These teachers may be the last of a generation who had been trained to use didactic, command-style methods of teaching reminiscent of my father's memories of his ex-army physical education teacher in the early 1950s. But, as Green points out, this can be attributed to the fact that the longer physical education teachers remain in the profession and the longer individual teachers remain at the same school, the more conservative their practices become and the less likely they are to leave (Green 2008; 225). Imagine teaching physical education in the same school for thirty plus years. In other words, despite decades of progress and change, there may still exist a small proportion of 'dinosaur' games teachers who walk the corridors bearing one ball and a bag of bibs, a description given of himself by former physical education teacher Gary Boothroyd in his account of his 27-year teaching career in an inner-city secondary school.

> I lift a set of bibs from the various row of colours on hooks along the storeroom wall, pick up a pile of marker discs on an aluminum pole and, with whistle round my neck, head out behind the stick-wielding cohort, locking all three doors after me as I go.
>
> *(Boothroyd 2004: 45)*

But all is not lost. Much progress has been made possible by those who have aspired to become physical education teachers having a particular mindset whereby they enter the profession as 'agents of change' (Hardman and Green 2011). As Armour and Jones put it:

> If sports are 'physical chess' then physical educators are the grand masters (and dames) with the awesome responsibility of enthusing and enabling young people to reach for the level of their own capabilities. Now that is a career worth having.
>
> *(Armour and Jones 1998: 141)*

Many physical education teachers have continued to work against the grain by offering a broad range of physical activities to enhance pupil motivation and participation. These are the next generation of physical education teachers who have the capacity and influence to make significant decisions and changes. For those who wish to 'join the club', this can be a life-changing moment but they need know and understand exactly why they want to become a physical education teacher. Ask yourself exactly the same question. Why do you want to become a physical education teacher? Can you describe the reasons? If high-quality physical education is to be taught in schools at all stages of education then it requires committed teachers who genuinely want to contribute to way in which the way physical education is taught. I hope that the following chapters of this book show how the professional development of physical education teachers is moulded, shaped and formed incrementally over a period of time and inform potential teachers of the journey that awaits them.

Notes

1 *Times Educational Supplement*, 28 February 2014: 31.
2 Armstrong and Miller, 'Heart Surgery on Old Teacher', Hat Trick Productions. Available online at www.youtube.com/watch?v=cJI2Ua4xhKs (accessed 23 September 2014).
3 The Smiths, 'The Headmaster Ritual'. Available online at www.youtube.com/watch?v=RgNfTx9pGzA (accessed 23 September 2014).

2

HOW TO BECOME A PHYSICAL EDUCATION TEACHER

The teacher that had the most influence on my life was Miss Kaye. She taught me at Chigwell County Primary School from the ages of 10 until about 12. She taught a lot of different subjects but, most importantly, she was the one who taught us sport and took us to all sorts of different gymnastics and running events. She encouraged me to take part in gymnastics from when I was about 10 and would put me in for competitions. When I was getting ready to leave the school, she told me that I was talented and that I should join a club. I was good at gymnastics and athletics at that stage and wasn't sure which way to go. I talked to her about which one I should follow up and she encouraged me to go down the athletics route, so I have a lot to thank her for. At primary school, we did a bit of everything – a bit of rounders, a bit of gymnastics – but lessons were much more structured when I went on to West Hatch High School in Chigwell.

Sally Gunnell, Team GB Olympic Gold Medallist,
400 m hurdles, Barcelona 1992[1]

The mechanics of 'how' to become a physical education teacher are discussed in this chapter and illustrate the different pathways and processes of achieving qualified teacher status (QTS). Before doing so, there are a number of essential requirements other than formal academic qualifications that would-be teachers must be able to meet. Anyone applying to teach must do so through the Universities and Colleges Admissions Service (UCAS). In the UK, whether it is PGCE, School Direct or undergraduate routes into teaching, admissions tutors in schools and universities assess the application before inviting prospective candidates to interview, subject to them having the appropriate academic qualifications and supporting statement and references. In the case of physical education, the interview typically consists of a practical assessment of physical literacy, a teaching scenario as well as a formal face-to-face interview and a written task. Candidates are usually made a 'conditional offer' based on the outcome of the interview. Candidates must pass two independent UK government tests in literacy and numeracy prior to commencement of their teacher training and are subject to a criminal background check. The Criminal Records Bureau and the Independent Safeguarding Authority have merged to become the Disclosure and Barring Service (DBS). All applicants for a teaching post must undergo a DBS clearance check, which involves a check of criminal convictions. The DBS is a centralised UK government agency that holds information about potential candidates which may prevent them from teaching in UK schools. Schools are required to have all current and new teachers as well as trainee teachers cleared through the DBS before taking up or continuing with employment or initial teacher training. Those individuals who are offered a university teacher training place must also be declared 'fit to teach' by an occupational health advisor.

The premise upon which this particular chapter is based is that, during my teacher training, my university tutors would always stress to me that anyone entering the teaching profession should never underestimate the influence that they will have on a child and the trust that a parent affords to them. In a 2013 Ipsos MORI poll,[2] teachers were ranked the second most trusted professionals next to medical doctors, with bankers and politicians ranked as the least trusted. As a parent myself, I hand over my prized possessions each morning and trust that they will be educated for five hours a day, five days a week for 38 weeks a year. Being a teacher, therefore, requires individuals who are committed practitioners and understand what it takes to have this privileged position in society. There are, however, a few exceptions to the rule. There have been news stories of 12 teachers raising money for their school's charity by posing semi-naked for a calendar, with each teacher appearing on a different page for each of the months of the year.[3] In another case, a female physical education teacher faced possible disciplinary action from her school after appearing in a range of 'completely inappropriate' poses on a modelling website, which caused anger among some parents from the school where she taught. Other high-profile legal cases have resulted in custodial sentences being given to teachers for having inappropriate relationships with pupils of the type referred to in the 1980 hit single 'Don't stand so close to me' by the British rock band, The Police.

The National Society for the Prevention of Cruelty to Children recommends that child protection and safeguarding policies in schools should provide guidance for all staff and trainees so that they clearly understand the need to maintain appropriate boundaries in their dealings with young people. The work of Brackenridge (2001) has also stressed the need for national governing bodies of sport to provide support for those involved in coaching, so that adults are aware that attitudes, demeanour and language all require care and thought, particularly when members of staff are dealing with adolescent boys and girls. Teacher training programmes stress that a member of staff or volunteer is in a position of power or influence over a pupil or student by virtue of the work or nature of the activity being undertaken. The critical message is that all staff should ensure that their relationships with pupils are appropriate to the age and gender of the pupils, and should take care that their language or conduct does not give rise to comment or speculation because, from time to time, some staff may encounter young people who display attention-seeking behaviour or who profess to be attracted to the teacher. Staff should be able to deal with those situations sensitively and appropriately but should ensure that their behaviour cannot be misinterpreted. In these circumstances, the member of staff should also ensure that a senior colleague is aware of the situation. It should also be noted that a teacher can be vulnerable to unintended misuses of electronic communications, such as email, text and social media, which may be misconstrued. All teachers should, therefore, give due care and attention to the ways in which they conduct themselves professionally.

Owing to changes in UK government policy, initial teacher education in higher education has been subject to significant cuts in the allocation of funded training places for teachers, signposting the UK government's intention of having more teachers trained by school-led initiatives. In the academic year 2013–14, the core allocation of these places to universities was 26,970. On 1 November 2013, the UK government announced the provisional allocation of training places for teachers for the following year. For the academic year 2014–15, this had been reduced by 15 per cent to 22,900, despite the prediction by the National Audit Office that an extra 256,000 school places would be needed by 2014–15 and an additional 14,000 teachers would be required. Meanwhile, for the same period, the numbers allocated to school-led initial teacher training via the 'School Direct' route had increased by 61 per cent from 9,586 to 15,400.[4] In some cases, university postgraduate courses for initial teacher training became unviable and had caused universities to abandon their provision entirely.[5] As a result, there are now various ways of becoming a physical education teacher in the United Kingdom, owing to changes to government policy with regards to routes into teaching in which aspiring teachers learn their craft and are initiated into their 'trade' (Green 2008: 210). The training of physical education teachers in England has undergone considerable changes over the years. From a certificated profession in the former polytechnics and teacher training colleges in the 1970s, teachers of physical education enter a graduate profession with university degrees in physical education, sport science, youth sport, sport studies, sport coaching and other sport-related subjects. Many complete a three-year degree and then go onto a one-year (36-week) postgraduate teacher training course in physical education and gain QTS. Others complete a four-year undergraduate degree in physical education with QTS, although very few UK institutions now offer this particular pathway into teaching. Kirk (2013: 221) reflects upon the changes in initial teacher education and asks who could have predicted that, by 2014, the four-year initial teacher education programmes would be more or less replaced by one-year (36-week) postgraduate certificates. Within the UK, university trained teachers could become a dying breed, as more initial teacher training moves towards school-led initiatives such as School Direct.

Successive UK governments have reconstructed the way in which teachers are prepared for the classroom, with trainee teachers spending more time learning their craft and gaining what Nutt and Clarke (2002: 158) describe as 'hands-on experience'. There has, however, been an even greater shift towards school-led as opposed to university-led initial teacher training placing the onus on schools and giving more responsibility to mentors in schools. In 2002, there were 31 providers of initial teacher training for physical education in the UK; 29 of them offered a post-PGCE, with 12 institutions offering a four-year bachelors degree and 10 offering both (Kirk 2013). In 2014, this number had been significantly reduced. The number of students who take the four-year undergraduate route into teaching has since been dramatically reduced with only three remaining universities in the UK offering this option. The post-PGCE course is for existing graduates, who usually hold a higher classification of degree. In most subject areas, including physical education, students with a first-class and second-class higher degree (2:1) receive a tax-free government bursary towards the costs of their training. At the time of writing, this has since been stopped for all non-shortage subjects. The course is partly academic (PGCE) and partly professional (QTS). Students take 120 level-six credits, 60 of which are assessed at level seven, leading to one-third of a master's degree. Over 36 weeks or 180 days, students work towards achieving QTS by providing evidence that they have met the *Teachers' Standards* (Department for Education 2013a). Sixty days are university based while 120 days are spent in two different training schools. Students monitor their own professional development, typically using an e-portfolio, and are assessed on their teaching competencies by their mentors in their respective training schools, which is quality assured by universities. There are eight standards for qualifying to teach that a trainee teacher must consistently show evidence of achieving during school-based training.

Since 2010, there has been an increasing emphasis on employment and training routes into teaching, with schools playing a leading role in replacing more traditional routes into teaching as highlighted by government advisor Charlie Taylor.

> In the past teachers were often parachuted into schools from on high without any direct school involvement in the content or the focus of their training course. Imagine this situation with any other profession. Imagine doctors having no input into the training of doctors. Imagine law schools where solicitors or barristers were not fundamentally involved in designing the courses. Yet this is the situation we have had with teachers. As a head you may have had no input in the training. But when that teacher has started with you, and Ofsted comes calling the second week of September, it is you who will be held to account. Some schools even refuse to take trainees – because they are worried that parents will complain, that their results will suffer, or that Ofsted will criticize them. I can understand this in schools under pressure where results are not good, but this happens even in schools that are rated outstanding by Ofsted. If outstanding schools refuse to get involved in training the next generation of teachers, I think there's something

very wrong with that. Now this situation is not universally the case, there are many examples of excellent partnerships between schools and providers of teacher training. However, I think things can get better and the introduction of School Direct last summer will change things significantly.

(Taylor 2013)

The Department for Education (2013b: 8) included statistics from the School Workforce Census (Department for Education (2013c), which found that 56 per cent of teachers in secondary maintained schools in England teaching physical education had a degree or higher, 16 per cent had a Bachelor of Education (B.Ed.) degree, seven percent had a PGCE and 2 per cent held an 'other' relevant qualification. Overall, 80 per cent of all teachers who taught physical education had a relevant post A-level qualification, while one in five teachers who taught physical education had no relevant post A-level qualification. The same report cited EACEA/Eurydice (2013), who reported that across Europe, physical education is taught by generalists and specialist teachers in primary schools, while in lower secondary education physical education teachers tend to be specialists. Specialist teachers at primary school usually have a bachelor's degree whereas in lower secondary education almost as many countries require a master's degree as well as a bachelor's degree. The secondary school curriculum and staffing survey in England (Charles *et al.* 2008) reported that the gender split of teachers was almost equal, with 49 per cent of physical education teachers being male and 51 per cent female. The majority of physical education teachers were in the youngest two age bands: 51 per cent were under 30 years of age and 27 per cent were aged 30–39. Fifteen percent of physical education teachers were aged 40–49 and 10 per cent were aged 50 or over. For many physical education teachers, the route into middle management positions in schools and colleges is a natural progression and this may account for the low numbers of physical education teachers in the 50 and over age bracket.

The 'graduatisation' of the teaching profession has been referred to as one of the most significant changes in physical education in recent decades (Green 2008: 210) but, it is claimed by Green, trainee teachers of physical education are frequently less prepared to teach practical physical education than those trained two decades or more ago, despite extended school placements. Nonetheless, the requirement to have degree-level qualifications to teach physical education and its overall degree-worthiness has been a major advancement for the subject since the first bachelors degree in physical education was offered by Birmingham University in 1949 (Bailey and Kirk 2010). I studied for four years at the former Borough Road College between 1982 and 1986, during a time when it became the West London Institute of Higher Education and subsequently Brunel University. I undertook a four-year B.Ed. honours degree in the days when physical education teachers were required to train to teach an additional subject, which, in my case, was English. I was trained in a mixed-sex cohort by some of the very best lecturers you could expect back in the days when you had to be at least a county athlete and score highly on the Western Motor Ability Test[6] to get on to the course. Some of the alumni included former 400-metre Olympic hurdler Alan Pascoe and 200- and 400-metre runner Kathy Smallwood, together with several very talented rugby players who played at the neighbouring Harlequins Rugby Football Club at what is now known as 'The Stoop'.

In 1998, the UK government introduced the Graduate Teacher Programme (GTP) designed for graduates who wished to attain the same QTS that was often awarded alongside a four-year teaching degree or a PGCE, while training and working for a year in a paid teaching role. The GTP programme was aimed at graduates who wished to change their career and train to become a teacher but needed to earn an income while they trained. It has since been replaced by the School Direct programme, which was introduced in 2012. Routes into teaching also included School-Centred Initial Teacher Training (SCITT) for graduates. A SCITT course is based in and run by a consortium of schools, where the trainee teacher is located in a school environment for an entire academic year. It leads to the award of QTS. Some SCITT programmes can lead to the award of PGCE validated by a university. In June 2012, the Teaching Agency announced that School Direct would become the main route for initial teacher training from September 2013. These routes were either salaried or training routes. One of the main differences with the School Direct programme compared with a more traditional PGCE programme is that trainee teachers train predominantly in one school with a shorter complementary experience at another school. School-led partnerships are overseen and governed by a decision-making body in which representatives of schools have a majority voice. School staff, rather than university staff, have key roles to play in the marketing, recruitment and selection of candidates, the development of the content of the programme, internal and external quality assurance and the training of mentors. The National Association for the Teaching of English conducted an online survey of members' views of the likely effects of the School Direct route into teaching;[7] 730 individuals completed the survey. Its report revealed a deep pessimism about this mode of teacher training and some of the reasons there had been problems in recruitment:

- Respondents doubt schools' capacities to resource key elements of teacher training.
- Trainees' subject knowledge, understanding of educational purposes and processes, and classroom preparedness will all decline.
- Trainees will be less well tutored and mentored.
- Employers will find difficulty in filling posts appropriately and the national/regional balance of job supply and demand will be affected.
- Regional provision of initial teacher training will be more variable and worse overall.
- Trainees desire University-led training that allows them to reflect on and learn from multiple teaching placements through contact with their tutor, their peers, and other learning communities.

Despite the initial pessimism and low recruitment figures, the School Direct route into teaching has been pursued by the Teaching Agency (since renamed the National College of Teacher Leaders and Leadership) as the main point of entry to the profession, a point reaffirmed by Education Secretary of State, Michael Gove, in 2010, when he said that teachers should learn their 'craft' in schools, rather like surgeons learn in hospitals based on the model of teaching hospitals and set up as showcases for good teaching allowing for more on the job training.[8] Other employment-based routes into teaching included Troops to Teachers, introduced in 2013 for exiting servicemen and women from the British Armed Forces, while more than 300 university-based teacher training courses in England were facing closure or merger, as funds were switched towards school-led training.[9] The Troops to Teachers initiative was introduced as a fast-track system into teaching exclusively open to ex-service personnel. It is a two-year, employment-based 'advanced standing' programme leading to an honours degree with QTS and is a cross-government initiative supported by the Department for Education and the Ministry of Defence.[10]

In a statement from the New Visions for Education group, Professor Sir Tim Brighouse stated that the provision of teacher education was undergoing an unpublicised crisis:[11]

> The first and most alarming issue is that the need to train teachers at all has come into question. Michael Gove has said that neither academies nor free schools have to have teachers trained to the qualified teacher status standard. Given that he wants most schools to be either one of these, it is clear that he does not prioritise the need for teacher training. The number of academies has increased dramatically so that now over half the secondary schools in England have academy or free school status and if Gove has his way this number will continue to grow. Coupled with this, Gove has given up the need to plan teacher training places nationally. We have now reached a position where qualified teacher status is no longer seen as a necessary requirement for teachers in the English public education system, unless they are in local education authority-maintained schools.

So incensed was Professor Brighouse that he went on to say:

> The question of the partnership between schools and universities is ever changeable but to divorce them completely is a mistake and to suggest that teachers need no training at all is a grave error. Teaching is a complicated business and you must have time to reflect on the pedagogical processes involved. It appears that Michael Gove considers subject knowledge enough. What he appears to fail to see is that you need far more than subject knowledge if you are going to stand up in front of 30 children and teach them stuff that they do not already know and inspire them to want to learn more.

Further political point scoring took place in January 2014, when the Labour Party announced proposals for the licensing of teachers with regular checks on performance and a system of re-licensing every five years. Similar to previous proposals, this scheme dubbed by the UK press as 'Classroom MOTs', was rather like having a medical check-up or having a car serviced. What the politicians failed to realise is that to teach know-how, you have to know how to teach.[12] Choosing a career can involve a great deal of thought and changing of decisions along the way. Inevitably, there will be soul-searching questions: Are you prepared for change? Do you know what you are letting yourself in for? Are you clear about the role? Are you sure you want to teach physical education? Are you more interested in coaching sport? How ready and prepared are you with respect to including children with additional learning needs and/or disabilities? Did you know that there are 451,000 full-time equivalent teachers working in UK state-funded schools? Ninety-six per cent of all teachers hold degree-level qualifications. Three out of four are female and are predominantly white. Within secondary schools there are approximately 26,000 secondary school physical education teachers (Department for Education 2013b). Did you know that physical education attracts approximately 3 per cent of trainee teachers from black and minority ethnic backgrounds compared with 11 per cent of new entrants to the teaching profession overall (Flintoff et al. 2008)? Do you realise that on average you will work 50 hours per week (Department for Education 2013b) and spend some of your time on what you might perceive to be unnecessary, meaningless and bureaucratic tasks? Are you happy to make a modest salary and never be wealthy? Are you capable of managing encounters with obnoxious pupils and difficult parents? Do you have the emotional intelligence to deal with insolent behaviour? Are you prepared to deal with dubious excuse notes and pupils who simply do not want to take part? Did you know that the School Workforce Census (2010–11) showed that 56 per cent (268,000) of all teachers took, on average, five days sickness absence per year? Do you really want to work in a profession where the assessment of pupil progress is often used as a stick with which governments can 'beat' teachers when comparing results between schools and even between teachers (Green 2008: 81)? Would you be happy to teach in an environment that might seem like working in an examination factory? Did you know that that 40 per cent of 'new' teachers quit their jobs within the first five years of their careers.[13] Has it ever crossed your mind that long hours, endless targets, data-hungry inspectors and worried children are making teachers leave the profession in droves? Are you aware that the BBC reported that more than one-third of school and college staff suffer from mental health issues, including disturbed sleep and stress-related illnesses as a result of working in a climate of fear caused by feelings of insecurity? Did you know that education professionals do more unpaid overtime than any other professional group, which has caused constant, intense pressure to meet targets, with excessive observations, changes in the curriculum and Ofsted inspections.[14] Are you prepared to answer people such as the Chief Inspector of Schools, Sir Michael Wiltshaw, who is reputed to have said that 'if anyone says to you that staff morale is at an all-time low then you know that you are doing something right'.[15]

The reality of being a physical education teacher is that you will be observed a great deal of the time either by your line manager, a school governor or an Ofsted inspector. You will be judged and your pay will be based on your performance. At times, you will feel as if your back is against the wall and that you are not trusted to do the job that you have been trained to do. It might feel as if the teaching of physical education is not being left in your capable hands. Physical education teachers have often complained to me that their daily routines often involve them in plugging holes rather than fixing the leak and this can cause feelings of stress and despair. You may feel that a child's education is more to do with achieving a set of results rather than their emotional wellbeing. It is possible that you may perceive your role as jumping through hoops and ticking boxes and that you are just a pawn in a game of political chess. All in all, it may make you feel 'punch drunk'.

The decision to teach physical education, though, is inevitably informed by positive experiences as a pupil and a willingness to share those experiences with other young people. Irrespective of the career choices and decisions young people make from becoming a police officer, fire fighter, midwife or paramedic, there are often underlying reasons for making such decisions which usually emanate from a philanthropic approach to life. For some, being a physical education teacher is a built-in vocation. For others it can be a baptism of fire (Armour and Jones 1998: 124). This book therefore intends to help people like this to make an informed decision and the right choice for them and to help them to deal and cope with the potential and inevitable pitfalls that may lie ahead.

In the following chapter, I expand upon debates related to changes in initial teacher training policy and how these might impact on what a physical education teacher is within the new policy structure. I am acutely aware, however, that there may be some readers who do not necessarily share a common set of values about learning to teach physical education and that some have different attitudes and beliefs about the training of teachers with respect to the teaching and learning of physical education in schools. There are many who have deeply felt and often polarised views of the subject (Green 2008: 1). Indeed, it is immensely difficult nowadays to champion one model of physical education (Green 2008: 28). If there is one certainty in education, it is change. I entered the teaching profession two years before the Education Reform Act was passed through the UK Parliament in 1988. Within three years, by 1991, the first National Curriculum for Physical Education for England and Wales was operational in schools. Even with the introduction of successive centralised policy documents such the National Curriculum, there has been little uniformity in its implementation and many dissenting voices within the profession. In this respect, there has not been universal support among some physical education colleagues in the profession with regard to the prescriptive and regulatory nature of its contents. I hope, however, that these different views might be worthy of discussion and might stimulate professional debate with respect to the lessons can be learned from the past. It is my intention in the next chapter, therefore, to attempt to explain what a physical education teacher is, what a physical education teacher does and what a physical education teacher of the future might be.

Notes

1   Sally Gunnell, 'My Best Teacher', *Times Educational Supplement*, 20 March 2009. Available online at www.tes.co.uk/article.aspx?storycode=6010473 (accessed 23 September 2014).

2   Ipsos MORI, 'Politicians trusted less than estate agents, bankers and journalists', fieldwork 9–11 February 2013, published 15 February 2013. Available online at www.ipsos-mori.com/researchpublications/researcharchive/3133/Politicians-trusted-less-than-estate-agents-bankers-and-journalists.aspx (accessed 23 September 2014).

3   'Nude Teachers: Harmless Fun or Bad Taste?' *BBC Newsround*, 18 June 2003. Available online at http://news.bbc.co.uk/cbbcnews/hi/chat/your_comments/newsid_2993000/2993990.stm (accessed 23 September 2014).

4   Parr, C., Else, H. and Elmes, J. (2014) 'Public Workforce Training Under Pressure', *Times Educational Supplement*, 15 May. Available online at www.timeshighereducation.co.uk/features/public-workforce-training-under-pressure/4/2013237.article (accessed 29 September 2014).

5   Universities UK, *Initial Teacher Training*, Parliamentary Briefing, 7 November 2013. Available online at www.universitiesuk.ac.uk/highereducation/Documents/2013/InitialTeacherTraining-Nov2013.pdf (accessed 23 September 2014).

6   The Western Motor Ability Test is a battery of skill-related physical fitness tests designed to measure an individual's level of co-ordination, speed, power, agility, balance and reactions.

7   National Association for the Teaching of English, *Surveying the Wreckage: The professional response to changes to initial teacher training in the UK*. Available online at www.nate.org.uk/cmsfiles/ite/Surveying_the_Wreckage_web_1.pdf (accessed 23 September 2014).

8   Jeevan Vasagar, 'Michael Gove Sets Tough New Targets for Secondary Schools', *Guardian*, 24 November 2010. Available online at www.theguardian.com/politics/2010/nov/24/michael-gove-tough-targets-secondary-schools (accessed 23 September 2014).

9   Angela Harrison, 'More Teachers to Learn in Classroom – Michael Gove', *BBC News*, 12 June 2012. Available online at www.bbc.co.uk/news/education-18427512 (accessed 23 September 2014).

10 Angela Harrison, 'University-led Secondary PGCEs Face Uncertain Future', *BBC News*, 8 February 2012. Available online at www.bbc.co.uk/news/education-16944873 (accessed 23 September 2014).

11 Professor Sir Tim Brighouse, 'Government Induced Crisis in Initial Teacher Education', New Visions for Education Group, 15 April 2013. Available online at www.newvisions-foreducation.org.uk/2013/04/15/government-induced-crisis-in-initial-teacher-education accessed 23 September 2014).

12 Sarah Simons, 'Classroom Practice: To Teach Know-How, Know How to Teach', *Times Educational Supplement*, 20 February 2014. Available online at www.tes.co.uk/article.aspx?storycode=6406285 (accessed 23 September 2014).

13 John Harris, 'Teachers: Life inside the exam factory', *Guardian*, 14 March 2014. Available online at www.theguardian.com/education/2014/mar/14/teachers-life-inside-the-exam-factory (accessed 23 September 2014).

14 Association of Teachers and Lecturers poll of 925 education staff in England, Wales and Northern Ireland. Katherine Sellgren, 'Teachers Report Rise in Mental Health Fears', *BBC News*, 14 April 2014. Available online at www.bbc.co.uk/news/education-26990735 (accessed 23 September 2014).

15 William Stewart, 'New Ofsted Chief Fires Warning Shots', *TES Magazine*, 2 December 2011. Available online at www.tes.co.uk/article.aspx?storycode=6145814 (accessed 23 September 2014).

3

WHAT IS A PHYSICAL EDUCATION TEACHER?

As a teenager, I wanted to play football, that's what I saw on TV. Watching my favourite team week in, week out. And I just wanted to be like them. I was good at running but I wasn't as good at controlling the ball. So thanks to the support of my PE teacher Alan Watkinson...I got into running...if it wasn't for him I don't think I would be running.

Mo Farah, Team GB gold Medallist 5000 m and 10,000 m,
London 2012 Olympic Games[1]

When legendary BBC commentator Bill McLaren, known as the voice of rugby union, passed away in January 2010, I read his obituary. I discovered that he studied physical education in Aberdeen and taught physical education in different schools in Scotland between 1959 and 1987. Many of the deserving tributes to him referred to his teaching career and his compassionate and inclusive approach to teaching physical education. On television, he had a 'knack' of explaining things using phrases that sparked the imagination. Combined together, his teaching and commentating skills, together with his dulcet Scottish tones, made him an effective communicator to both children and adults. I also discovered that the BBC track and field athletics commentator Ron Pickering also studied for a diploma in physical education at Carnegie College of Physical Education in Leeds and then a Master's degree in education at Leicester University. He then became a teacher of physical education at Stratford Grammar School and then Wanstead County High School. I can recall the way in which he described the last 50 metres of a race. It was difficult not to get enthused by his passion and excitement as the event reached its climax. It was quite simply infectious.

If Bill McLaren was the voice of rugby union and the late Ron Pickering was the voice of athletics then the late David Coleman was the voice of BBC sport. Coleman's ability to describe and explain any sporting context made the viewer sit on the edge of their seat and listen intently to the events as they unfolded on their television screens at home. His life has since been celebrated in a 2014 BBC documentary film that paid tribute to his contribution to British sport. Like the many sporting advocates of my generation, McLaren, Pickering and Coleman inspired me to play sport, listen to sport, watch sport, study sport, understand sport and eventually teach sport. They had the qualities that form the genetic make-up and DNA of a physical education teacher. This chapter attempts to define exactly what is a physical education teacher, which is not an easy task, even for someone who has been in the profession for 30 years. The task is made even more difficult as physical education teachers increasingly work in a landscape of consortia, free schools, academies and denationalised curricula, where the outsourcing of the subject to corporate coaching and sport industries or health providers is fast becoming the norm (Evans 2014: 319).

To some, the professional identity of a physical education teacher is synonymous with that of a sports coach, where performance-related outcomes and marginal gains matter a lot. For others, there are distinct differences between being a sports coach and being a physical educator. Branson (2014), for example, believes that while a sports coach can undoubtedly develop skills, a physical education teacher is the facilitator in physically educating future generations of children and young people. Being physically educated rather than being physically active is what counts. Being able to play sport is simply not enough. Understanding the concepts, theories and benefits of being physically educated is what matters. According to Green (2008: 19), many physical education teachers believe that sport, and especially team sport, has a worthy place in the secondary school curriculum as a valued cultural practice and lies at the heart of many physical education teachers' views about their subject and their habitual preferences. Ward (2014: 570) has shown that the socialisation of physical education teachers is dominated by competitive sporting discourses, often resulting in them teaching through performance-based coaching models. Alternatives to this are subordinated by notions of excellence in sport performance enthusiastically endorsed by politicians. Moreover, sporting practices, under the banner of physical education, have resulted in physical education teachers suffering from an identity crisis born out of its relationship with sport (Ward 2014: 571). To others, being a physical education teacher is about being an educator of children through the medium of physical activity (Capel and Whitehead 2010). Such extremes of views have led me to ask a number of questions of myself. Who am I? What am I? Why am I? During my career, my professional identity has undergone somewhat of a tug-of-war and has been pulled from pillar to post. As such, I have constantly tried to gain deeper and more profound insights into how and why I teach and how and what pupils learn. So, who did I actually teach when I was physical education teacher? Certainly not a class of 30 talented athletes every time I entered the gymnasium. I did teach some talented athletes but I also taught pupils who actively hated taking part in physical education lessons. Many of the pupils I taught were either participants who actively enjoyed physical education lessons, passengers who came along for the ride and went through the motions, prisoners who would rather not be there but did as they were told or protesters who did not want to be there and would do anything to avoid taking part. In addition, I taught pupils with additional learning needs such as physical impairments, behavioural, social and emotional difficulties or language and communication difficulties. In mainstream schools, the chances are that a physical education teacher will have to plan to differentiate the learning in accordance with one or more of those needs. That is why in my role as a teacher educator I have tried to ensure that a focus on adaptive and inclusive physical activity is an integral part of university-led initial teacher training.[2]

David Brown defines the professional journey of becoming a teacher as one that has political origins, which in many ways is equivalent to gaining a driving licence in that a series of lessons leads to a test and a licence is issued.

> Becoming a teacher is when the teacher becomes 'qualified'. 'Qualified' is taken to mean certified by the state that they are 'legitimate'. In short, the student teachers have the legitimate knowledge and skills to become teachers and pass on the kinds of knowledge the state deems appropriate.
>
> *Brown (2005: 15)*

Rather like learning to drive a car, the qualified teacher only begins to learn how to teach once they have 'qualified' and are left on their own. There are, however, some who believe that merely being an expert in a subject automatically qualifies them to teach without any formal training. This may be a moot point; some have recognised teaching as a profession but not in the same sense as a medical doctor, dentist or veterinary surgeon. Rather than being viewed as impersonal civil servants with formal qualifications, teaching has been likened to parenting. Great teachers are seen to be forged because they pick it up as they go along, akin to being a parent, and do not need a university certificate to do so.[3] This has become a topical issue for political satire since the introduction of free schools and academies[4] by the UK Coalition Government in 2010, with respect to the numbers of teachers without formal teaching qualifications. Ros Asquith's cartoon depicting a parent and child being spoken to by the child's head teacher sums it all up in terms of the irony: 'He failed. No worries. Not having any qualifications never did me any harm'.[5] Even Ofsted's Chief Inspector of Schools agreed that head teachers should be allowed to have 'untrained' staff if they believed they were the right candidate, a practice that he admitted to during his time as a head teacher in an East London comprehensive school.[6] During a television debate on the BBC political affairs programme, 'Question Time', on 24 October 2013, Tim Farron, Liberal Democrat Member of Parliament for Westmorland and Lonsdale, recognised the importance of being qualified as a teacher but also suggested that it was acceptable to have unqualified teachers in free schools, as many of these teachers were experts in their fields. He suggested that Luis Suarez (the Liverpool footballer suspended for biting Chelsea defender Branislav Ivanovic in April 2013) could teach physical education in schools on the basis of his ability to play football at the highest level.

> I agree with the proposals and policies of this government in terms of the decisions to give teachers and Head Teachers more freedom and autonomy that is absolutely right, and he's absolutely right to use experts in the classroom, to bring them in. Use Lord Sugar to talk about business on a one-off occasion. Now, for your PE lessons bring in Luis Suarez, just don't let him teach a course in citizenship.[7]

While Mr Farron's comment may have been flippant, even tongue-in-cheek, this suggestion about a multi-million pound footballer found guilty of committing an act of violence that would have carried a custodial sentence had it been committed off the field merely served to reinforce the marginal status that physical education had within the curriculum. Suarez received a ten-match ban and went on to receive the Professional Footballers Association's player of the year award and the Football Writers Player of the Year award for 2014 just one year later. Then, incredibly, on 24 June 2014 during a World Cup game against Italy, Suarez committed an identical act of violence against Italian defender Giorgio Chiellini and was banned from taking any further part in the competition. Shortly afterwards, reports emerged of a seven-year-old pupil who was facing expulsion from his primary school for biting a classmates wrist during a playground game of football.[8] Whatever next? Disgraced Newcastle United football team manager, Alan Pardew[9] as a future curriculum leader of physical education in a department consisting of Joey Barton,[10] Nicholas Anelka,[11] Marlon King,[12] Lee Bowyer,[13] Malkie Mackay,[14] Richard Scudamore[15] and Ben Flower?[16] Now there's a thought!

I began my teaching career in 1986, at a secondary school that was adjacent to a very large council estate where over 50 per cent of the pupils were entitled to free school meals.[17] One of many things I remember from my university training was that children from lower socio-economic backgrounds were less likely to participate in physical education and out-of-hours sport. I was going to prove that wrong and do something about it. During my career, however, I have reluctantly accepted that the importance of young people participating in physical activity is not always recognised, given the relatively low and marginal status with which physical education has historically been characterised by at all levels of the UK education system (Green 2008: 218). McCullick *et al.* (2003) showed that the US public perception of physical education teachers is that they are less intelligent than other teachers and are lightly regarded in contemporary society. Indeed, the marginality of physical education in relation to more academic school subjects often leads to a feeling of isolation among physical education teachers (Green 2008: 80). One thing I have learned is that to successfully negotiate a career in the physical education profession, teachers need to be adept in addressing a myriad of contextual workplace, status and support issues (Armour and Jones 1998: 123). UK Secretary of State for Education Michael Gove's reference to subjects such as physical education (among others) as 'soft' subjects,[18] reinforced the view that seemingly non-serious subjects such as physical education are likely to be viewed by governments and schools as expendable in favour of more academic and examinable subjects (Green 2008: 60) reinforcing the perception of physical education as a practical subject and teaching as a technical process. Mr Gove's comments did the physical education profession very few favours in raising its academic standing as an examination subject. Matters were made worse on 4 June 2014, when the UK government announced a major shake-up of the examination system in secondary schools and colleges which included the scrapping of performing arts after the age of 14,[19] causing the head teachers leader Brian Lightman to comment that 'we need to finally let go of this toxic discourse about "soft" and "rigorous" subjects'.[20] For a number of years I had to convince my colleagues in schools that General Certificate of Secondary Education (GCSE) examination physical education, for example, was actually worth the paper it was written on and still have the same enduring debate with trainee physical education teachers.

The fact that low professional status, lack of recognition and the educational downgrading of practical physical education has been (and still is) an accepted part of many physical education teachers' lives (Armour and Jones 1998) is perhaps a reflection of its position in contemporary education. And yet, physical education teachers themselves have been complicit in the low status afforded to their subject, insofar as they have perceived physical education to be less serious and a release from the academic aspects of formal schooling (Green 2003: 61). While things have moved on since Armour and Jones (1998) carried out their fieldwork, the fact remains that physical education teachers are still seen as good disciplinarians and good with kids in the eyes of other teachers but not valued for anything else. The image of the physical education teacher portrayed by one teacher in Armour and Jones's study as an 'old phys edder, sweaty jock type' may still be true in the minds of some teachers. In US popular culture, the embedded stereotype of the physical education teacher as a 'dumb jock' continues to be perpetuated (McCullick et al. 2003). Other subject teachers may perceive physical education teachers as 'punching above their weight' in the world of academia: physical – yes; education – no! During my career as a secondary school physical education teacher, senior pupils would frequently approach me and ask for permission to be excused from non-accredited or 'core' physical education lessons as other subject teachers had suggested that the time would be better spent revising for their forthcoming public examinations. Pupil participation rates in 'core' physical education lessons were low. Many would bring excuse notes, forget to bring kit or simply not show up. This was perhaps indicative of the way in which parents, pupils and teachers perceived the subject and accounts for the reasons why pupils excuse themselves so often from physical education lessons (Lamb 2014). I would often sit at formal parent evenings twiddling my thumbs in the hope that I might actually meet and speak to one of my year 10 or 11 pupils' parents about their child's progress in physical education. There was the odd sarcastic comment from other subject teachers that physical education teachers did not have the marking that other subjects had and that there was no academic rigour in what they did. Other members of staff would tease me by asking why the physical education department stopped teaching pupils after the age of 14. The title of Gary Boothroyd's (2004) book and his account of 27 years of teaching physical education in an inner-city comprehensive school in Birmingham perhaps says it all – *Are You Are Proper Teacher, Sir?*

The lack of status afforded to physical education compared with other curriculum subjects is partly self-inflicted by physical education teachers. I have realised that some physical education teachers may have been their own worst enemies, in that they have continued to promote the delivery of activity choice or 'option' physical education otherwise known as 'core' physical education for upper-school pupils. Quite often, physical education teachers justify the place of non-accredited physical education for pupils in years 10 and 11 as it provides pupils with a break from the serious work of education, giving the impression that cognitive functions are not used in physical education (Capel and Whitehead 2013). What physical education teachers have tried to achieve in keeping the subject in a very overcrowded curriculum has actually had the opposite effect, as the time devoted to physical education can be as little as 60 minutes a week (Ofsted 2009). Kirk (2013; 228) confirms that while physical education teachers have themselves recognised that the subject does not deliver the benefits it aspires to, there has been little taste for radical reform among them, leaving the middle- to longer-term future of the subject looking bleak and in crisis. Within core physical education lessons, there has always been a tendency for schools to staff these lessons with non-specialist teachers, who turn up without appropriate clothing or footwear, usually carrying a single ball of some description and a whistle ready to stand on the touchline and bark instructions to the pupils. This has always been an enduring issue in physical education, even when I was at university, and I ask myself today whether I would be satisfied for my own children to be taught physical education, or any other subject for that matter, by a teacher who had not been trained to teach the subject, as is sometimes the case. Armour and Jones (1998: 96) believe that the problem lies in the physical education profession saying the 'right things' but 'doing the wrong things' and that, in a nutshell, is the profession's crime.

Despite different approaches to show that physical education is more than 'mere' sport, some physical education teachers have never taken the next step and distanced themselves from the academic nature of their work. They have been the silent majority. Without putting too fine a point on it, I have always felt that physical education teachers were signing their own death warrants by retaining 'core' non-examinable physical education and responsible for the low status often associated with it as a secondary school curriculum subject. In other words, the low status was self-inflicted by physical education teachers themselves, who were 'digging their own graves' by keeping recreational-types of activity on the curriculum in the senior years of secondary school. Some physical education teachers have tried to convince me that when taught well, 'core' physical education lessons are as educational as accredited courses in physical education. While that may be true in some cases, based on my observations and discussions with trainee teachers after returning from periods of school-based training, I do not believe that this is always the case. On one occasion, while trying to arrange a visit to a school to observe a trainee physical education teacher, I was told not to come in on Tuesday afternoons as it was 'only' year 10 core physical education lessons. The situation today is vastly different, as there has been a groundswell of interest among physical education teachers in introducing more forms of accredited physical education to pupils after the age of 14. It has been difficult to ignore the rapid growth of accredited physical education courses and it is testament to the increasing popularity of this type of approach to the teaching to pupils aged 14 to 18, where learning 'about' rather than learning to do has become increasingly more important for teachers. In 2012, 16 per cent of all final-year pupils were entered for the GCSE for physical education with 71 per cent of entrants achieving a grade A★–C (Department for Education 2013b). Green (2008: 54) acknowledges that the advent of an educational marketplace has substantially increased the pressure of time for non-examinable subjects. At best, the physical education profession can hope for a stabilisation of the time allocated for physical education. At worst, the time could disappear altogether. By retaining 'core' physical education, is it simply a better use of the time available to educate pupils about physical education? Like Green (2008: 54), I have always believed that one of the more realistic avenues open to physical education teachers seeking to increase the time allocation for physical education lies in the 'academicisation' of the subject'; that is, increasing the number of academic and vocational qualifications offered through physical education to pupils after the age of 14.

In the foreword to this book, Professor John Sugden highlighted his own experiences of physical education teacher training in Liverpool in the 1970s and described his namesake, Mr Sugden, played by the late Brian Glover in the iconic 1969 film, *Kes*. This brought back memories of the novel *A Kestrel for a Knave* written by Barry Hines (1968), from which the film was adapted and which was a core reading text in my English literature lessons when I was at secondary school. Based on his own observations, it would seem that the film's director, Ken Loach, was not too far from the truth in portraying the standard physical education teacher of the time. One particular scene, used extensively by teacher educators, shows Mr Sugden proudly leading his boys out to the field, appointing himself as one of the captains, taking it in turns to pick individual pupils, stripping off into his Manchester United kit, refereeing the game while playing and awarding himself and scoring a penalty. The public perception of physical education teachers is often magnified, reinforced, even exaggerated by portrayals of bullying male physical education teachers such as Mr Sugden teaching appalling lessons. Brian Conley's depiction of the fictional physical education teacher Dynamo Doug Digby in the 1990s nostalgic comedy-drama *The Grimleys*,[21] written by Jed Mercurio, is a sad indictment of the media perception of male physical education teachers as aggressive, cruel and vicious, but perhaps there is no smoke without fire. After all, it is claimed that physical education teachers internalise attitudes, behaviours and customs which make up the subculture of physical education (Green 2008). These are passed on from generation to generation, where certain attitudes and practices become part and parcel of physical education teacher's personalities or second nature (Green 2008: 208). It is, in effect, a self-perpetuating cycle whereby aspiring physical education teachers enter their training and the profession with philosophies that are heavily influenced and dominated by sport and fitness ideologies based upon their own experiences of physical education (Cale and Alfrey 2013). There can be no excuses, however, for the types of practices that simply humiliate young people prompting them to post their feelings through online blogs:

> In PE, we had a football lesson where we had to get the ball, hold it, THEN kick it; it was pouring down with rain that day so it was hard to hear the teacher, so I just got the ball and kicked it back to the person. Then, he started YELLING at me and said I had to HOLD the ball. He treats me like I'm stupid and then in cricket he said 'am I teaching special needs cricket?' he then yelled at me saying 'IS THAT BAT TOO HEAVY FOR YOU?' and called me an idiot. I don't think my Headteacher knows about this. I'm in the UK by the way.[22]

Most alarming is the characterisation of male physical education teachers as chauvinistic, sadistic, control freaks who have failed to achieve sporting excellence themselves, which was highlighted in one episode of *The Grimleys*, when English teacher Miss Titley (played by actress Amanda Holden) retorts to Dynamo Doug Digby: 'Has it ever occurred to you that teaching PE is the most suitable job in the world for you? Think about it, Doug. You love sport, you're academically inept and you're a sadist'.[23]

Even the way in which (male) physical education teachers are portrayed on British children's television reveals the stereotype that broadcasters want children to see. The infamous Mr 'Bullet' Baxter played by actor Michael Cronin in the BBC's 1970s and 1980s children's series *Grange Hill*, written by Phil Redmond, epitomised the way in which children viewed their physical education teachers at that time. He was the only teacher in the school who could end a reign of terror and he eventually became the deputy head teacher. When Mr Robson, played by Stuart Organ, arrived as Grange Hill's new physical education teacher, he was the complete antithesis to 'Bullet Baxter', having a philosophy that sport should be about taking part not winning. His caring attitude helped him to build a good relationship with pupils and he became Grange Hill's seventh head teacher in 1998. His role as head of physical education was taken over by the terrifying ex-military Welsh physical education teacher Mr Dai 'Hard' Jones, played by Clive Hill, who had a novel way of encouraging basketball accuracy – he would answer questions about his bodyguard career to those who scored a free shot at the basket. Many of these perceptions continue to be exacerbated by other portrayals of the stereo-typical male physical education teacher, such as the character Trevor Gunn, played by actor Philip Glenister, in the 2013 BBC situation comedy, *Big School*. He describes the character he plays as 'a dysfunctional, unfit, lothario physical education teacher who is quite grotesque'. In one episode, Trevor Gunn exclaims that physical education is one of the hardest degrees to do, having covered modules on learning how to pump up a football and how to blow a whistle. Glenister's own recollections of his school physical education teachers provided him with material in order to develop his character for television:

Question: Any memories of your time at school that has helped flesh out the character?

Answer: You know PE teachers were always fairly sadistic creatures, although they weren't at my school from what I remember. They were always quite good blokes. We used to get caught round the back of the mobiles having a sneaky fag and rather than confiscating our cigarettes off us our PE teacher used to give us money for them, then confiscate them. So it was quite a good deal.[24]

Studies of how physical education teachers are portrayed by the movie industry and Hollywood screenwriters, in particular, have shown that they are represented as incompetent teachers. In a study of 18 cinematic images of physical educators by McCullick *et al.* (2003), there were repeated inferences that physical education teachers and athletic coaches were the same as each other. Male and female physical education teachers are frequently type-cast and seen as 'butches, bullies and buffoons'. Often, physical education teachers were portrayed as brutal drill sergeants, heartless taskmasters and the proverbial 'bully from hell' who enjoy seeing pupils humiliated (McCullick *et al.* 2003). This is exactly the way that director Craig Gillespie chose to cast Billy Bob Thornton in his role as a sadistic, no-nonsense gym teacher in the 2007 movie *Mr Woodcock*. Readers may wish to view the trailer to the film to realise exactly the way in which the media enjoy portraying the physical education teachers' personae. McCullick *et al.* (2003) also found that characterisations of physical education teachers are highly gendered, with female physical education teachers portrayed as butch and lesbian while male physical education teachers are devoid of any masculine leadership qualities. Sue Sylvester, played by actress Jane Lynch in the American comedy-drama *Glee*,[25] is the epitome of how television producers wish the general public to see those that teach in schools and specifically in sport. Flintoff *et al.* (2008) suggest that the centrality of the body and the link to the perceived low status of the subject are influencing factors in perpetuating stereotyped attitudes and images of physical education teachers' identities. The bottom line is that school administrators in general could hardly be blamed for voting for the elimination of physical education as a curriculum subject after viewing these cinematic depictions of physical educators. Films such as those studied could seriously devalue physical education teaching as a career and seriously affect recruitment of physical education teachers (McCullick et.al: 14). Unlike the portrayal of Dynamo Doug Digby and his own assertion that he was 'born to teach PE', that his pupils were 'weak and worthless' and that the abbreviation 'PE' stands for 'punishment exercise', the modern-day physical education teacher has an array of skills that go a long way towards challenging that perception. Being a physical education teacher today is a far cry from the days of Dynamo Doug Digby and Trevor Gunn. It is and should be a profession to be proud of, despite the views that some non-specialist physical education teachers in the profession still have:

> I'm doing my A-levels at the moment – PE, biology, English and psychology. I have to drop one subject this year and carry on the rest. I chose to drop English and when my English teacher asked why, I explained that I am not enjoying the course. She then asked me what I want to be when I'm older and I said 'a PE teacher', and she glared at me and said 'that explains all . . .', and then walked away!!!!!!!!!!![26]

What saddens me more is the way in which journalists recall their own secondary school physical education lessons with deep disdain and the way in which their physical education teachers simply provided them with an escape route to either go through the motions or opt out completely from their physical education lessons. In the wake of the controversy about girls' low participation rates in sport caused by the Sports and Equalities Minister Helen Grant, Rachel Cooke wrote in the *Sunday Observer*:

> Physical education lessons meanwhile became a convoluted exercise in avoidance. The slothfulness soon spread among the girls like a contagion. Cross-country runs began with a truculent jog until we were out of sight of the teachers, at which point we would repair at the nearest newsagents for sweets and fags. Rounders involved making sure your team was out as soon as possible, the better that you might field and get to sunbathe and gossip in the long grass. Athletics meant hiding in the loos until it was 'too late to change, Miss'.[27]

It is also concerning to know that physical education teachers can make pupils withdraw from physical education lessons as described by journalist, Phoebe Doyle:

> When I was at school I hated PE. Dreaded it. Not only that, I thought I was rubbish at it, in fact I was rubbish at it. I was the one running away from the hockey ball (they're hard those balls, y'know). Once I'd tired from the years of humiliation from being last to be picked, I took to bringing letters (a combination of fake and real) getting me out of it. I had all manner of ailments and injuries which rendered me too poorly for PE yet remarkably sparky in English and history. I'd sit on the field with the other twice-weekly rebels; we'd talk about boys and doodle on our class books about who we loved 4eva that week – it wasn't physical, or educational. It was at best passing the time, and at worse learning that exercise just wasn't for us. I remember cross-country too. A regime seemingly invented purely to put us off ever wanting to run. We'd do it January, we'd don our PE pants and aertex tops

and off we'd go – no stretching, no training – just straight out for a three mile run/jog/walk/smoke around our local town as an act of sheer humiliation. On return the fast boys who'd win effortlessly would be lined up at the finish line waiting to laugh at us as we ran in.[28]

On 21 May 2014, the *Independent* newspaper reported the findings of the Virgin Active research[29] which showed that more than one-third of 8–16-year-old girls avoided playing competitive sport because they felt self-conscious and embarrassed while taking part. Even more disconcerting was that 39 per cent of 16-year-old girls said that they never undertook any strenuous activity while at secondary school. These are not groundbreaking findings but the research asks a serious question about the state of affairs within secondary school physical education. As my career has developed, I have become increasingly concerned by the numbers of pupils who are put off physical education because of an underlying belief that 'physical education' is synonymous with 'sport' or who avoid taking part because of a perception that it is not a real subject. This is hardly remarkable, given that pupils do not recognise the educational purpose and view physical education in recreational and less serious terms (Green 2008: 20). In other words, physical education does not do exactly what it says on the tin. This is particularly true at independent fee-paying schools, where 'pupils just do sport' (Chappell 2013: 39). Ofsted (2014) argued that state-funded schools can learn a lesson or two from the way in which the public (private) schools teach and organise sport while other have suggested that state schools should adopt a model similar to the way in which sport is organised in private schools as if it as some sort of miracle cure to a terminal illness.[30] Indeed, there is a suspicion among some researchers that the recruitment of sports coaches rather than qualified teachers (similar to many English private schools) may become the sole or main providers of school sport (Green 2008), particularly in the new academies and free schools set up by the UK Coalition Government since 2010. The privatisation of physical education as a public limited company (Evans 2014) has led me to question whether the UK Coalition Government's intentions meant that I should be training sports coaches rather than specialist teachers of physical education. After all, it is widely accepted by academics and researchers (Brown 2005; Green 2008), albeit demoralising for teacher trainers, that by the time many teachers reach the training stage they have become so accustomed to associating physical education primarily with 'sport' that is difficult for teacher educators to teach 'old dogs new tricks'. In this respect, sport clings to the trainee physical education teacher whereas physical education falls away. Was I being asked to condone the type of practice where physical education lessons were just an arena for the selection of school teams or representation at the annual school sports day, swimming gala or inter-school sport competitions? My role was and is to train physical education teachers who are capable of developing physically literate pupils through meaningful and purposeful physical activities, not to train sports coaches whose sole purpose is to integrate elite pupils into competitive sports programmes. Was physical education simply being used as a guise for promoting elitist competitive school sport? Would an overemphasis on sex-stereotyped team games leave the vast majority of pupils in secondary schools disillusioned and disaffected? As such this posed other vexed questions with regards to the content of the physical education curriculum and the educational rationale behind decisions made by teachers on behalf of their pupils.

Green's (2003) recollection of his own schooldays perhaps epitomises the experiences that most pupils either recall or are currently encountering in that physical education in practice is quite removed from physical education in theory. For Green, physical education was about doing sport, playing sport rather than understanding sport (Green 2003: ix). Like Green, this has led me to question what the expectations of physical teachers are, how do they think and justify what they do and why they teach in they way that they teach. Is it also the case in other subject areas such as art, music, dance and drama that pupils merely do and play rather than understand? Laker (2002:5) has observed that a commonly held perception is that physical education means playing games which unfortunately is the prevalent interpretation of the school subject. Keech (2012b: 177) asks the questions: What is school sport about? Why sport and not physical education? Why do we want to encourage participation? What is the role of schools, our physical education teachers and their partners in provision? His response is that the purpose of school sport has been to expand a broader experience not only of sports themselves but of physical activities associated with health and physical literacy. Researchers (Green 2003; Capel and Whitehead 2013, for example), have consistently highlighted the misnomer between physical education and sport. For example, there are some physical education teachers who bask in the reflected glory that a bulging trophy cabinet brings without thinking twice about the role school sport plays in the development of a well-rounded approach to education. Schools, and particularly head teachers, have been urged to support the education of parents and others in that a successful school sport programme is one which engages all pupils in a full range of sports and activities. Cups, medals and records have been the operative words put into the mouths of head teachers but a full trophy cabinet does not equate to success if a high percentage of pupils drop out at 16 (Marchant 2013: 42). This contradicts the widely held view of physical education professionals who have consistently referred to the holistic development of the whole child through the medium of physical activity (Green 2008: 17).

Physical education teachers have worked hard to shed the sports label that has long been associated with the profession. More schools, for example, are prepared to diversify their physical education curriculum to include activities such as kinball, double-dutch skipping, cheerleading and the physical education teacher's trump card and secret weapon – street surfing (Stidder and Binney 2011). Having said that, my observations would also suggest that in secondary schools coaching sport remains a priority for some physical education teachers where the success of their school teams is often used as a measure of how successful a physical education department is within the school and the wider community. But Armour and Jones (1998) warned us that the professional socialisation of physical education teachers via sport may well bring with it problematic baggage and this prediction has proven to be true. This level of ambiguity has continued as my own career has evolved. On the one hand, physical education teachers claim that their subject specialism promotes healthy active lifestyles and, on the other hand, they claim that pupils' achievements in competitive representative team sports are the best way to achieve and quantify this. Pupils are confronted with many mixed messages – do I play sport to get fit or do I get fit to play sport? In this sense, boundaries have been blurred, corners have been rounded and rules have been bent. Even for the most ardent and committed of all physical educationalists, competitive school sport may still be seen as a type of elasticated 'tripwire' that may be tentatively crossed to an extent but without selling the core, fundamental values that underpin the teaching and learning of physical education. At their best, physical education lessons are inclusive forums where all pupils can succeed in a broad range of physical activities irrespective of what they are or who they are. At their worst, physical education lessons are time trials for the school's track and field team and a selection process for the identification of the most able and elite performers. Who can run the fastest? Who can throw the furthest? Who can jump the highest? Over the years, nothing much has changed. It took me a while to reach the conclusion that providing pupils with opportunities to achieve and record their personal best times or distances through a range of Olympic-style adult events as portrayed on television was not the best way to teach pupils. The reality of this type of approach was that the lessons were often teacher-centred, usually delivered in a very formal command style. This often resulted in pupils standing in long queues waiting their turn and having as little as three attempts to run, jump or throw in a one hour lesson. Pupils would also be taught the same sprinting, javelin or long-jump lesson, for example, each summer during the first three years of secondary school. It was not uncommon to hear pupils say 'Sir, we did this last year'.

Physical education and school sport have been, and continue to be, kicked about like a political football despite the Education Select Committee's promise of 'no more political football', published in October 2013 and their recommendations to government:

> The balance of evidence to our inquiry supports the view that competition in school sport deters some young people from participating in sport and physical activity. We therefore recommend that the Department for Education makes clear to all schools that they must offer both competitive and non-competitive sporting opportunities to their pupils.
>
> *(Education Select Committee 2013, para 30)*

Just eight months later, Ofsted (2014: 9) recommended that all maintained schools and academies should 'embed competitive school sport firmly in the school culture and ethos and make it a central part of school life'. Despite the tireless efforts of teacher educators in higher education institutes, it seems that physical education initial teacher training has very little impact on the largely established beliefs of policy makers who may have very fixed views of physical education when they were pupils at school. So, physical education teachers have been, and are being, led to believe that their ability is not to be judged on their achievements inside the formal physical education curriculum but more on the accolades and trophies won on the sports field. Rather than celebrating the success of the grades achieved by pupils in formal public examinations in physical education or public exhibitions of pupils work in curriculum time, physical education teachers promote themselves through the announcement of the results of *their* school teams in school assemblies, newsletters, local newspapers or in glossy school brochures. They proudly display silver sports trophies in polished glass cabinets as the centrepiece of the school's main reception area, reminiscent of the halcyon days of physical education before the teacher's strikes in the 1980s. Physical education teachers compete for overall bragging rights over other schools in their local communities, reinforcing the fact that a structural feature of networks such as physical education teachers is competitive rivalry (Green 2008: 28). That is not to deny the place or value of sport in schools but, at the same time, sport creates a perception that it is the sole purpose of physical education teachers to produce successful teams. I have noticed, for example, that secondary schools are often defined as either 'rugby-playing', or 'football-playing' schools and become synonymous within local community folklore, where physical education is often overlooked at the expense of the achievements of school sports teams. Some pupils become strangers in their own land – a footballer in a rugby playing school, as depicted by John Evans:

> To play soccer was to go looking for trouble, to court instant ignominy and invite the status of deviant. It was, especially if one had the ability to play The Game (Rugby Union), a denial of ones' duties, a betrayal of one's school, friends, community and country. After all it was The Game that celebrated our school's and county's status, that demarcated the boundaries and announced the qualities of our subculture and our precise class position. It was The Game that would help us mingle with the posh and the proletariat, that told us we were the 'tidier' (the more respectable) *within* our working class.
>
> *(Evans and Bairner 2012: 145)*

You might be forgiven for thinking that contemporary physical education has moved on and come a long way since the days of John Evans' mining valley grammar school in South Wales. And yet, you may wish to think again as physical education and school sport is still a symbolic representation of gender and social class, as confirmed by Alan Bairner's superlative account of his own schooldays in Scotland (Evans and Bairner 2012), where six lashes across the palm was the standard punishment for any boy who dared to play football in the playground.

In an area traditionally renowned for producing talented footballers, including John Thomson and George Connelly of Celtic and Scotland and

Jim Baxter of Rangers and Scotland, to name but three, boys at our school were denied the opportunity to play our favourite game. Instead we learned to play rugby union. Even at the time, it was obvious to us that this was part of a wider agenda to enhance our social standing. But this project backfired spectacularly when we visited Edinburgh's merchant schools (George Heriot's, George Watson's, Daniel Stewart's) and saw what real middle-class education looked like. More sobering still was the realisation that often they would ask their second fifteen to play our firsts and so on down the fixture list. In rugby, as in life, we were beneath them. Even further above us were the really posh schools such as Edinburgh Academy, Tony Blair's *alma mater* Fettes College, and Glenalmond in Perthshire against whom we were not even allowed to play.

(*Evans and Bairner 2012: 146*)

In many cases, the types of team games that pupils play at school and subsequently into adulthood reflect and confirm not only the expectations of their gender development but also their socioeconomic status. This is reflected at the top end of elite sport by the disproportionate numbers of privately educated pupils who go on to represent national teams and achieve international sporting success (Tozer 2013), albeit in predominantly the sitting-down sports of rowing, cycling, sailing, rifle shooting and equestrian events. While only 7 per cent of all school-aged children are privately educated, more than one-third excel in elite international sport, rising to 50 per cent if association football is excluded (Ofsted 2014). Evans and Bairner (2012: 145) concluded that achieving Olympic success may seem infinitely more accessible when viewed from Wellington College's 400 acres of English countryside (an independent school in Berkshire, England, where the annual fees are £30,000 a year in a country where the average working wage is £25,000 a year). Rather than being more naturally gifted, inherently and genetically better endowed with academic and sporting talent, pupils attending independent fee-paying schools are just better equipped than the rest of the population by virtue of their upbringing in relatively richly resourced families and schools, which brings access to resources (knowledge, skills, values, opportunities). The result is that recognition and success in education and sport is simply more achievable. Chappell (2014) reaffirmed this in his small-scale case study of independent and state school physical education and concluded that physical education and sport in independent fee-paying schools is simply better resourced in terms of staffing, facilities, finance, time and status. As Chappell states: 'The problem lies in the fact that in independent schools sport is part of the school day in which staff are expected to contribute whereas in the state-sector it is optional and very few staff are willing to contribute' (Chappell 2014: 58).

The same could also be said of the selective single-sex grammar schools[31] introduced after the Second World War for children deemed to have innate intelligence at the end of their primary schooling. As a result of the 1944 Education Act, 11-year-old children were effectively creamed off on the basis of a one-off examination and life-changing judgements were made which had far-reaching implications and ramifications for the physical education and school sport I had experienced as a child. In this respect, Evans and Davies (1986) noted that 'physical education conditions and re-conditions class, culture and power structures. The price which has to be paid by many for their meagre receipt of knowledge is the heavy cost of knowing more sharply one's lowly place' (cited in Evans and Davies 2002: 20).

My experiences at the secondary comprehensive school I attended were indicative of the way in which physical education was used to socially engineer children, as we tended to be taught the value of purposeful exercise through certain team games considered to be suitable for our position within the education system. Meanwhile, boys at the single-sex grammar school were being educated through games that emphasised strategic thinking and complex movements that would prepare them for their future leadership roles in society. Just as the elite independent fee-paying schools were preparing their pupils to become the future 'captains of industry', so the grammar schools were preparing their pupils to become their 'vice-captains'. Pupils attending state-funded schools were being prepared as 'factory fodder' and would have to remain on the sidelines and compete for the remaining positions in society. I am now more acutely aware that being middle class offers massive advantages if your goal is either to achieve health longevity or to perform in top level sport (Evans and Bairner 2012: 144). In other words, if I want my son or daughter to play test-match cricket or international rugby union then I had better pick their independent school very carefully. Perhaps there was an element of truth after all, when Secretary of State for Education, Michael Gove, publically acclaimed to the Commons Education Select Committee two years before the start of the London 2012 Olympic Games that 'Rich thick kids will always do better than clever poor ones'[32] – a phrase that I have often cited to a number of head teachers, who have retorted through gritted teeth, that, unfortunately, he is right. When viewed in these terms, physical education and sport might just be seen as a commodity to be traded on the open market.

Becoming and being a physical education teacher then, is not necessarily what the general public might expect, even though Alan Tomlinson's description of his own physical education teacher may exacerbate many of the images that many people have:

> One of the legendary PE teachers of my grammar school days was known for two things. Not the sophistication of his lesson plans. Not even his smile as he forced boys to heave themselves up the rope to the roof of the gym, thighs reddening on each tortuous pull. He was a minor celebrity, as son of the local Member of Parliament. And he was sunburnt every summer term, stripped down to his shorts for much of the day and lazing on the edge of the playing field.
>
> *(Tomlinson and Allison 2012: xvi)*

The role of the physical education teacher, however, has changed significantly and the repertoire of skills now required is very different compared to the 1980s when I taught physical education in schools. Nonetheless, Allison's recollections of his own schooldays in post-war Lancashire is perhaps the epitome of what some may think of physical education in schools and how the curriculum was arranged:

> When you are young you take on board the existing social arrangements and work with them, only later realising how bizarre they were; there is a kind of social osmosis that tells you that whatever is, must be. PT was 'physical training'; during my time it changed to PE – 'physical education', though we didn't notice any change in content. OG was 'organised games', primarily cricket and rugby. It was what gave meaning and purpose to life. We played games more or less all the time whereas PT was an irksome chore which occurred twice a week. The idea that they could be merged and called 'sport' or 'sports' did not occur to us.
>
> *(Tomlinson and Allison 2012: xiv)*

As you will read in other chapters of this book, Tomlinson and Allison's trips down memory lane may not be too dissimilar to the way in which contemporary physical education in some schools is delivered reflecting the current UK Coalition Government's intentions of reintroducing more 'proper' competitive team sports into the physical education curriculum. To me, the politicians had scored a political own goal by rejecting high-quality physical education in favour of an obsolete and dysfunctional model, trialled in the fifties, which had caused many to suffer injury and pain and to opt out of physical education lessons, as confirmed by Jim White's recollections of his school physical education lessons:

> Lacrosse is a game, as I recall it, that involves not much more than being whacked around the knuckles by someone wielding a wooden-framed net as if he had been a gladiator in a former existence. In a damp Mancunian winter, when the hands are raw with cold, it seemed a particularly unnecessary game.
>
> *(White 2007: 11)*

Look no further than the school physical education experiences of British comedian and actor Stephen Fry and the creative excuses he made up to get out of them:

> I do not think there has ever been a schoolboy with such overmastering contempt, fear, dread, loathing, and hatred for 'games' – for sport, exercise, gymnastics and physical exertions of all or any kinds. Every day I would wake up with a sick jolt wondering just how I might get out of that day's compulsory rugby, cricket, hockey, swimming or whatever foul healthy horror was due to be posted on the notice-board that morning. The

catalogue of multiple lies, evasions, self-imposed asthma attacks and other examples at what Edwardian school fiction characterised as 'lead-swinging', malingering and 'cutting'. All the acts of a cad, a swine, a rotter, an outsider and a beast.[33]

So what exactly is a physical education teacher? There are no shortcuts in trying to answer the question of what physical education teachers are. An understanding of the educative value of physical education is needed if teachers are to be true believers in themselves and understand their roles. For many years, I have sensed that there have been 'silent screams' within the physical education fraternity as sport has taken over the teaching and learning of physical education as if a military coup has occurred. One might ask, whose fault it is? Who is to blame? Have physical education teachers been asking for trouble without even realising it? Armour and Jones (1998) suggest that it is time to call a truce between physical education and sport because, like it or not, physical education teachers are closely identified with sport. The next chapter explains that it is fundamental misconceptions about what physical education is that has caused a number of false interpretations of what a physical education teacher is. Therefore, having a conceptual understanding about the definition of physical education is essential to becoming a physical education teacher.

Notes

1   '"Where It All Began": Mo Farah Goes Back to School', *ITV News*, 24 September 2012. Available online at www.itv.com/news/2012-09-24/mo-farah-goes-back-to-school (accessed 23 September 2014).

2   University of Brighton, School of Sport and Service Management, 'Students organise inclusive sports festival' YouTube, 24 July 2013. Available online at www.youtube.com/watch?v=ilK-VhMDnbk&list=PL9036FECA22DB89CD&index=23 (accessed 29 September 2014).

3   Anthony Seldon, 'Teaching is Like Parenting: You don't need a Qualification'. *Guardian*, 28 October 2013. www.theguardian.com/commentisfree/2013/oct/28/teaching-qualification-nick-clegg-course (accessed 23 September 2014).

4   New Schools Network, 'Free Schools – International Evidence'. Available online at www.newschoolsnetwork.org/set-up-a-free-school/resources/free-schools-international-evidence (accessed 23 September 2014).

5   Ros Asquith, 'Headteacher Quality' [cartoon], *Guardian*, 28 October 2013. Available online at www.theguardian.com/education/cartoon/2013/oct/28/headteacher-explains-qualifications-don-t-matter (accessed 23 September 2014).

6   Christopher Hope, 'Untrained Staff are Fine to Teach in Schools, Says Ofsted Chief Sir Michael Wilshaw', *Telegraph*, 8 December 2014. Available online at www.telegraph.co.uk/education/educationopinion/10504452/Untrained-staff-are-fine-to-teach-in-schools-says-Ofsted-chief-Sir-Michael-Wilshaw.html (accessed 23 September 2014).

7   David Dimbleby, Chair, debate with Conservative Education Minister Liz Truss, Labour's Shadow Energy Secretary Caroline Flint, President of the Liberal Democrats Tim Farron, author Owen Jones and *Mail on Sunday* columnist Peter Hitchens. *BBC Question Time*, 24 October 2013. Available online at www.youtube.com/watch?v=5oQZ5dHuVxg (accessed 23 September 2014).

8 Joseph Layton, 'Luis Suarez Bite: Child of Seven "expelled from primary school for copying Uruguayan striker"', *Mirror*, 28 June 2014. Available online at www.mirror.co.uk/news/uk-news/luis-suarez-bite-child-seven-3778782 (accessed 23 September 2014).

9 Newcastle United Football Club manager Alan Pardew was banned by the English Football Association in 2014 for seven games and fined £100,000 for publically head-butting David Meyler, an opposing player from Hull City, in front of 30,000 witnesses and watched by millions of television viewers. In 2012, he was also given a two-match ban for pushing an assistant referee.

10 Premier league footballer Joey Barton was jailed for assault and affray in 2008.

11 Nicolas Anelka was fired by premiership football club, West Bromwich Albion, for using an anti-Semitic and racist gesture known as a 'quenelle', best described as an inverted Nazi salute, after scoring a goal against West Ham United on 28 December 2013.

12 Former professional footballer Marlon King was convicted and jailed for dangerous driving in May 2014. He was also jailed in 2009 for sexual assault.

13 Lee Bowyer was seen on television fighting fellow Newcastle United teammate Kieran Dyer during their three–nil home defeat to Aston Villa in April 2005.

14 Former Cardiff City Football Club manager, Malkie Mackay, was accused of sending racist, sexist and homophobic text messages in August 2104.

15 Premier League Chief Executive Richard Scudamore was criticised by politicians and sports executives for inappropriate, unacceptable and deeply disappointing sexist comments about women's football in May 2014 – a criticism he accepted as 'an error of judgement'.

16 On 11 October 2014, in the first two minutes of the Rugby League showcase final at Old Trafford, Manchester, Wigan's Ben Flower committed an act of violence against opposing St Helens player Lance Hohaia in front of 70,000 spectators and a multi-million TV audience and was sent off the field of play. As a result of punching Hohaia twice, the second whilst Hohaia was on the floor, Flower received a six-month ban from the game. A similar assault off the field of play would be regarded as grievous bodily harm with intent, a crime that could result in up to eight years' imprisonment. See 'Ben Flower: Wigan prop banned for Lance Hohaia punch', BBC Sport, 14 October 2014. Available online at www.bbc.co.uk/sport/0/rugby-league/29612687 (Accessed 22 October 2014).

17 Free school meals are available to those who are eligible, from lower socioeconomic backgrounds. See www.gov.uk/apply-free-school-meals (accessed 24 September 2014).

18 Neil O'Brien, 'Michael Gove Plans to Chop Back Soft Subjects in Schools: He Could Keep Chopping', *Telegraph*, 28 October 2011. Available online at http://blogs.telegraph.co.uk/news/neilobrien1/100114146/the-end-of-soft-subject (accessed 23 September 2014).

19 Richard Adams (2014) 'Home Economics GCSE set to be scrapped', *Guardian*, 4 June 2014. Available online at www.theguardian.com/education/2014/jun/04/home-economics-gcse-scrapped-a-levels (accessed 24 September 2014).

20 Sean Coughlan, 'GCSE and A-Level Subject Range Set to be Cut Back', *BBC News*, 5 June 2014. Available online at www.bbc.co.uk/news/education-27680893 (accessed 24 September 2014).

21 *The Grimleys*, television drama series set on a council estate in Dudley, West Midlands, in the mid-1970s. First broadcast by Granada TV for ITV in 1999–2001.

22 'I Hate My PE Teacher?', *Yahoo Answers*. Available online at https://uk.answers.yahoo.com/question/index?qid=20120825143810AAQ8BUM (accessed 24 September 2014).

23 'Dynamo Digby', *YouTube*, 6 July 2012. Available online at www.youtube.com/watch?v=l4FZ4Yz2nA8 (accessed 24 September 2014).

24 BBC One, Big School, 'Interview With Philip Glenister'. Available online at www.bbc.co.uk/programmes/profiles/2ygtR1f76V0KVCRLJKrFsGy/interview-with-philip-glenister (accessed 24 September 2014).

25   *Glee* is a US musical comedy-drama television series, created by Ryan Murphy, Brad Falchuk, and Ian Brennan, aired on the Fox channel, May 2009 onwards.

26   'Is being a P.E teacher a crap job?', *Yahoo Answers*. Available online at https://uk.answers.yahoo.com/question/index?qid=20090521065153AATrZay (accessed 24 September 2014).

27   Rachel Cooke (2014) 'To bring girls into sport, get rid of old ideas of femininity', *Sunday Observer*, 22 February 2014. Available online at www.theguardian.com/commentisfree/2014/feb/22/girls-school-sport-femininity (accessed 24 September 2014).

28   Phoebe Doyle (2012) 'PE Teachers Made Me Bunk Off PE', *Guardian*, 11 February 2012. Available online at www.theguardian.com/teacher-network/2012/feb/11/pe-teaching-competitive-sports (accessed 24 September 2014).

29   Survey of 2006 young people aged 8–16 years, conducted by Springboard UK, May 2014: 'Virgin Active and leading organisations launch Active Inspiration campaign to tackle "black hole" of youth inactivity' [press release], Virgin Active Health Clubs, 21 May 2014. Available online at www.virginactive.co.uk/press/2014/Virgin-Active-launches-active-inspiration (accessed 24 September 2014); Chris Green, 'A third of young girls believe exercise is socially unacceptable', *Independent*, 21 May 2014. Available online at www.independent.co.uk/life-style/health-and-families/health-news/a-third-of-young-girls-believe-exercise-is-socially-unacceptable-9405338.html?dm_i=14DE,2H7EY,5PBAYU,90MZN,1 (accessed 24 September 2014).

30   John Claughton (2013) 'Don't get mad, get even: How state schools can emulate the private sector's sporting success', *Independent*, 18 September 2013. Available online at www.independent.co.uk/news/education/schools/dont-get-mad-get-even-how-state-schools-can-emulate-the-private-sectors-sporting-success-8825115.html (accessed 24 September 2014).

31   Grammar schools are selective secondary schools which base their pupil intake on the results of an entrance examination called the 11 plus.

32   John Humphreys, 'What's Wrong With Our Schools?' *BBC News*, 19 September 2010. Available online at www.bbc.co.uk/news/education-11331574 (accessed 24 September 2014).

33   'Should There be More Sport in Schools?', *Guardian*, 9 August 2012. Available online at www.theguardian.com/commentisfree/2012/aug/09/should-there-be-more-sport-in-schools (accessed 24 September 2014).

4

WHAT IS PHYSICAL EDUCATION?

I came from a council estate, a background that could have really put me off
on the wrong tangent. I was in a group who weren't very focused or driven,
were always getting into trouble. But two people I really wanted to do proud
were Kenny Deans, my PE teacher, and my karate instructor, Dave Wilson.
The willingness of PE teachers to run extra-curricular sports clubs was a
crucial factor in creating success.. If someone's just doing the timetable, that's
what they're there to do, but if they go into that volunteering role, you know
they're passionate, and that rubs off. PE teachers could be the foundation of
a massive change in health in this country. If they can inspire people into
sport, it's going to reduce obesity and diabetes. There's a much more powerful
message than just creating Olympians. Hopefully, my path will take me into
PE teaching. I'd be tremendously honoured to part of a teaching group that
I hold massively high in esteem.

> *David Smith won gold in the adaptive mixed coxed four at the World Rowing*
> *Championships in Slovenia then, in London, he took gold at the Paralympics.*
> *Now, he is preparing for the Rio 2016 Paralympic Olympic Games,*
> *where he hopes to compete in cycling*[1]

The aim of this chapter is to provide an overarching view of what physical
education has been and what it has become. In other words, what physical
education is and more importantly what it is not. I realise that, in writing this
chapter, I am, to all intents and purposes, a hostage to fortune to those who have
idealistic objectives of what physical education can achieve. Indeed, put ten physical
education teachers in a room and ask them to define their specialist subject and you
are likely to get ten different responses. Thorburn and Horrell (2014: 622) maintain
that despite physical education being a familiar curriculum presence in the lives of
most pupils, the educational contribution of the subject has often been open to

doubt and uncertainty, giving many pupils confusing, opaque and distant messages about the subject. Many politicians in successive UK governments have made sweeping claims that physical education and (competitive) school sport can entrench character-building qualities in young people, combat youth crime, cure the obesity crisis, develop responsible citizens, lead to success in school examinations and even contribute to the numbers of medals won by British athletes at international sporting events. The Secretary of State for Education, Michael Gove, suggested in 2014 that running – among other more traditional forms of punishment in schools, such as writing lines, picking up litter or cleaning graffiti – could be used as an adequate sanction for bad behaviour.[2] During the 1990s, I recall a government campaign to have all school children engage in one hour of team games every day, based on the premise that more team games would mean fewer 'thugs' and fitter children, despite advice from leading sport scientists that recommended better ways of helping children to be fit. This lends credence to Green (2008: 41) and his assertion that the public has been led to believe that physical education is 'a panacea or wonder drug, that if administered sufficiently, would rid society of a breadth of social ills'. Just like any prescription drug, however, there are often side effects and a serious danger of overdosing, as British comedian Peter Kay will testify:

> I was never a fan of PE at school and don't ever recall asking to be physically educated . . . If it had been up to me physical education wouldn't be on the curriculum. It would just have to be something you did after school if you hadn't got a life. PE was just an opportunity for the fit kids to show up the fat kids. I was the last to get picked for any kind of sports and then even that usually resulted in a heated argument between the two captains. 'We're not having him, we had him last week. And anyway, it didn't matter because whoever got me I'd still always end up being put in goal of some kind.
>
> *Kay (2006: 112–13)*

It seems that physical education does not come with the proverbial bells and whistles that it purports to possess. Ask some adults about their childhood memories of school physical education lessons and you are likely to get a response that conveys images of cold, wet days, traipsing through muddy fields in little more than a vest and shorts or climbing ropes in the gym as confirmed by Finlo Rohrer: 'For many people PE encapsulates their unhappiest memories of school. They look back to blasted, windswept sports fields where shouting PE teachers in ill-fitting tracksuits marshalled unwilling pupils'.[3]

This is perhaps reminiscent of scenes from the musical video *Love Lost* by the group the Temper Trap.[4] Equally, it may be indicative of the findings by Ofsted (2013a) with respect to primary school physical education and the high levels of inactivity within physical education lessons. These findings are not new or unknown to the profession and have even been portrayed in one scene in Joanna Trollope's (2013) contemporary reworking of Jane Austen's classic novel *Sense and Sensibility*:

Miss, I would just like to say that physical education in this school is a disgrace. I mean, standing in line for 40 minutes is hardly aerobically effective. I doubt that I have worked off the calories in a stick of care-free gum.

If we look back at history, the emergence and development of the team games and the notion of muscular Christianity that originated in the Victorian public schools of England and the teaching of aesthetic movement-type activities that emanated from the Ling system of Swedish gymnastics formed the two staples of secondary school physical education in the second half of the twentieth century (Mangan 1981). Capel and Whitehead (2013) remind us that the teaching of physical education after the 1944 Education Act took a militaristic approach, where drill, marching, parading and standing exercises, combined with strict discipline, were performed in unison under the command of a teacher. This was also a time when men joined the physical education teaching profession en masse, bringing with them a combination of skills that focused mainly on competitive team games and outdoor and adventurous activities, which subsequently developed in the separate male teacher training colleges in the 1960s and 1970s. The mass influx of male physical education teachers made a significant contribution to the way in which physical education evolved in schools (Kirk 1992). As a result, physical education as a curriculum subject in secondary schools evolved with two quite distinctive identities: one for boys and one for girls. The separate male and female physical education teacher training colleges were eventually phased out and merged into coeducational initial teacher training institutions in the late 1970s, although this did not have universal support. Despite attempts to experiment with coeducational or mixed-sex physical education in secondary schools and the merging of physical education departments together male and female physical education teachers have remained remarkably resilient against any form of gender amalgamation. Kirk (2013) maintains that the dominant form of physical education in schools today is more or less the same as the 1960s, taught predominantly in single-sex groups by same-sex physical education teachers through directive, command styles of teaching where learning progression seldom occurs. Ward (2104: 569) confirms that sport has traditionally formed the subject matter through which physical educators have attempted to achieve the objectives of education, health and child development. Physical education teachers might be accused of being stuck in reverse and going full circle back to the days when their predecessors taught physical education in exactly this way to separate groups of boys and girls, respectively. So, what is going on? Despite five revisions to the national curriculum for physical education since the 1988 Education Reform Act, little has changed in that skill-based learning through games and sport remains in a dominant position on the physical education curriculum and has been spectacularly resistant to change (Kirk 2013: 223). Moreover, it is common knowledge that only a small minority of adults continue to participate in the types of activities they had experienced at school. David Kirk maintains that most concerning of all is that physical education remains the most sex-segregated and gender-differentiated subject in the secondary school:

> Given a past dominated by gender differentiation, by skill learning and by the surveillance and regulation of pupils' bodies from the drilling and exercising form of the subject, there has been a remarkable level of continuity in the practice of the subject despite the proliferation of aims over the years.
>
> *(Kirk 2010: 23)*

Defining physical education is not an easy task, as many individuals will have different experiences and 'as its terrain develops its borders become more contested and nebulous' (Green 2008: 2). Fisher (2003: 141) suggested that the bulk of the population of most countries and almost all politicians would be hard pressed to differentiate between physical education and sport, as would most physical education teachers, and are more likely to support rather than resist the sportisation of physical education (cited in Green 2008: 229). Heightened political debates regarding the purpose and content of the physical education curriculum dominated much of the 1980s and 1990s. Physical education teachers were seen at best as well-meaning but essentially confused, while politicians lauded sport as promoting positive personal and social values and outcomes. Houlihan (2000) observed that the political division between sport and physical education seemed to legitimise the marginalisation of physical education teachers in the curriculum design process and the strong political lead from government resulted in a 'traditional' curriculum dominated by competitive team games. Physical education teachers were essentially served a 'gagging order' by the policy makers from above and became merely pawns in a highly political game (Ward 2014). Penney and Evans (2013) stated that definitions of physical education vary a great deal among professionals, with conflicting opinions on the content and scope of what physical education should and could be. Moreover, academics in the field are quick to state what physical education is *not* but hesitate to state what physical education *is* (Penney and Evans 2013). Green (2008: 229) suggested that the vast majority of the population in most developed countries would be unable to tell the difference between physical education and sport, as would physical education teachers and politicians, and therefore people would be more likely to support rather than resist the promotion of sport within the physical education curriculum. Burgess (2013:19) makes a case for rebranding physical education to move away from the confusion brought about by the use of physical education and sport by many, including physical education teachers themselves, to mean the same thing. Keech (2012b: 177) explains that political interference has resulted in a continuing ontological and practical debate about the purpose of physical education and school sport. He questions whether politicians understand what has to be achieved. For Keech, serious questions about physical education and school sport remain unanswered:

> With competitive school sport at the forefront of the current policy agenda, I wonder if I would have been a (physical education) teacher that embodied that winning mentality or whether I would have been sufficiently reflective to develop the broad and balanced PE curriculum needed to develop

physical literacy and contribute to developing the health of young people. Despite everything that has been written, significant questions remain.

(Keech 2012b: 177)

Green (2008: 21) asserts that attempts to define physical education reflect a misplaced tendency to view the subject as made up of some kind of timeless essence. For Green (2008), teachers and academics of the subject appear to be romantic conservatives and assume that physical education is a good thing but have failed to find out exactly why. Ward (2014: 571) talks of an implicit agreement among physical education teachers, which results in them providing physical education lessons based on a sporting model typically consisting of learning repetitive techniques associated with traditional games that are reflective of neither pupil needs nor interests outside school. In this context, the content of physical education lessons is regurgitated and focuses on the mastery of performance skills in short lessons through blocks of sport- and teacher-directed learning where pupil progression throughout their years at school remains very limited. In this sense, physical education is merely the window dressing of the secondary school curriculum whereas sport is essentially the substance. In this vein, I had always been led to believe, by other (male) physical education teachers, that the role of the physical education teacher involved talent identification and performance development. Now I realise that while physical education teachers can give pupils self-confidence and point potential athletes in the right direction, as shown in each of the introductory testimonies to the chapters in this book, they cannot claim to have invested 10,000 hours of their own time to produce an Olympic champion (Syed 2010). I have heard physical education teachers compare themselves to *X-Factor* judges, boasting about how their former pupils had gone on to pursue a professional career in sport, as if they could claim sole responsibility for this feat. I have never heard a science teacher claim to have produced a Nobel Prize winner, an art teacher claim to have produced a Turner Prize winner, a music teacher claim to have produced a Brit Award winner or a drama teacher claim to have produced an Oscar-winning actor or actress. After all, what can physical education teachers in state-funded schools possibly achieve in 76 hours of formal curriculum time a year,[5] other than the development of physical literacy skills and a desire to continue with physical activities outside of the school environment? And yet, failure on the international stage in major sporting events is often attributed to poor teaching of physical education in schools, as highlighted by Boothroyd's (2004) poem 'He's the Man':

Yes. He's the man. He's the one to blame.
He's the reason England hardly ever win a game.
It's his fault; Eriksson (Taylor, Venables, Hoddle, Keegan) has a dodgy football team,
And why our batsmen cower like rabbits in a headlight's beam.
He's at the root why Tim never wins a crown, The reason Kiwis, Boks and Aussies trample us into the ground.

Now if you want to know this villain And like the pundits spit upon his name,
There he is…Clowning in a tracksuit, PE teaching is his game.

(Boothroyd 2004: 3)

It may be just a coincidence but on the day that the English national football team learned that their achievements at the 2014 FIFA World Cup finals in Brazil was the worst in 50 years, Ofsted (2014) reported that too many state schools were letting down the next generation of professional sportsmen and women. One wonders whether England's premature exit in Brazil could be attributed to the poor teaching of physical education in state schools and whether their poor performance might be due the fact that too many of the players were educated in state schools. The irony here is that the national football team of England that competed in the World Cup finals in 2014 was managed by a former physical education teacher who taught in state schools in South London before his own rise to fame. But some parents truly believe (and indeed expect) that state school teachers can produce Olympic champions, as highlighted by Jim White's account of his own son's non-competitive primary school in North London.

In other countries, a talent like hers would have been nurtured, trained. But, in an inner London school in 1994 it was dismissed as a social embarrassment, the equivalent of picking your nose in public. Far from offering encouragement to help develop her natural ability, here was the girl's educational mentor telling her that her skill was unwanted, worthless. And then we wonder why Britain does not produce its share of athletes.

(White 2007: 17–18)

Green (2008: 42) refers to the physical education curriculum as the 'meat in the sandwich' (the what) that sits between the nature and purpose of physical education (the why) and the actual delivery of the physical education curriculum by teachers (the how). In this context, what goes into the sandwich (the physical education curriculum) and the means through which it is made (the management of the physical education curriculum) depends upon individuals and groups within and beyond the immediate policy network of physical education. There will, of course, be different interpretations of the recipe and ingredients between teachers, departments and schools in terms of the physical education curriculum and the pedagogic methods and content based on locality, intake, expertise, facilities and resources. Convincing others, however, to adjust and consider alternative ingredients is not necessarily an easy task and is perhaps akin to getting children to eat vegetables, as highlighted by Ken Green:

Recruits to PE teaching who share a common background – typically consisting of sport and team games – may have great difficulty envisaging alternative curriculum models for the subject. Since so few recruits have experience in models other than that of 'traditional' PE (with its emphasis on sport and games), few may accept that such alternatives can exist except in the minds of textbook writers and teacher educators. This merely serves to reinforce the already existing values and beliefs of new PE teachers.

(Green 2008: 213)

My own stance of what physical education represents is based upon an inclusive approach to teaching and learning but I also have a particular standpoint with regards its position in the wider educational profession. The term 'physical education' is often abbreviated to 'PE'. Other secondary school subjects are also referred to in an abbreviated form such as RE (religious education), CDT (craft, design and technology) and ICT (information and communications technology). This reinforces the marginal status and value of these subjects compared to other curriculum areas. I have, therefore, chosen not to abbreviate 'physical education'. I have, however, found it increasingly difficult to limit my use of the term 'school sport' in the context of providing a definition of the term 'physical education' in this chapter. The term 'school sport' has been increasingly used in government policy documents alongside 'physical education' in the title of the subject, thus giving the impression that school sport is synonymous with physical education. This may be a reflection of trends in physical education, where there has been an increasing drive to push physical education to the margins of the school curricular and to replace it in the guise of school sport (Green 2008: 228). The Department for Education (2013b) reported their key findings from evidence on physical education and school sport and repeatedly used the term 'physical education' alongside 'out-of-hours school sport' as if the two were joined at the hip. While a concerted effort to define the term 'physical education' and 'school sport' was evident, the report soon lapsed into using the term 'school sport' rather than 'physical education' as an all-encompassing term, thus reinforcing the popular and misguided notion that physical education and school sport are synonymous, resulting in inaccurate media headlines (Hawman 2013). This is extremely confusing to the general public, given other ambiguous terms used in public policy since 2000, such a sports college, school sport partnership, school sport coordinators and sport education. Laker (2002: 6) defines school sport as organised competitive contests between groups of pupils either within a school, as in house or tutor group matches, or between schools in the form of representative teams. This definition is much the same meaning that sport has in a wider societal context, the major difference being that school sport claims an educational component. I believe that to refer to 'school sport' alongside 'physical education' is misleading and may cause some confusion among readers of this book. In this respect, a clear message needs to be sent identifying what physical education is and what it is not. My use of the term 'physical education', therefore, refers specifically to the UK government's intended offer of at least two hours of high-quality physical education *in the formal curriculum* to all pupils.

In defining physical education, a good starting point would be that it is a statutory entitlement of children and young people and, for many pupils, curriculum physical education remains their only guaranteed exposure to physical activity during the formative years of schooling (Association for Physical Education 2013). In most westernised countries, physical education is a foundation subject with timetabled space on the formal curriculum and it is reasonable to suggest that young people aged between 5 and 16 experience it on a regular basis (Green 2008: 1). In 2009–10, the average curriculum time spent on physical education in primary schools was 127 minutes and in secondary schools it was 107 minutes (Quick *et al.* 2010). In state-funded schools, five per cent of the available curriculum time is allocated to formal physical education teaching during the academic year or 380 hours across five years in secondary schools. This equates to 76 hours per pupil per academic year, with as much as 56 hours devoted to competitive team sports (Ofsted 2013a). Typically, pupils learn physical skills through human movement and participate in a range of planned physical activities designed to improve physical fitness, gross motor skills, coordination, problem solving, decision making and evaluative techniques. Within physical education lessons, pupils engage predominantly in a range of competitive team games but also in physical activities such as gymnastics, dance, swimming, athletics and outdoor education, all of which have a health-related focus. And yet, Cale and Alfrey (2013) claim that health promotion is perceived by physical education teachers to have marginal status, who afford it less attention than other aspects of physical education – namely sport and competitive team games. Within the national curriculum for physical education (2008), programmes of study provide the basis for teachers to plan their intended learning outcomes which allow pupils to select and apply skills, tactics and compositional ideas, acquire and develop these skills and evaluate and improve their own and others performance. The content of what will be taught in physical education lessons is determined by government policy, which dictates a statutory entitlement for all pupils. Teachers have a legal obligation to implement these policies in state-funded schools and to formally assess the progress of pupils against nationally set attainment targets at particular ages. Consequently, there seems to be very little variation between schools in terms of what pupils experience in their formal physical education lessons, which invariably have an overemphasis on sex-segregated, gender-specific team games (Ofsted 2013a). Overall, the place of physical education on the formal secondary school curriculum has got to the point where it has become almost untenable in its current form. As (Kirk 2013: 228) states: 'physical education is shoehorned into a timetable just like any other subject even when this arrangement clearly does not suit the requirements of many of the physical activities that constitute programmes'.

Laker (2002: 5) defines physical education as 'an educational process that uses human movement as its medium particularly through the teaching of games'. For many physical educationalists, the term 'physical literacy' has particular resonance with the teaching and learning that takes place in schools. The Association for Physical Education (AfPE) has defined the aims of physical education as follows:

The aim of physical education is to develop physical competence so that all children are able to move efficiently, effectively and safely and understand what they are doing. The outcome – physical literacy – is as important to children's overall development as literacy and numeracy.

(Association for Physical Education 2013)

Researchers, such as Margaret Whitehead, have discussed the concept of physical literacy as an integral part of the teaching and learning of physical education in schools. She provides the following concise definition: 'Physical literacy can be defined as the motivation, confidence, physical competence, knowledge and understanding to maintain physical activity throughout the lifecourse' (Whitehead 2010: 204).

For Green, physical education is based upon a humanistic approach and the development of the child as a whole:

The concept of physical literacy is based on the monist approach to human nature which stresses the importance of holistic development and provides a clear rationale for the importance of the development of individuals as a whole. As such physical education teachers should not only provide opportunities to learn and practice pre-requisite skills of games and sport but social aspects of co-operation, team work, deferred gratification, respect and fair play.

(Green 2013: 56)

Capel and Whitehead have argued that while physical education, recreation and sport are closely related to each other, they are distinctly different: 'Definitions of physical education that have been formulated in key literature focus on the centrality of the movement experience in physical education and/or on the subject as contributing to the education of the whole child' (Capel and Whitehead 2013: 5).

Hardman (2007) also refers to physical literacy as being an integral outcome of teaching physical education and has defined a physically educated person:

Physically educated persons might be described as being physically literate, having acquired culturally normative skills enabling engagement in a variety of physical activities, which can help to maintain healthy wellbeing throughout the full life-span; they participate regularly in physical activity because it is enjoyable; and they understand and value physical activity and its contribution to a healthy lifestyle.

(Hardman 2007: iii)

The consensus of opinion among academics and educationalists is that physical literacy is a core component of physical education and is linked directly to the development of fundamental movement skills, which provide the tools that children need to take part in a wide range of physical activities. Jo Harris, former chair of the Association for Physical Education, commented at the Westminster Forum in November 2013:

> Physical education is about education. That is why it is called physical education. The lessons are not there to be endured or suffered or tolerated as might have happened in the past. Having a boot camp approach to this does not work.

Yet, defining contemporary physical education remains a mixture of confusion and misinterpretation, causing many young people to doubt its importance in their lives. Thorburn and Horrell (2014) suggest that physical education lessons which are based on energy expenditure and fitness indices are often to the detriment of achieving more rounded educational goals and should not be viewed as a vehicle for the transmission of biomedical messages. A common working definition of physical education is clearly distinguished physical education away from school sport. This vision is one that is shared by professionals in the field of education both in the UK and elsewhere and it is this underpinning philosophy that dictates the structure, content and modes of delivery that exist in different schools. For Green (2008: 113), physical education is about health awareness in terms of increasing levels of activity during the school day and increasing pupil's adherence to sport and exercise in a manner that will lead to lifelong participation. Ofsted (2013a: 4) have also stated that the nature and purpose of physical education in schools is to inspire young people to participate in physical activity:

> Physical education (PE) is part of every child's entitlement to a good education. It is unique in that it is taught through physical activity in weekly practical lessons both indoors and outdoors, in a wide range of physical, creative and aesthetic settings. It provides pupils with the generic skills, knowledge and understanding they need to become physically literate, and at the same time gives most of them their first regular experiences of sport. When taught well, physical education enthuses and inspires pupils to participate fully and develop a lifelong love of physical activity, sport and exercise.
>
> *(Ofsted 2013a: 4)*

Proposals announced under the UK Coalition Government in July 2013 stated that:

> A high-quality physical education curriculum inspires all pupils to succeed and excel in competitive sport and other physically-demanding activities. It should provide opportunities for pupils to become physically confident in a way which supports their health and fitness. Opportunities to compete in sport and other activities build character and help to embed values such as fairness and respect.
>
> *(Department for Education 2013b: 220)*

The consensus of opinion among physical educationalists is that a physical education curriculum with an overemphasis on formalised competition is unlikely to engage and motivate pupils. Kay's (2014a: 11) premise is that that wherever one teaches physical education in the world there are four overarching constants that hold true as to why physical education is taught in schools – health, human qualities, physical literacy and intelligent performance. However, Kay (2014b: 20) maintains that there is a lack of understanding among present policy makers to make this model of physical education a reality because they themselves do not understand the difference between physical education and sport, indicating a 'benefit of the doubt' view of the subject. Schools have the flexibility to provide a physical education curriculum that has breadth, depth and balance, incorporating aesthetic and individual opportunities, as well as formalised competition for pupils who are motivated by competition. The reality, however, is that physical education in one-third of primary schools and one-quarter of secondary schools in England is poorly taught (Ofsted 2013a). In Wales, a similar picture is apparent in secondary schools, where significant shortcomings in the progress of pupils in physical education lessons were reported in one-third of all schools (Estyn 2012). In some primary schools, pupils are often inactive in lessons and are rarely challenged to achieve their full potential. a's catchphrase that 'there is not enough physical in physical education' encapsulates their general findings. For example, Ofsted (2013a) found that:

> In some schools, there is not enough physical education in PE. In other schools, PE is not taught in enough depth and there is only limited access to a high standard of competitive sport. PE requires further improvement in about one third of primary schools and one quarter of secondary schools. In primary schools, some teachers lack the specialist knowledge needed to teach PE well and outcomes for pupils are not as good as they could be. More able pupils are not always challenged to achieve their very best, levels of personal fitness are not high enough and not all pupils are able to swim 25 metres before they leave school.
>
> *(Ofsted 2013a: 4)*

For the purpose of this book, the guidance provided by the AfPE with respect to the definitions of physical activity, physical education and school sport are acknowledged as the basis for teaching physical education in schools. While physical activity, physical education and school sport are similar, in that they all include physical movement, there are important differences between them, as clarified in their descriptions:

> Physical activity is a broad term referring to all bodily movement that uses energy. It therefore includes physical education and sport.
> Physical education is the planned, progressive learning that takes place in school curriculum timetabled time and which is delivered to all pupils.

> School sport is the structured learning that takes place beyond the school curriculum (i.e. in the extended curriculum), sometimes referred to as out-of-school-hours learning.
>
> *(Association for Physical Education 2013)*

The European Parliament Policy Department states that:

> Generally physical education (PE) is a phase of education, which aims through a balanced and coherent range of physical activities to contribute to the optimum development of an individual's potential including growth and development, physical and psycho-social competencies. PE makes a unique contribution to the education of all pupils; it provides them with the knowledge, skills and understanding necessary to perform a variety of physical activities, maintain physical fitness, and to value as well as enjoy physical activity as an ongoing part of a healthy lifestyle.
>
> *(Hardman and Marshall 2007: iii)*

Many of the reasons for including physical education as a core foundation subject in schools would include increasing fitness levels, addressing rising obesity rates and improving basic movement skills. In addition, the development of personal, social, moral, spiritual and cultural education through physical education should not be underestimated as one of the main objectives. I would also add that an important component of any physical education curriculum must be the provision of swimming to all pupils across primary and secondary ages. Alongside reading and writing, swimming is one of the most important life skills a school can give to young people. A survey of 3501 primary schools, for the Amateur Swimming Association (2013), found that 51 per cent of 7–11-year-olds (just over one million children) could not swim 25 metres, the length of a standard pool. Only two per cent of schools surveyed delivered the government's recommended 22 hours a year of swimming lessons. The report recommended that Ofsted should focus physical education inspections on swimming as 'it is the only sport that can save lives'. And yet, secondary schools continue to offer a staple diet of games-related activities that has little or no appeal to the vast majority of pupils in schools. Green (2008: 143) notes that physical education teachers have very distinct views as to what types of physical activities are appropriate for boys and girls. Despite research which has shown that pupils prefer a varied and broad experience of physical activities, the physical education curriculum continues to be dominated by gender-specific, sex-segregated, competitive, physically vigorous traditional games. Quick *et al.* (2009), for example, reported that schools in England provided 19 different sports to pupils in schools of which football, cricket and rounders were the most common. Across Europe 'ball games' occupy the vast majority of curriculum time for physical education with 27 countries providing children under the age of 14 years with these activities as a mandatory part of their compulsory schooling (EACEA/Eurydice 2013). This was confirmed by Ofsted's 2013 report based on evidence from inspections of physical education in 120 primary schools and 110 secondary schools between September 2008 and July 2012:

> Traditional team games tended to dominate the curriculum at the expense of aesthetic and athletic activities. For example, it was not unusual for the schools to allocate more than two thirds of the PE programme in key stages 3 and 4 to games such as football, rugby, hockey, netball, basketball and volleyball, and in the summer term tennis, rounders, softball or cricket. This had two effects: it left only minimal time for activities such as gymnastics, swimming, dance and athletics, and it reduced the time spent studying specific outdoor games in greater depth in order to generate high standards of performance.
>
> *(Ofsted 2013a: 38)*

In Wales, a similar picture is evident where boys in particular are exposed to a physical education curriculum that is predominantly games-orientated:

> Generally, schools allocate a larger proportion of time at key stage 3 to competitive activities than to other areas of activity. This is particularly true for boys. However, schools are increasing the emphasis on creative and adventurous activities and health, fitness and wellbeing activities and this has helped to engage girls more successfully. Most schools promote healthy lifestyles well. A few schools have well-designed cross-curricular arrangements to develop pupils' awareness of healthy lifestyles. However, few schools co-ordinate this work systematically enough across subject areas.
>
> *(Estyn 2012: 3)*

Green's study of 35 practising physical education teachers in the North-West of England during the 1990s found that physical education was camouflaged as sport because many physical education teachers continued to view sport rather than physical activity as the most suitable and likely vehicle for achieving other educational goals (Green 2003: 143). The evidence suggests that, in a British context, sport (and in particular traditional team games) is taught in the majority of secondary schools, even though other activities are available to pupils such as athletics, swimming, outdoor and adventurous activities, gymnastics and dance. This begs the question as to the reasons why children are socially conditioned to believe that physical education equals sport. Laker (2002: 6) argues that it is authorised versions of physical education that are imposed by governments that create a public perception which physical education and sport are like Siamese twins. Green (2008: 209) offers an answer and suggests that it is previous experiences of traditional games and sport-based curriculum models which has led to prospective physical education teachers having custodial orientations. Physical education teachers tend to emulate the physical education they have themselves experienced. For male physical education teachers, this would have typically involved them becoming skilled in the games of football (soccer), rugby and cricket, while, for female teachers, this would have meant becoming skilled in netball, hockey and rounders. Subsequently, therefore, they become accustomed to associating physical education primarily with those particular sports in schools. Alternative models and curricula have been suggested to have greater appeal to a broader population of pupils. These models have included activities ranging from an 'A' list of aesthetic, artistic, athletic, adventurous, aquatic, aerobic and alternative activities (Stidder and Griggs 2012), an inclusive 14–19 physical education curriculum (Stidder and Wallis 2012) and an alternative physical curriculum for key stage three based upon two hours of physical education per week (Stidder and Binney 2011). Alternative activities such as skateboarding, for example, may not at first glance seem to be the best use of time within a physical education lesson but if we consider that it is not just activity itself but the outcome of the activity that is equally important, these types of activities may go some way towards convincing teachers that increasing confidence and self-esteem by learning something that would not otherwise be available to pupils is a justifiable reason for including these types of activities.[6] There is little evidence to suggest, however, that physical education teachers are willing to teach anything other than traditional types of team games both in the UK and Europe, despite the fact that fewer than one in four children, particularly girls, participates in regular moderate to vigorous exercise in schools (Department for Education 2013b).

It is widely accepted within the physical education profession that the teaching of physical education promotes physical literacy, health-related fitness, skill acquisition, skill development, decision-making skills, evaluation skills, education about the body and water confidence. In contrast, sport develops outside of physical education lessons. It focuses on performance, tactics and strategies, is competitive by nature and can involve team representation and training sessions. This, arguably, adheres to the national curriculum for physical education that published in 2013.[7] Some physical education teachers, for example, might argue that a games–centric curriculum does ensure that all pupils develop competence to excel in a broad range of physical activities, are physically active for sustained periods of time, engage in competitive sports and activities, which therefore might contribute to them leading healthy, active lives in the future. The increasing focus on sport, and competitive team games in particular, among physical education teachers is perhaps a reflection of the failure of teacher training institutions to develop future recruits to the profession who are reflective practitioners and advocates of breadth, depth and balance of experience. Academics have suggested that initial teacher training has little impact on trainee teachers of physical education, who are fundamentally unresponsive, during their training, to reflecting critically on their established beliefs and practices (Green 2008: 211). Indeed, the long-term impact of initial teacher training on future teachers is even less effective, as they revert to stereotype once they have officially qualified to teach.

In order to make sense of physical education and what it represents, Green (2008) uses a series of shorthand terms (isations) to explain the notion of role conflict and the tensions created among physical education teachers. Green (2008) explains that quite often physical education teachers are torn between these multiple roles, such as health promotion (healthisation), competitive sport (sportisation) and the educational development of pupils (academicisation). Many of these multiple roles are often exacerbated by UK government policy, which is moving very firmly in the direction of school sport (rather than physical education), in order to motivate more young people to take part in competitive sport. Green (2008: 227) explains that it is the sportisation of physical education that has led to a loss of identity and ultimately to the subject redefining itself. In this respect, physical education has surrendered to a process by which sport becomes more prominent in the justification for the practice of physical education. This has led to a transformation of physical education into school sport from something normally focused upon education to something essentially focused on leisure, recreation and high performance, to which educational outcomes are purely incidental. Some of the reasons associated with this cause and effect is the competition-isation of physical education, as evidenced in the School Games Initiative introduced by the UK Coalition Government in 2010. In addition, school sport, together with the economic and symbolic value of extracurricular sport and interschool competition, has reflected the marketisation of education, otherwise referred to as 'bums on seats'. As a result, physical education departments sell themselves to pupils, parents and communities by increasingly turning to sports coaches to deliver aspects of curricular and extracurricular physical education, despite the fact that it is widely accepted that sports coaches have sporting rather than educational priorities and tend to prefer working with more able pupils (Green 2008). Ward (2014: 571) alludes to the fact the sportification of physical education simply serves to confirm its peripheral role in the curriculum, subordinating it as a short-handled tool to solve long-term national health concerns. In this respect, physical education merely acts as a sweetener to the medicine required to increase pupil attendance, behaviour and achievement.

In comparing the provision of competitive school sport as opposed to physical education, it is evident that physical education and school sport in other countries are seen as two quite separate components of school life. In the United States, for example, school sport and physical education are totally detached from one another while in the UK they are inextricably linked together. Keech explains that, in contrast to the United States, while there are pronounced differences between what constitutes physical education and school sport in the UK, it is evident that many politicians and policy makers have misled the public by integrating physical education and school sport and, therefore, they are perceived as synonymous:

> A crude distinction would be that school sport is the extended curriculum as PE is more concerned with the education of the physical and the more that sport is prioritised the less educative the activity. So if the current thrust is on sport then the educational value of activities and opportunities has to be questioned. While they are clearly not the same, PE and sport have

> become integrated into an increasingly significant but complex and 'overcrowded' (Houlihan, 2000) policy network in which PE has become the initial focus of engaging young people in PE, physical activity and sport for socially inclusive concerns.
>
> *(Keech 2003: 376)*

However, cynics have described the structure of high-school and college sport in the United States as a reflection of US society in general, which is often characterised by the 'highly competitive, capitalistic, authoritarian, patriarchal, product-orientated culture where winning is everything' (Schempp and Oliver 2000: 145). In this sense, sport does have its ugly side and a propensity for children to be corrupted by parents and others who see that winning is the most important outcome of any competition, to the point where children are encouraged to cheat, even in something as innocent as an egg-and-spoon race (White 2007: 20).

That is not to deny the valuable contribution that competitive school sport makes to the physical education curriculum in providing extension and enrichment in a number of recreational and competitive activities, as it can provide a springboard for involvement in sport throughout life (Hardman and Marshall 2007). In most cases, however, these are experiences usually reserved for elite performers often in single-sex teams and have performance-related outcomes associated with them. In the UK, extracurricular sport is often organised voluntarily by (same-sex) physical education teachers (and sometimes by non-physical education specialist teachers) who have a keen interest in a particular sport. While many pupils in the UK have similar perceptions of physical education and sport compared to those in the United States, it is girls who have fewer opportunities than boys to participate in extracurricular school sport and girl's access to competitive after-school sport is significantly better in the United States compared with the UK (O'Sullivan *et al.* 2002).

UK inspection evidence has shown that sport is often considered to be the main focal point within school physical education departments, where the ability of teachers are often judged on their achievements outside the formal physical education curriculum and more on the accolades and trophies won on the sports field (Ofsted 2013a). In the UK, the overemphasis on competitive team sports within the formal physical education curriculum can perpetuate sex differences where the content of lessons and the organisation of the physical education curriculum and departments overall reflect the single-sex context of modern contemporary sport. This is representative of a central UK government policy that considers physical education as synonymous with particular forms of sport and perpetuates a privileged curriculum that is of much greater relevance to boys than it is to girls (Williams and Bedward 2001). At ministerial level, it was claimed on 20 February 2014 that women were put off by 'unfeminine' sports and might prefer to take up cheerleading. Gymnastics and ballet would also leave them looking 'absolutely radiant', according to Helen Grant, the Sports and Equalities Minister.[8] Consequently, boys are encouraged to participate in sports that have a greater cultural status whereas girls are more likely to follow activity programmes that are less prestigious. Research suggests that many girls in the UK have historically been deprived the opportunity to participate in the national sports of football, rugby and cricket, on the grounds that they were born female (Harris 1993), while boys' participation in traditional female sports has been negligible. As a result, some schools have provided privileged (competitive team game) experiences for boys in contrast to girls, where success, satisfaction and self-esteem are often the direct outcomes of such experiences (Penney 2002).

Green (2003: 143) claimed that while real change may well have occurred in the ideologies and practices of physical education teachers, such change may not be as transformative as one might want or be inclined to believe as widespread continuities persist alongside the occurrence of such changes. This has made it impossible to capture the essence of physical education in one single perspective and even harder to define the subject with any sense of finality. My observations would confirm that sport and team games continue to provide the nucleus of most curricular activities in secondary schools with a focus on performance-related outcomes. Capel and Whitehead (2013; 19) shared their concerns about the notion of physical education teaching today expressing their worry that so little has changed, despite several revisions to the national curriculum for physical education and radical changes to society. Historical traditions and the reluctance of teachers to change together with public expectations has left physical education as a subject area that appears to be orientated towards sport and recreation and for various reasons unable to move with the times. Rather like school dinners, very little has changed in the world of physical education teaching over the years. The recipe and ingredients have remained untouched for generations. Pupils are dished up the same menu of physical activities their own mothers and fathers experienced years before them. In this respect, using the terms 'physical education' and 'sport' synonymously is very dangerous, as they are complex concepts with contested meanings. While there may be a marginal overlap, physical education uses competitive sport as elements within a much broader sphere of study in order to achieve some of its aims. Capel (2000) has argued that sport and physical education are interrelated, as each one makes a contribution to the other but the dominance of competitive team sports within the physical education curriculum, however, reinforces the belief that sex-appropriate team games, sex-segregation and same-sex staffing is taken for granted as this is the norm in the world of competitive adult sport. In this respect, there have been limited opportunities for pupils in schools to extend their sporting interests or aspiration outside of predetermined sex boundaries. Ward (2014: 576) suggests that sporting activities should be seen as the medium through which physical education seeks the achievement of its educational aims but there is a need to make physical education reflective of the era of second modernity, as opposed to the era of first modernity in which it was conceived. Clarke reminds us that physical education is neither a neutral nor inclusive arena. It is an arena that continues to marginalise and exclude those who do not match stereotypical expectations of being male or female including pupils and teachers alike: 'Physical education remains largely a male preserve where status and privilege is ascribed to hegemonic forms of masculinity and others are subordinated. To transgress traditional gender norms is to risk censure and harassment' (Clarke: 2012: 97).

In its broadest sense, national, regional and school physical education policies reflect the polarisation of policies and practices and the outcomes of such practice on the experiences of pupils in schools. The next chapter pays particular attention to ways in which education policy influences the teaching of physical education in schools and how the interpretation of such policies can enhance or restrict the experiences of pupils within the context of formal curriculum provision. It is time to explore the political dimension in which physical education and school sport sit and time to consider the rhetoric and reality of policy into practice. The next chapter aims to put meat on to the bones.

Notes

1   Henry Hepburn, 'Physical education – "Every Olympian, it's been down to a PE teacher"', *Times Educational Supplement*, 15 November 2013. Available online at www.tes.co.uk/article.aspx?storycode=6374329 (accessed 25 September 2014).

2   Eurosport, 'BBC expert Foster slams Gove for "demonising" running', *Yahoo! Sport*, 6 February 2014. Available online at https://uk.eurosport.yahoo.com/blogs/world-of-sport/bbc-expert-foster-slams-gove-demonising-running-142511691.html (accessed 25 September 2014).

3   Finlo Rohrer, 'PE Heaven or Hell', *BBC News*, 24 November 2010. Available online at www.bbc.co.uk/news/magazine-11814633 (accessed 25 September 2014).

4   Temper Trap, Love Lost [official video]. *YouTube*, 10 May 2010. Available online at www.youtube.com/watch?v=VLTPKKt-pMs (accessed 25 September 2014).

5   In state-funded secondary schools, physical education occupies five per cent of the total curriculum time, equivalent to two hours per week over 38 weeks. Thus, each pupil receives 76 hours of physical education during each academic year.

6   Beau Lambert, 'My Left-Field Lesson – Ramp Up Self-Belief', *TES Magazine*, 9 January 2014. www.tes.co.uk/article.aspx?storycode=6389570 (accessed 25 September 2014).

7   The national curriculum for PE at key stages 1 and 2 was disapplied with effect from 1 September 2013 and is no longer statutory. See http://webarchive.national archives.gov.uk/20130802151201/www.education.gov.uk/schools/teachingandlearnin g/curriculum/primary/b00199167/pe (accessed 30 September 2014).

8   Radhika Sanghani, 'Get more women into sport through cheerleading – It's feminine says sports minister Helen Grant', *Telegraph*, 20 February 2014. Available online at www.telegraph.co.uk/women/womens-politics/10652074/Get-more-women-into-sport-through-cheerleading-its-feminine-says-sports-minister-Helen-Grant.html (accessed 25 September 2014).

5

WHAT IS PHYSICAL EDUCATION POLICY?

Dave King was the Principal at the David King Nautical School, where I went on a course when I was 17. I was immediately put at ease by Dave's teaching manner, the result of the quiet confidence he had, due to his knowledge and seamanship. What I was learning with Dave was interesting to me, as it sat quite outside any of the subjects I'd learned at school. What I loved about it was everything seemed so relevant. Dave taught me things that I didn't even realise until recently. He taught me the obvious things such as how to navigate and how to manoeuvre a boat. But he also taught me to be confident, to stay calm and to always be organised. He taught me that on a boat everything has a place, and that the boat is almost run as an operation. Dave was quiet, but confident, and always managed to keep his sense of humour even when things were going pear-shaped. He had pride in what he did and a very professional manner. He would consider everything before speaking or acting and could get on with anyone, whether it was the boys from the barges on the River Humber or the wealthy owner of a property company who had come to learn to navigate. He was a natural leader, but led by example and experience. Dave was great at building confidence, and working with a team. He would get the most out of people, and this is a skill I have tried to take with me in my life. He always encouraged me to do my best, and as professionally as I could.

Dame Ellen MacArthur: sailor and founder of the Ellen MacArthur Foundation and the Ellen MacArthur Cancer Trust[1]

In this chapter, the significance of government policy is discussed with respect to the daily practices of physical education teachers. The development of physical education as a curriculum subject has been and continues to be highly influenced both by legislation and education policy. Many of the decisions that schools and teachers make are influenced by decisions that are made way beyond the gymnasium, the changing room and the school gates (Green 2008) and are invariably prescriptive and regulated. It stands to reason that practitioners of physical education will be equally influenced by the intended outcomes of particular policy objectives. Therefore, it is important for aspiring teachers of physical education to have conceptual knowledge and understanding of how physical education policy can shape and mould both their professional identity and day-to-day practices in schools. Teachers who teach in state-funded schools in the UK are governed in their practice by national policy in the form of a national curriculum, funding, school denomination and the examinations system or what Green (2008: 225) refers to as 'the ubiquitous league tables'. At a local level, the school catchment area, traditions of the school, the governing body and head teacher's ideology, resources, timetabling, grouping arrangements and class sizes are but a few of the influences that impact and affect the way in which teachers present their subject to pupils in schools.

Green (2008) refers to 'policy' as a statement of intent to achieve, maintain, change or modify something, whereas Penney and Evans (2005) define policy as an authoritative decision about how things should be done. Lamb (2014) suggests that, in simple terms, physical education lessons are structured around policy and practice but it is at the departmental level in schools that is most crucial in relation to the lasting memories that pupils have about their physical education lessons. Education policy refers to official government texts and subject agency documents that provide guidance to teachers on the development and implementation of specific subjects in state-funded schools and provide the reference point for the development of physical education in schools. Houlihan and Lindsey (2013) have shown how these policies allow teachers to work legally within certain parameters of legislation while providing a degree of flexibility within the context of individual schools. Governments define us all as merely consumers of their policy products, which has resulted in a sizeable wedge between politicians and teachers where there should be synergy between them (Evans and Davies 2002: 18). It has been suggested, however, that putting policy into practice is not necessarily a straightforward process, as it fails to acknowledge the power of practitioners to amend policy in its implementation and influence both the outcome of current and future policy initiatives (Penney and Evans 2005) even though few physical education teachers have knowledge of, let alone play an active role in, the policy process (Penney and Evans 1999). As teachers are invariably the final link in a chain between policy and practice, this inevitably results in Penney and Evans's (1999) notion of '*slippage*' in the implementation of policy or a disparity between the actual practices of school physical education departments and the principles outlined in particular policies. Curtner-Smith *et al.* (1999) found exactly that. Green (2008: 43) maintains that what physical education teachers do in practice is often at odds with official policy and they have often been found to persistently modify policy frameworks to fit with their own personal views about physical education and make it manageable within their own particular school environment. The introduction of a national curriculum for physical education (NCPE) has had, therefore, little impact on teacher's instruction. Research suggests that policy frames and forms the fabric of the personal and professional lives of teachers and therefore it is important to consider those which are relevant to teachers and affect their practice (Penney and Evans 2005: 21).

Since the 1944 Education Act, the teaching of physical education in schools has been statutory. After the Second World War, British society embraced the idea of promoting leadership, physical fitness and moral citizenship through physical education. As a result, the benefits of physical exercise were recognised by the British government and became an integral part of the education system and has remained an integral part of a statutory national curriculum in schools in England. The structure of post-Second World War schooling left a significant social and political imprint in terms of its impact on physical education. Many exiting soldiers from the army were recruited into the teaching profession and took up teaching physical education as a profession. This was characterised by regimented drill-type activities and games, which emphasised the concept of invasion, occupation, warfare and conquest, particularly for boys, in the same way that the public school games came to symbolise what Parker (1996: 146) has described as 'a muscular elite at war; a site of moral upbringing, and a basis upon which the imperial forces of the British Empire might flourish' – a reference to the belief that competitive sports could contribute to the formation of a nation's character. Many of these principles also had relevance to the notion of adventure training, where young boys could be trained and educated in the outdoors essentially used to promote leadership and character-building but also to cultivate morality and citizenship.

Even with the introduction of comprehensive education during the 1950s, the separate male and female physical education teacher training colleges reinforced gender stereotyping by training future teachers in 'feminine' and 'masculine' appropriate activities in which boys and girls were taught separately, often by a teacher of the same sex as the group (Fletcher 1984), a trait that has continued to characterise physical education over the years. In this respect, Evans has commented that the reorganisation of secondary schooling in the 1950s failed to challenge the established content, organisation and gender-differentiated practices in physical education and therefore 'exacerbated rather than dissipated processes of gender differentiation within the subject, helped to announce the divide and the differences between male and female "traditions" of physical education, privileging the form and sustaining its position of dominance within the subject' (Evans 1990: 146).

It was not until the 1960s that educationalists began to recognise the importance of scholarly debates surrounding physical education and the value of alternative models of teaching physical education. Educationalists began to realise that child-centred learning based on the individual needs of each pupil was more effective than those grounded in the athletic tradition and 'muscular Christianity' of the elite British private schools. New and innovative approaches began to emerge, such as Bunker and Thorpe's (1982) games for understanding, Mosston and Ashworth's

(1986) spectrum of teaching styles, Siedentop's (1994) sport education model and the introduction of educational gymnastics. A move towards mixed-sex and mixed-ability teaching groups in physical education was even considered at one point during the 1970s and 1980s as a means of breaking down gender inhibitions and increasing pupil progress. Dyson and Casey's (2012) cooperative learning, values-based teaching and learning (Stidder *et al.* 2013) and thematic physical education (Stidder and Hayes 2010) have all added to what is an essentially a pedagogical model-based approach to physical education as an alternative to the multi-activity, sport-technique-based physical education that can still be seen in many secondary schools today, which may be extremely unpalatable for some physical education teachers and for many secondary school-aged pupils.

Following the Education Reform Act 1988, a UK working party (Department of Education and Science 1989) was established to assess the provision of physical education in primary and secondary schools. Subsequently, an NCPE was introduced in 1991 to but failed to produce any notable change (Talbot 1993). After subsequent revisions to the legislative requirements (Department for Education 1995), sex-differentiated practices, for instance, continued in schools and remained largely a marginalised issue within physical education (Penney and Evans 1999; Flintoff and Scraton 2001). Most notably, the process by which the NCPE was formulated was based on the hidden agendas of a few key government ministers and national governing bodies of sport, who, according to Houlihan:

> engineered a situation through which they were able to juxtapose the practice of competitive sport with physical education and argue that the former would lead to positive social, economic and personal outcomes, whereas the latter, at best, lacked clarity of purpose, and at worst, undermined competitive values.
>
> *(Houlihan 2002: 202)*

Consequently, the Conservative government sports initiatives such as 'Sport: Raising the Game' (Department of National Heritage 1995) insisted that schools should focus on traditional sex-stereotyped team games, to raise levels of physical activity among children without addressing the need to de-stereotype the physical education curriculum. British Prime Minister at the time, John Major, made it perfectly clear that 'competitive sport teaches valuable lessons which last for life . . . and should be one of the great pillars of education alongside the academic, the vocational and the moral' (Donovan *et al.* 2006). Clarke and Nutt (1999) highlighted the significance of this and suggested that 'Raising the Game' did little to dispel concerns regarding gender, since traditional male competitive team sports were placed at the heart of weekly life in every school. Similarly, the revised NCPE in England (Department for Education 1995) may not have advanced the curriculum in the direction of 'PE for all' and had particular significance to issue of girls' participation in physical education (Evans and Penney 2002). For example, the maintenance of traditional sex-stereotyped games undermined, rather than enhanced, the quality of girls' experiences, particularly in mixed-sex physical education groups (Green and Scraton 1998). The third NCPE in England (DES and QCA 1999) aimed to provide effective learning opportunities for all pupils and to increase opportunity, entitlement and access for all pupils and yet 'there remained damaging disparities in the resourcing of education, the design of the curricula, the teaching methods and grouping strategies used within and between schools' (Penney and Evans 1999: 14), thus adding credence to the claims of Green and Scraton that: 'the restoration and "privileging" of team games in the NCPE has potentially significant consequences not only for co-educational PE but also girls post-school physical activity and thus, their likely commitment to health-related exercise' (Green and Scraton 1998: 282).

Many of the reasons why girls' participation in physical education lessons has been historically lower than boys may be attributed to the design of secondary school physical education, which has traditionally been shaped by policies and practices that have highlighted the differences between the sexes while ignoring the similarities. Likewise, Green (2008) has shown how teachers' perceptions of physical education in schools is often based upon their own previous school experiences as pupils and therefore competitive performance-orientated sport, team games and fitness constitute the vast majority of the secondary school physical education curriculum. This has led to a male-centred physical education curriculum for girls and may have discouraged many of them from active participation in physical education. While much has been publicised about the 'gender gap' between boys' and girls' literacy, hitherto there has been less attention paid to the disadvantages experienced by girls in comparison to the provision of physical education for boys. In this respect, it would seem to be an anomaly that has continued to limit the opportunities of young people, particularly girls, to participate in activities outside traditional feminine and masculine boundaries (Williams and Bedward 2001).

A change of UK government in 1997 resulted in a greater emphasis on social inclusion and became a prominent part of policy development. The terms 'equality' and 'equal opportunities' took on the colloquial term 'inclusion' and included meeting the needs and interests of girls and boys but, while the opportunities for boys and girls in contemporary physical education could be considered as more equal, there still remained damaging disparities in the provision of curricular physical education. Consequently, the UK government's concern with social inclusion in many aspects of educational policy generated much professional debate and exchange among teachers in terms of what the new policy directives meant for their practice. The additions of both general and subject-related statements on inclusion within the revised NCPE (DES and QCA 1999) made many of these issues even more relevant to that practice and was mirrored by corresponding Labour government sport policy initiatives such as 'A sporting future for all' (Phillpots 2012). Exactly what a fully inclusive physical education curriculum would look like was difficult to say and how teachers would face the challenges of meeting the needs and interests of pupils from such a wide range of backgrounds was not fully known.

Following the introduction and subsequent revisions of a NCPE in England (DES 1991; Department for Education 1995; DES and QCA 1999) a number of UK policy initiatives were introduced into schools to address the falling standards in physical education and participation rates of young people. In 2002, the Department for Culture Media and Sport launched the national Physical Education, School Sport and Club Links (PESSCL) strategy and began to transform the landscape of physical education and sport in schools. Through it, a national structure was created, enabling more children and young people to take part in a wider range of sports for more time. The PESSCL strategy aimed to provide new opportunities in physical education and sport as part of an overall national strategy (DES 2002). Part of this strategy saw the introduction of specialist sports colleges and the school sport coordinator programme, which aimed to provide a broader balance of activities to young people outside traditional games activities. Specialist sports colleges were state-funded secondary schools that received increased funding from the UK central government for the purposes of raising standards in physical education within their own schools, as well as a cluster of schools within the local community. Subsequently, the school sports coordinators programme along with the revised NCPE (2005) aimed to promote sporting opportunities for young people through a partnership arrangement with other schools within a sports college partnership. It also aimed to provide support from secondary school specialist physical education teachers to primary schools as a compensatory measure for the inadequate preparation of primary school teachers to teach physical education. During this time, the physical education profession was entering a period of transition and significant change, as physical education teachers prepared for yet another major policy change under the Labour government with the introduction of a fourth revision of a NCPE (DCSF and QCA 2007), implemented in September 2008 alongside the 'Physical Education and Sport Strategy for Young People' (PESSYP) (DCSF, DCMS, Sport England and YST (2009). Key concepts and processes through a range of content and attainment targets were the operative words of physical educationalist. In this respect, the goalposts had been metaphorically moved.

Green (2008) provides an example of the policy outcomes of the NCPE which did not have identical results in both male and female physical education departments in secondary schools which he attributes to the social dynamics of gender among other things. For example, while girls and boys had the opportunity to experience the 'same' curriculum, the provision of different team games, did not necessarily mean an inclusive or identical programme and learning experience. In this respect, sex-differentiation in physical education and the appropriation of certain activities for girls and boys highlighted the need for a more reflective physical education curriculum and a need for teachers to confront existing prejudices and myths concerning boys and girls participation. It is acknowledged, however, that because physical education is affected by gender in so many ways that policies in physical education are complex, contradictory and seldom straight-forward to implement. Moreover, the failure to acknowledge gender issues in physical education has continued to influence the NCPE and has remained a key feature of both teaching and training within physical education.

The election of a UK Coalition Government in May 2010 resulted in further change of education policy and the re-emergence of competitive school sport as a major area of policy development in order to reverse a perceived decline in competitive sport brought about by left-wing councils that scorned it as 'elitist' and insisted on politically correct activities with no winners or losers. Voices from within educational circles in the UK began to drive the place of competitive school sport and physical education on to the political agenda, particularly since London achieved the rights to hosts the 2012 Olympic Games. In June 2010, the UK Coalition Government announced plans for the introduction of a 'schools Olympics' and endorsing this particular initiative education secretary of state Michael Gove said: 'We need to revive competitive sport in our schools. Fewer than a third of school pupils take part in regular competitive sport within schools and fewer than one in five take part in regular competition between schools',[2] echoing his previous sentiments at the Conservative Party conference in October 2007 when he pledged to make it easier once more for children to do 'proper' competitive team sports in schools.

The 'one size fits all' policy or what Kirk (2013: 225) refers to as the multi-activity, sport-technique-based approach to physical education received a lukewarm reception and his subsequent public letter to Baroness Campbell at the Youth Sport Trust dated 20 October 2010 reaffirmed his intention of introducing more competitive team sport in schools. In his correspondence, Michael Gove confirmed that 'The Coalition Government will encourage more competitive sport, which should be a vibrant part of the life and ethos of all schools through the creation of an annual Olympic-style school sport competition'. This was a sad indictment of the way in which physical education was viewed, reflected by Michael Gove's use of the term 'sport' 32 times compared with 'physical education' once and the abbreviated term 'PE' on five occasions. In her response, dated 29 October 2010, Baroness Campbell referred to the change of government policy as 'deeply disappointing'. She pointed out that the change would potentially exclude pupils with special needs, disaffected teenage girls, pupils on the verge of exclusion and those where sport is not culturally embedded. While offering support for competitive sport, Baroness Campbell also stressed her commitment to ensuring that young people who do not enjoy team sports are provided with opportunities to engage in an activity that they can pursue throughout their lifetime. Eileen Marchant, chair of the Association for Physical Education at the time, also corresponded with the Secretary of State for Education on 2 November 2010, expressing concern about the impact of the intended policy on the teaching and learning of physical education in schools:

> I know that the National Curriculum is shortly to be reviewed and AfPE is very much committed to keeping physical education as a statutory subject. We are aware that competition will feature strongly in the revised curriculum

but without an effective grounding in a high-quality physical education curriculum competition will suffer at all levels.

On 24 November 2010, the UK government's White Paper, *The Importance of Teaching*, was announced in the House of Commons, signalling the beginning of a radical overhaul of the education system in England. In terms of physical education, it was clear that the vision for physical education was firmly embedded in competitive team sport as a means of providing moral fibre and personal toughness to pupils in schools:

> 4.28 Children need access to high-quality physical education, so we will ensure the requirement to provide PE in all maintained schools is retained and we will provide new support to encourage a much wider take up of competitive team sports. With only one child in five regularly taking part in competitive activities against another school, we need a new approach to help entrench the character-building qualities of team sport.
>
> *(Department for Education 2010a: 45)*

It was extraordinary that two years before the Olympic Games and, ironically, on the same day as announcing the government reforms to teaching, Prime Minister David Cameron attempted to justify the government's decision to axe the Schools Sport Partnership (SSP), together with £162 million of previously ring-fenced funding, on the basis that it was a poor use of public money. The efforts of teachers through the SSP programme were not in vain, making the dismantling of the SSP's even more painful by being thought of as ill conceived. In September 2012, the 'Olympic legacy' was unveiled and nowhere did the term 'physical education' appear. Even the announcement of a school games programme[3] was criticised. Instead, the Olympic-style school games was to form the centre piece of the Coalition's physical education strategy, with pupils competing at district and national level against children from other schools. In 2013, the Department for Culture Media and Sport revealed that almost three-quarters of children under 10 and half of children aged 11 to 15 had said that the Games had not inspired them to take up a sport (Association for Physical Education 2013: 59). While the Olympic and Paralympic Games may have inspired half a generation to engage in more competitive sport, the same could not be said of physical education in schools. Much of this can be attributed to the lack of and quality of facilities, the lack of suitably qualified teachers, lack of time devoted to physical education and the way that curriculum content is presented to pupils in schools. Prior to the London 2012 Olympic and Paralympic Games, physical education was said to be, at best, minimal and at worst non-existent, reflecting the diminishing status of the subject (Green 2008:45). Mo Farah's former physical education teacher branded the government's lack of investment into physical education as an 'insult', while Lord Moynihan, British Olympic Association Chairman at the time, attributed the lack of an Olympic legacy as being responsible for poor quality teaching and a lack of space and time for physical education in schools. It was shameful that that there is very little evidence of an Olympic legacy and even less evidence of its impact on the teaching of high-quality school physical education, particularly at the primary phase of education. Instead, the use of public money had been directed to fund 'elite sports' ahead of the Rio De Janeiro Olympic Games in 2016 and one might argue that this was simply an act of 'wilful neglect'.

Keech (2012b) explains that there has been a policy explosion in physical education and school sport and has become the nexus of three important policy sectors with complex and overlapping relationships: talent identification and development; education and raising standards and the development of school and community sport and health. All of this leaves physical education professionals confused as to what they are actually expected to do.

> School sport is the structured learning that takes place beyond the school curriculum (i.e. in the extended curriculum), sometimes referred to as out-of-school-hours learning. Again, the context for the learning is physical activity but with the publication of 'Creating a Sporting Habit for Life' ... the latest youth (and community) sport policy document, one may be forgiven for feeling dizzy.
>
> *(Keech 2012b: 177)*

In 2013, ring-fenced public money was pledged by the UK government to all primary school head teachers specifically for improving the provision of physical education. All schools with 17 or more pupils were to receive a lump sum of £8,000 plus a premium of £5 per pupil. The government's announcement on 5 December 2013 to extend the primary physical education premium[4] to 2016 may have been perceived as too little too late and a way of saying sorry to the general public for the lack of an Olympic legacy in schools. A further sweetener was added on 5 February 2014, when it was announced that a further £150 million would be shared among primary schools up until 2020,[5] which may have been more than a coincidence considering that a UK general election was less than a year away. While the funding to all primary schools to improve physical education was to be welcomed, it simply did not go far enough. It was merely a drop in the ocean compared with what needed to be done to improve the state of physical education in primary schools. To some, the new primary physical education premium may have been the equivalent to adding a sticking plaster to a gaping wound. The public might have been placated but the politicians stood accused of 'mass child neglect' because of decades of poor physical education lessons, particularly in primary schools and the rising levels of obesity among young people. Research conducted by the UK Coalition Government between April and June 2014 (Lloyd *et al.* 2014) found that up-skilling and training of existing staff, buying new equipment, increasing extracurricular activity and employing an external sports coach were the main priorities for head teachers in primary schools when it came to spending the primary physical education premium. Of some concern was that some primary schools chose to employ external sports coaches when changing their curriculum physical education staffing rather than specialist physical education teachers and even more preferred to employ external coaches for their extracurricular physical education. This may have been a case of physical education on the cheap.

There were more significant things that could have been done to improve the teaching of physical education in primary schools so that enough 'physical' aspects could be included in physical education lessons allowing teachers to teach it more in depth. And yet there were no government announcements to invest public money into building fit for purpose indoor sports facilities in all primary schools. Instead, from 2014 onwards, primary schools across England would be able to benefit from National Lottery funding to improve existing sports facilities in schools rather than replacing them. The new funding pot announced by the Chancellor of the Exchequer during his 2013 Autumn Statement was to help primary schools which had little or no outside space to get more young people active. There were no suggestions that taxpayers money would be used to invest in primary school initial teacher training for physical education despite research that primary teachers received as little as 12 hours of physical education subject knowledge training during their initial teacher training (Kirk 2010). Nor was there any mention of having specialist physical education teachers, who were not required to teach mathematics, English or science, in every primary school until, on 2 June 2014, it was finally announced that there was to be a £360,000 funding boost to expand the number of primary physical education training places that would eventually provide 240 primary schools.[6] Kirk (2010) concluded that, together with modern foreign languages and music, a physical education subject specialist should be introduced into every primary school nationally requiring specific undergraduate programmes in primary physical education which would feed into existing PGCE, School Direct and SCITT entry routes into teaching. In the aftermath of the UK government's drive away from traditional university-led training routes to more school-centred training, this could well alleviate some of the problems caused in its wake. Among primary teachers there were silent screams for help, as depicted by Kate Townshend:[7]

> If you're a primary school teacher, and an honest one, you'll admit that there is at least one subject that fills you with the kind of cold dread usually reserved for injections, spiders and traffic wardens. For me, it's physical education. Through a cunning combination of luck and working part-time, I have for the past few years managed to evade the humiliation of having to confess that I have all the co-ordination of an intoxicated duck, because PE has fallen on one of my days away from school.

There was no acknowledgement that the time and status given to physical education in primary schools needed to be increased. For years, it has been acknowledged that the root cause of poor-quality physical education in primary schools is due to a lack of attention during initial teacher training courses and the correspondingly low levels of confidence among primary school teachers in teaching physical education. On some courses, trainee primary school teachers receive the equivalent of a day's training in physical education (Ofsted 2013a). Prior to the 2010 UK General Election, the answer to improving primary school physical education was found with the advent of the school sport partnerships linking specialist secondary school physical education teachers with clusters of primary schools. There was no suggestion of reintroducing and neither were there any official comments that the content of the physical education curriculum was way past its sell by date and in need of serious attention. The politicians could be accused of selective hearing. The silence was deafeningly loud!

The solution was not rocket science. The answers were blatantly obvious but needed spelling out. Kirk (2013: 229) did exactly that by stating that there is strong evidence from a variety of sources to suggest that specialist physical education teachers need to be working in both primary and secondary schools. Ofsted (2014) seemed to have all the answers when it announced how they would assess and report on how effectively the new funding was being used to improve physical education and sport provision when making judgements on the quality of the school's leadership and management. While it was up to schools to determine how best to use the additional funding 25 examples were provided including the employment of specialist teachers of physical education so that primary-school-aged children could learn the fundamentals of human movement. But what would the equivalent of £9,000 a year achieve and more importantly what would it buy? Would it prevent some primary schools from sidelining key subjects such as art, music and physical education in the race to hit government targets for literacy and numeracy? Would it address the fact that 50 per cent of all primary school pupils were being denied the opportunity to take part in two hours of school physical education per week, as highlighted by Eileen Marchant during the BBC 'You and Yours' Radio 4 broadcast on 15 December 2011? Would it help teachers with little training to teach high-quality physical education lessons in school halls or dining rooms in less than 30 minutes a week? Would it increase the total of 19 hours per year for physical education which for some children is the only form of physical activity they ever do? For two-thirds of the year, primary physical education lessons take place indoors due to the British climate but, all too often, the indoor spaces available to teachers are taken away to facilitate rehearsals for Christmas nativity plays, music concerts or other whole school events at the expense of physical education. How would £9,000 a year stop this from happening?

A coach with specific knowledge of one sport without a pedagogical background was not the answer. The answer it seemed was to address the teaching of physical education in the primary schools where specialist teachers of physical education, who had received high-quality training, were most needed so that pupils could be physically educated to a high level by the time of transition to secondary school. Two hours of high-quality physical education per week in primary schools in appropriate facilities would do the trick. Time could be spent creating far stronger links to clubs and to promoting clubs within the school. Non-competitive activities should be given greater prominence. Health issues such as obesity should feature strongly as part of a whole school programme linked to physical activity. Years of research that showed that the physical education curriculum in primary and secondary schools were dominated by a narrow version of competitive sports, in particular invasion games, and asked a serious question about the rationale for this and whether research had any value in the eyes of policy makers and think-tanks. Physical educationalists were so incensed with the government's expectation for physical education teachers to provide more competitive school sport for elite performers that an alternative model was published in the national UK physical education journal. It suggested that secondary schools should drastically reduce interschool competition and phase it out altogether at key stage four (Marchant 2013: 44). This fell on deaf ears and was completely ignored by policy makers, despite the research that consistently found that competitive sport was a deterrent for most young people when taking part in physical education lessons. Sport Scotland (2005) had shown that self-confidence was linked to competition. Although most pupils enjoyed the competitive element of physical education and sport, many pupils, particularly girls, were turned off physical education and school sport because it was too competitive. Girls found competitiveness more of a problem in mixed-sex groups, where boys raised the level of competitiveness through making negative and sexist comments and through bullying. This is one of the reasons why activities such as orienteering, skateboarding, aerobics, cheerleading and yoga had become increasingly popular in secondary schools, and why some traditional team sports were less popular. To cater for all pupils, research had suggested that a range of alternative activities, such as street dance, outdoor pursuits and golf, had captured the interest of those not suited to team games or were at risk of disengaging from traditional physical education lessons (Ofsted 2013a: 4). Stidder and Binney (2011) suggested that disability sports such as boccia and goalball for able-bodied pupils could help pupils appreciate the different learning needs that some children have. Vickerman and Hayes also contributed to the debate and highlighted that pupils with additional learning needs were often left out of any policy discussion highlighting the need for teachers to apply policy decisions effectively into their departments and lessons.

> In summary, PE teachers and schools must ensure that inclusion is reflected within policy documentation, as a means of monitoring, reviewing and evaluating delivery. The critical factor, however, is the need to move policy through into the pedagogical practices of PE teachers. While philosophies and processes are vital for schools and teachers, they must ultimately measure their success in terms of effective inclusive practice, which is embedded within a 'person centred' approach to the education of pupils with SEND.
>
> *(Vickerman and Hayes 2012: 64)*

Nonetheless, on 11 September 2013, the government published the fifth set of revisions to the NCPE (DFE 2013). Two hundred and twenty four pages were devoted to writing the entire national curriculum for England. Physical education appeared on the last four pages of the document and was written on exactly 90 lines in 856 words. It was as if physical education had been pencilled into the national curriculum rather than engraved. As with previous versions of the NCPE, long-established discourses were retained with little to prompt teachers away from a physical education curriculum dominated by traditional team games. In this respect, the proverbial new broom was not sweeping clean the traditions of the past and seemed to strengthen the importance of elite sporting performance. Just as before, new and alternative approaches that consciously would challenge stereotypical views and practices remained largely a matter of potential (Penney 2002:123). Attainment targets, key concepts and processes were a thing of the past. Face-to-face competition rather than 'outwitting opponents' through 'proper' team and individual games alongside competitive sport were now the popular educational catchphrases being shared among politicians. The continued focus on competition in the revised NCPE (2014) and the requirement to 'master', 'perform', 'play', develop', compare' rather than 'create' led some educationalists to predict that a reliance on sports coaches rather than teachers in primary schools would potentially become the norm, as performance rather than creativity ignores the pedagogical aspects of teaching provided by the teacher (Lavin 2008). Moreover, even though there were no legal requirements to include the named games that appeared in the square brackets within the national curriculum for key stage three and four, the fact that they appeared in the document said it all and put traditional team sports back at centre stage. Perhaps that is what the politicians meant when they announced in June 2014 more regulation in the teaching of British values in all schools. Mission accomplished!

Notes

1   Ellen MacArthur, *Times Educational Supplement* 14 December 2012. Available online at www.tes.co.uk/article.aspx?storycode=6309572 (accessed 25 September 2014).
2   'Ministers to announce launching of school "Olympics"', BBC News, 26 June 2010. Available online at www.bbc.co.uk/news/10423816 (accessed 25 September 2014).
3   Department of Culture Media and Sport, 'Olympic-style Sports Competition for Young People launched as part of 2012 Legacy', 28 June 2010. Available online at www.gov.uk/government/news/olympic-style-sports-competition-for-young-people-launched-as-part-of-2012-legacy--2 (accessed 25 September 2014).
4   'Getting more people playing sport'. Available online at www.gov.uk/government/policies/getting-more-people-playing-sport/supporting-pages/school-pe-and-sport-funding (accessed 25 September 2014).
5   James Kirkup, 'David Cameron to announce extra sports aid for pupils until 2020', 5 February 2014. Available online at www.telegraph.co.uk/news/politics/david-cameron/10620747/David-Cameron-to-announce-extra-sports-aid-for-pupils-until-2020.html (accessed 25 September 2014).
6   R. Vaughan, 'PE Specialist in Primary Schools to Double', *TES Connect*, 2 July 2014. Available online at http://news.tes.co.uk/b/news/2014/07/02/pe-specialists-in-primary-schools-to-be-doubled.aspx?dm_i=14DE,2LO43,5PBAYU,9I017,1 (accessed 25 September 2014).
7   Kate Townshend, 'Sporting Chance', *TES Magazine*, 14 March 2014. Available online at www.tes.co.uk/article.aspx?storycode=6413988 (accessed 25 September 2014).

SECTION TWO

The journey ahead

6

BECOMING A TRAINEE PHYSICAL EDUCATION TEACHER

I would have to nominate my old PE teacher, Graham Hatch, at St Augustine's High School in Kilburn, North London. He was from Wigan and by far and away the nicest of the bunch. I wasn't brilliant at school, although I excelled outside the classroom at cycling or playing football, rugby and basketball. Mr Hatch recognised that I was a fairly good cyclist and he encouraged me. When I told most other teachers that I wanted to win an Olympic gold in cycling, they dismissed it as crazy. They said: 'How many inner-city kids do that?' Mr Hatch was different. He took an interest, asked me about my cycling and generally encouraged me. Mr Hatch is still at the school, although now as deputy head. My brother, who is eight years younger than me, is a teacher there now as well, so I still have a link to the school. I went back there about ten years ago to hand out Duke of Edinburgh awards and saw Mr Hatch then.

Sir Bradley Wiggins[1]

In this chapter I have drawn upon case study research to illustrate the experiences of trainee teachers during their school-based placements and the anomalies that sometimes exist when training to teach physical education. For over a decade, I have been particularly interested in researching the 'gendered' dimension of initial teacher training in physical education and how male and female trainee teachers of physical education have been shrouded in a gendered straitjacket during their training in preparation for the world of teaching physical education and remain totally oblivious of the consequences for themselves and for their pupils. In British schools, there are a number of male-associated games (such as soccer, rugby and cricket), which are predominantly practised by boys and are often taught in sex-segregated groups by male physical education teachers. Similarly, there is a variety of activities that are generally associated with female participation (netball, hockey, rounders and dance), which are invariably taught to girls in single-sex groups and are often considered to be the preserve of female physical education teachers. This is frequently re-enacted by male and female trainee physical education teachers within formal school-based initial teacher education programmes and consequently reaffirms the appropriateness of gender-divided activities, groupings and staffing among prospective physical education teachers (see Flintoff 1998 and Stidder 2002 for further discussion of these issues). It has often occurred to me that single-sex secondary schools rarely have opposite-sex physical education teachers or trainees within their physical education departments. Likewise, mixed-sex secondary schools often have sex-segregated physical education departments staffed respectively by male and female physical education teachers, sometimes situated at opposite ends of the school or even on different campuses. During my own training in secondary schools this was the case. I was trained exclusively by male mentors and learned how to teach single-sex boys classes a prescribed diet of gender-appropriate activities. I never actually questioned this at the time and assumed that this was normal. It was not until I taught in North America that I began to ask critical questions of these types of practices which were completely alien to the teachers with whom I worked in North America.

My initial interest in the sex-role stereotyping of physical education teachers started during my postgraduate studies in the 1990s when I began to investigate the way in which secondary schools advertise for full and part-time physical education teachers. I found that schools perpetuate gender bias in terms of the vocabulary used in advertisements for teaching posts. For example, the use of the terms 'head of boys PE' or 'teacher of girls' PE' suggest that the post is only open to one sex and that the other sex need not apply (Stidder 2002, 2005; Stidder and Hayes 2006). Most recently, my research has focused on the actual training experiences of trainees in opposite-sex secondary schools (seven schools for boys and three schools for girls). I have consistently found that the sex of the physical education teacher or trainee physical education teacher makes little or no difference to pupils in secondary schools nor does it negatively impact upon a physical education trainee teacher's professional development (Stidder 2009b, 2012a, 2014). I have since documented the experiences of male and female physical education trainee teachers and their reflections of training in an opposite-sex secondary school which has subsequently been the topic of a 15-minute documentary entitled 'Does Sex Matter?', produced in 2013.[2]

What I have chosen to focus on in this particular chapter are the experiences of one male trainee physical education teacher, using previously unpublished data. What follows highlights the school-based training experiences of a male trainee teacher of physical education at a secondary school for girls. The male trainee teacher of physical education provided a continuous commentary within a secondary school for girls while undertaking the final stage of his statutory school-based training over a 75-day training period in south-west England. Using narrative reports and accounts through critical self-reflection, computer-mediated data were generated. The findings showed that these training experiences provided the trainee physical education teacher with subject knowledge enhancement outside of traditional gendered boundaries. This could, therefore, inform future strategic placements for other male trainee teachers of physical education in secondary schools for girls.

In England, there are 219 secondary schools for girls representing six per cent of all state-funded secondary schools.[3] The physical education departments of these secondary schools for girls have historically been staffed by female teachers of physical education who have tended to teach a physical education curriculum specifically designed according to the perceived appropriateness of particular physical activities for girls (Kirk 2002). Single-sex secondary schools are, therefore, central players in binding past, present and future gendered physical education discourses and practice which include same-sex teaching and same-sex training in single-sex schools (Brown and Evans 2004).

This is not unique to England. In other countries and regions, such as Scandinavia, studies have shown how the physical education teacher and gender are constructed and how the (Swedish) state has explicitly designed and trained the physical education teacher as the constructor of boys and girls as separate species (Olofsson 2005). In Finland, Berg and Lahelma (2010) have also shown that boys and girls are taught physical education separately, with a male teacher usually teaching the boys and a female teacher usually teaching the girls. It remains unclear from the research, however, why the teaching of physical education in secondary schools should take place in single-sex groups with a teacher of the same sex. In some cases, it has been shown that female secondary school physical education teachers prefer to teach girls because they believe that male physical education teachers command more authority as their teaching skills are ranked higher by boys than their female counterparts (Berg and Lahelma 2010). Similarly, female teachers of physical education in secondary schools favour teaching girls as it is difficult for female teachers (and trainee teachers) of physical education to gain the respect of boys, unlike the automatic respect that male teachers (and trainee teachers) of physical education tend to be given (Scraton 1992). In other cases, there is an assumption among secondary school teachers of physical education that boys prefer to be taught by male teachers and girls prefer to be taught by female teachers. Research has shown, however, that for most boys and girls, the teacher's gender or biological sex has no bearing on their preferences for a teacher. In this respect, the vast majority of boys and girls prioritise the teacher's individual ability as a teacher and their level of care for their pupils, rather than a teachers' gender or biological sex (Department for Children, Schools and Families 2009: 5). Research within primary schools[4] has also shown that the sex of the teacher has little bearing on the learning of pupils. For example, Francis et al. (2006) found that the substantial majority of pupils (aged between seven and eight) and teachers rejected 'gender matching' as a salient issue in pupil-teacher relations and learning outcomes, prioritising instead the abilities of the individual teacher irrespective of their biological sex.

To explain the gendering processes in physical education and how it can influence staffing (and training) patterns in physical education, Berg and Lahelma

(2010) borrow Hirdman's (1988, 1990) concept of the 'gender system' – a system that arranges males and females into their respective biological sexes. This results in a 'gender contract' or a set of invisible rules governing each gender – rules that determine what men and women should do, think and be. In this context, maintaining sex segregation and gender hierarchies in physical education is an active professional practice in which male and female physical education teachers are complicit in the construction of gender. Thus, security is based and maintained in the familiar, repeated and continuing practices in the school. Green (2008) has shown that physical education teachers are inclined towards replicating traditional (gender-associated) sport and games-orientated physical education as this is what they are most familiar with and is part and parcel of becoming and being a (male and female) teacher of physical education. Prospective (male and female) teachers of physical education, therefore, become most comfortable in teaching (coaching) the more traditional (gender-associated) games and sports-based models with custodial orientations, which they themselves grew up with. Becoming and being a male teacher of boy's physical education and a female teacher of girls physical education is therefore almost a rite of passage (Brown 1999, 2005; Brown and Rich 2002; Brown and Evans 2004).

Brown (2005) explains that trainee teachers of physical education in England have to demonstrate traditional gender-legitimate dispositions first and foremost, such as an expertise in particular gender-associated physical activities, as this is what they are anticipated to be teaching (coaching) for most of their careers, such as males teaching (coaching) football (soccer), rugby, cricket and females teaching (coaching) netball, (field) hockey and, rounders. This is exacerbated by head teachers and school governors,[5] who look to appeal to their customers (parents) by giving them what they want by ensuring that their physical education teachers (and by implication their trainee teachers of physical education) do not deviate too far from the popular gendered social scripts that have been laid down in physical education and school sport over the decades. In this context, a very rigid set of gendered behaviours for boys and girls has been promoted as accepted practice in secondary schools, where there has always been an expectation that men train to teach (gender-specific) sport in secondary schools to boys, while women train to teach (gender-specific) sport in secondary schools to girls (Laker *et al.* 2003). Physical education departments in single-sex secondary schools, therefore, have tended to consist of teachers of the same sex, with little if any critical analysis of the reasons why such practices exist. Moreover, it is claimed that staffing in physical education departments is often dependent on the after-school coaching expertise that teachers have to demonstrate alongside their formal curriculum duties, rather than their pedagogical competence. Given the gendered nature of sport, it is hardly surprising that staffing and training in physical education departments in single-sex schools has been largely driven by narrow perceptions of gender and its association with sex-segregated competitive team sport.

Green (2008) suggests that physical education curriculum leaders (heads of department) in secondary schools are often the linchpin between continuity and change, as they tend to be involved in the selection of new physical education teachers to their schools. In this respect, Green (2008) explains that physical education department managers co-opt physical education teachers like themselves to teach what they already have in place on the curriculum and within the after-school sports programme. In single-sex secondary schools, where there have always been same-sex teachers of physical education, it is likely that a gendered status quo is maintained. Green notes that consecutive generations of physical education teachers, therefore, absorb newcomers into what amounts to a very similar physical education network whereby physical education departments reproduce and regenerate themselves as a type of 'old boys' and 'old girls' alumni. As Green explains:

> Because established groups of physical education teachers have a tendency to close ranks when confronted by new policies and new teachers, differences between old and new often tend to exaggerated and the outsiders perceived and portrayed as not only different but in some way inferior.
>
> *(Green 2008: 215)*

The training of physical education teachers, therefore, continues to be influenced by a tendency for single-sex secondary schools to specifically request same-sex trainee teachers of physical education within 'partnership training agreements'[6] for periods of statutory school-based training. The extent to which the training of teachers of physical education is dependent on the sex of the trainee is not fully understood by researchers or academics, nor has it been sufficiently researched to make any conclusive judgements. Nonetheless, there are some emerging issues that warrant further academic analysis, as a series of email communications related to the allocation of placement schools to trainee teachers of physical education reveal:

> Sorry to spring this on you last minute but I have only just realised the student you are sending us is female! I assumed we would get another male since (Male Teachers' name) will be the mentor again. I'm really sorry but we don't have a female member of staff available to mentor, so unless you can send us a male, we won't be able to take one!
>
> Let me know asap!
>
> *(Email correspondence received 21 May 2010)*

> On a placement note, would it be possible for us to have a female ITT as we will have a new head of boys in the department. I don't want to overload the 'male' side and it would be unfair on the kids.
>
> *(Email correspondence received 20 September 2010)*

While these comments demonstrate the extent to which secondary schools privilege one sex over another within physical education initial teacher training, there are some physical education teachers who are beginning to question whether schools should specifically request a trainee teacher of physical education for periods of school-based training based upon their sex. For example, a male physical education teacher with responsibility for mentoring trainee teachers of physical education in a mixed-sex secondary school was asked whether he would prefer to mentor a male or female physical education trainee teacher for a period of statutory school-based training. His correspondence highlighted the extent to which some mentors now view the gendered nature of initial teacher training in physical education:

> I find the idea of schools specifically asking for male or female PE trainees extremely unethical. It has no benefit to both the trainee and the profession in the long run. For the trainee, it slows down their professional development, puts up social barriers and limits their chances of employment in the future. For the profession it merely promotes an archaic philosophy, stops children gaining diverse learning experiences and further segregates PE from other subjects on the curriculum.
>
> *(Email correspondence received 9 August 2010)*

Despite such progressive professional perspectives, the legacy of single-sex training institutions in the latter part of the twentieth century still influences physical education teachers. Berg and Lahelma's (2010) study showed that some female physical education teachers believed that the physicality[7] of the male teacher–male student relationship, more evident in physical education compared with other curriculum subjects in schools, was a justifiable reason for same-sex instruction (and training) in physical education, where mutual respect could only be achieved between male physical education teachers and male pupils through competition over the proper ways of using one's (male) body. Laker *et al.* (2003) refer to the idea of hegemonic influence,[8] where isolated dominant groups (such as male and female physical education departments) or social political structures (single-sex schools) maintain their hegemonic dominance through the covert transfer of gendered practice within physical education initial teacher training. The compliance of teacher training institutions in maintaining these types of gendered practice is an integral part of the relationship between these dominant groups and the relationship between groups and assumptions. When knowledge is recognised as being socially constructed, there is continued validation by subsequent generations who take for granted their practitioner knowledge without recognising that it is socially constructed practice. Thus, hegemonic domination works so that it appears as common sense that gender-specific roles are assigned to males and females within physical education initial teacher training during periods of school-based training and is maintained by training same-sex trainee teachers of physical education in same-sex schools. Laker *et al.* (2003) have therefore concluded that 'Gendered environments (in physical education) are continuing to thrive despite claims of an equitable learning environment' (Laker *et al.* 2003: 76).

Berg and Lahelma (2010: 41) argue that the masculine body unites boys and male physical education teachers in the same way that the feminine body unites girls and their female physical education teachers. This could, therefore, provide a rationale for maintaining same-sex staffing (and training) in same-sex schools and might explain why so few male trainee physical education teachers undertake their statutory school-based training in opposite-sex schools. Moreover, Berg and Lahelma (2010) maintain that a common argument for same-sex teaching and same-sex training in physical education is that boys and girls need same-sex role models as 'father' and 'mother' figures who understand the male and female body, respectively.

While there has been a research focus on the numbers of newly qualified female teachers of physical education gaining employment and promotion within secondary schools for boys (Rees 2012), there is little or no research to suggest that the same has been true for male trainee teachers of physical education. The focus of this chapter, therefore, is upon one male trainee teacher of physical education and his experience of being trained in a professional environment into which males have not been routinely encouraged or welcomed. The research reported here assesses whether these types of training experiences are educationally and professionally beneficial to the pupils, the trainee teacher and the staff within the school. In doing so, the aim of the research is to reach an informed judgement as to whether this can facilitate critical self-reflection while making pre-service (male) teachers of physical education conscious of gender influences so that they are better prepared to contribute to a broad and balanced physical education curriculum free from exclusion zones in their future teaching careers (Laker *et al*. 2003: 76).

Ben's story

Ben (a pseudonym) is a 24-year-old male university undergraduate physical education student. His ethnic background is 'white English'. Ben had attended a mixed-sex secondary school as a pupil and then trained to qualify as a secondary school physical education teacher following a four-year bachelor of arts degree in physical education with qualified teacher status (QTS) between September 2007 and June 2011. As part of his training, Ben was required to spend 32 weeks (160 days) within two placements schools during his four-year degree programme. His first training school was a mixed-sex comprehensive secondary school in south-east England at the beginning of the third year of his course (September 2009 to January 2010) following an initial ten-day placement at the same school in June 2009. The majority of his teaching experiences were with single-sex boys classes. He had not taught any parallel single-sex girl's classes but had taught some mixed-sex groups. His final school-based placement was at a secondary school for girls in south-west England in the final semester of his fourth year (February to June 2011).

The physical education department was staffed predominantly by female teachers but also consisted of one full-time male physical education teacher and a male physical education technician.[9] The school had trained a male trainee teacher of physical education from the same institution in the previous academic year (February to June 2010). The fact that the school had already appointed a full-time male physical education teacher and had trained another male trainee teacher of physical education suggested that there was a willingness to continue with this trend.

This particular study draws upon established methods to collect data, using critical self-reflection drawing upon narrative accounts and assessing ways in which philosophies and practices evolve. Critical self-reflection and pedagogy in physical education can contextualise and illustrate various topics of educational debate as well as inform research and provide the impetus for innovation and change. This can enable the researcher (and the researched) to view the art or science of teaching through a different pedagogical lens so that training, mentoring, instruction and learning can be (re)-assessed in terms of the selective tradition of practices that are ideological and political in nature (Macdonald 2002).

The method of data collection within this study involved critical incident writing through the use of an electronic online diary as a means of recording computer-mediated data. This has been shown to be an effective means of data collection within sport pedagogy and physical education, particularly owing to its propensity to provide illuminating data from a small number of subjects (Curtner-Smith 2002). In this respect, data were collected through writing-up of incidents which were particularly significant during the time of the research, based upon guidance provided before the placement. This included individual reflections of physical education lessons and experiences of daily practice. This allowed for the evaluation and assessment of the experiences of training to teach in an opposite-sex setting. Ben was able to access his own secure personal diary through the university's virtual learning environment[10] and record his reflections for the researcher to access on a weekly basis and store electronically. Ben was asked to critically reflect upon his experiences before, during and after his final period of school-based training and to record any significant incidents which aimed to elicit his perceptions, thoughts and experiences of training to teach physical education in an opposite-sex secondary school. A post-placement interview conducted 'in situ' was video-recorded and transcribed and included Ben's individual reflections of his experiences of daily practice at the secondary school for girls. This allowed his experiences to be evaluated and brought together a database from which analytical themes and categories could be identified. Ethical protocols were adhered to according the British Educational Research Association (2011) guidance in respect to insensitivities of the power relationship between researcher and researched, gaining informed consent, making the research findings available to participants and ensuring confidentiality.

Discussion

Before the placement, Ben had initial anxieties about training to teach physical education in a secondary school for girls. In this respect, Ben highlighted the following concerns he had before the period of school-based training. These included the issues of motivating girls and building effective professional relationships with his female pupils:

> I found out on my previous placement that, in my opinion, girls are harder to teach than boys; this is because if a boy is stubborn and doesn't want to particularly do something you can have a laugh and a bit of banter with them and nine times out of ten you can persuade them to take part in what you want them to do. Whereas, with girls, as a male teacher the opportunity to have that relationship is much harder. To act like this with boys is building relationships but acting like this with girls is deemed unprofessional and frowned upon, so I have to find other ways of motivating pupils that are possibly disengaged with physical education.

Ben's initial anxieties highlighted a number of important gender issues for male trainee teachers of physical education within school-based training. The issue of male trainee teachers of physical education having 'banter'[11] with the boys compared with building professional relationships with the girls is an important consideration as some male physical education teachers may prefer not to teach girls, because of anxieties related to parents and pupils misinterpreting working relationships, which may change the working practices of male teachers of physical education in opposite-sex schools. Ben's perception that building working relationships with girls could be deemed as 'unprofessional' and 'frowned upon' was further highlighted:

> I have a few initial concerns about my upcoming placement at the school for girls; firstly, I am more than aware of how female pupils respond to new young male teachers, I am slightly concerned that some of the older girls will try to push their luck and become flirtatious. I will need to remain professional throughout and nip this in the bud at the first opportunity.

Ben's comments suggested that he was unprepared for training to teach physical education to girls and that he had to rely on his instincts rather than any particular strategies he may have learned during his previous school placement or within his university training. His assumption, even expectation, that some of the older and more mature female pupils might 'push their luck' and 'become flirtatious' had clearly made him feel anxious, resulting in him adopting a defensive mechanism and strategy. This meant that he had to be on his guard so he could 'nip this in the bud' – an expression used in the English language to prevent something from growing. Flintoff (1998) initially cited how male trainee teachers of physical education had to deal with girls 'crushes',[12] which were both flattering but difficult to deal with, resulting in them changing their working practices and adopting a 'fatherly approach' to establish good working relationships with their female pupils. This was evident in Ben's account of an incident that took place at the start of one of his physical education lessons.

> I have noticed that recently the older girls try to flirt with me. An example of this was when I was using miniature whiteboards to assess pupils learning and a girl in one of my classes wrote that 'she loves Mr X'. When I saw this, I gave her a disapproving look, she rubbed it off quickly. I then set the pupils off on a task and spoke to the girl in question one on one and told her it was inappropriate and I didn't expect to see that kind of behaviour again. She then apologised.

This particular issue recurred during his placement. On another occasion, for example, Ben recalled how he had to involve the senior managers within the school, to prevent these types of incidents from escalating and happening in the future.

> There are a few girls that have developed a crush on me and have had to be told to stop by senior management. An example of this was at a recent cake sale at break time one girl in particular bought me a cake and got someone to bring it to the PE office to give to me. I didn't accept this cake as I felt it was unprofessional, especially as she just had her pencil case confiscated because she had written 'I LOVE MR X' on there. I have always done my utmost to remain professional but certainly needed some senior management to get across the seriousness of the point and that it has to stop.

Ben also highlighted his concerns regarding the management of the physical education changing area and that for a male trainee this would present both practical and logistical problems within a secondary school for girls:

> I am slightly concerned about what happens in regards to the changing rooms; i.e. what if there is a problem in the changing rooms or if a pupil is unwilling to come out for PE If anything happens I will have to wait for assistance from a female member of staff.

The issue of changing room management clearly had implications for Ben and made him feel anxious. This presents a male physical education trainee teacher with a series of awkward dilemmas that impact on daily practice and may, therefore, explain why the training of male teachers of physical education in secondary schools for girls is an unusual occurrence, owing to the apprehension and fears regarding the perceived difficulties of working and training in such environments. With regard to the issue of the changing rooms, Ben indicated that he had to rely on the availability of his female mentor or another female member of the physical education teaching staff, which had logistical implications for the preparation of his teaching:

> My main concern was about the changing room situation and every time I walked past them I felt the need to look the completely opposite way just to

be safe. The only problem is there is some equipment stored in the changing rooms, which I obviously can't access, so I have been informed to either get it out before the start of the day or to ask a female member of staff to get it out while I watch their class.

During a post-placement interview, Ben was able to reflect upon the challenges that this particular issue presented and explained how he devised a strategic approach which helped him to manage and deal with the situation.

There is a corridor from the PE department to outside and you have to go past the changing rooms so every time there is a door open I'd actually literally make sure that I was facing the other way. Even if there was nothing on the wall I'd pretend there was something on the wall just to make sure that there was no question. I still look the other way near the changing rooms but I don't feel half as nervous now. After lessons I'll wait in the corridor, not outside or near the changing rooms but jut down the corridor so that the girls can collect their valuables and things like that so I don't have a problem with it anymore.

For a male trainee teacher training to teach physical education at a secondary school for girls the issue of subject knowledge was also a concern for Ben. Training to teach a female-orientated physical education curriculum presented Ben with a number of challenges that tested his pedagogical capabilities. In this respect, Ben commented:

I am aware of the aesthetic activity that surround girls PE, such as gymnastics, as I have little experience in teaching this in comparison to football, rugby and cricket. Although this will benefit my professional development, I am still nervous about teaching these activities.

Training to teach physical activities traditionally and historically associated with female participation had clearly placed Ben outside of his comfort zone. This had exposed his own masculine sporting ethos and gendered habitus.[13] Ben's lack of expertise and experience of teaching these types of activities also reflected his own socialisation as a trainee teacher or what Lawson (1986) has described as a process of 'acculturation'.[14] Within the context of single-sex schooling, many of the assumptions that teachers hold often results in stereotypical expectations of their pupils' behaviour and for girls this has been shown to be reinforced by the content of the formal physical education curriculum transmitting covert messages to girls about the acceptability of particular forms of physicality through feminine-appropriate physical activities. Ben's comments indicated that the physical education curriculum at the secondary school for girls reflected ascendant values and ideologies associated with girls' physical education and what a typical physical education curriculum for girls should include.

During the course of the placement, Ben highlighted other challenges that he had encountered. Shortly after his school-based training had begun, the physical support for girls during physical education lessons had posed a number of professional dilemmas for Ben. Physical contact between a teacher and a pupil of the same-sex presents similar problems to that of contact between a teacher and pupil of the opposite-sex but it presents a very different context for men working with girls as highlighted by Ben:

> At the start of the week, I had a year 8 gymnastics lesson in which we were doing vaulting. In the vaulting lesson some of the girls needed supporting to get from the trampette up on to the box. To support and assist the pupils I obviously had to touch them. I asked them if they minded me supporting them (to which they said they didn't mind). I told each pupil I supported that I was going to put my hand on their shoulder and the other hand on their waist in order to help them get their hips up and spring onto the box. At the beginning this felt awkward and I wouldn't support pupils unless they really needed it, but the girls didn't seem to mind at all, and to be honest they seemed glad of the help. Maybe it was only me with the problem because of society today.

Ben's reference to 'society today' reflect the apprehension (and perhaps even paranoia) that some male physical education teachers have when working directly with girls and how this might be perceived and even misconstrued. It has been suggested, for example, that the physical nature of physical education, which often involves the touching of pupils' bodies, places male teachers and trainee teachers in a compromising and vulnerable position. This is a complicated and difficult issue for male trainee teachers of physical education in situations with female pupils and could therefore, be the rationale for dividing physical education groups and staffing these groups according to sex (Berg and Lahelma 2010: 39). Male physical education teachers and trainee teachers are considered to be more prone to these types ethical issues compared with women as, in some cases, their masculinity can be a threat to girls, unlike a female's femininity to boys (Berg and Lahelma 2010). As the placement progressed, many of Ben's concerns regarding the physical support of girls in physical education lessons when working with girls were eventually overcome. For Ben this was a matter of confidence and professionalism:

> These feelings of awkwardness have completely disappeared now and I have even helped with the year 11 girls swimming lessons and assessment over the past 3 weeks. The girls really responded well to me whereas at the start I had thoughts of 'is this allowed?' and 'is this OK?' I wasn't sure how I could help or how I would be perceived. I now don't have any queries with supporting or teaching swimming as it benefits the pupils and doesn't matter if they are male or female.

For Ben, training to teach physical education in a secondary school for girls meant that it was also potentially more difficult for a male to encourage the participation of girls when there were requests to excuse themselves from taking part in the lesson. Ben's initial concerns were that he might be perceived as insensitive and unsympathetic if he were to deny such requests but his experiences of dealing with these issues suggested otherwise. Dealing with pupil requests for permission to be excused from physical education lessons was a key issue highlighted in Ben's narrative account but were pragmatic rather than pedagogical. The comments provided by Ben suggested that these issues were less affected by the fact that he was male.

> Of course there are always notes from parents saying their daughter can't take part in PE because of their period pains. I know for a fact that I was uncomfortable with talking about this in my last placement (at a mixed school) and it usually got dealt with by a female member of staff, but now I can happily be professional and mature enough to be able to deal with it myself because I have had to. I can now talk to pupils about it, get them changed and get them taking part. I tell them that if it hurts they can stop but when we are out there they usually participate in the lesson fully.

Having completed the 75-day school-based training experience in a secondary school for girls, Ben overwhelmingly had a sense of achievement and self-fulfilment. In this respect, his comments were positive with regards to his professional development and his future employability as a specialist teacher of physical education. For example, as a male trainee teacher of physical education, his experiences of training exclusively with girls had enhanced his subject knowledge and helped him to understand the pedagogy of physical education in a very different context:

> I can see no reason whatsoever why male PE teachers shouldn't be employed or train to teach PE in all girls schools. I think to myself why is it ok for a male maths teacher to work in an all girl's school but not a male PE teacher? At the end of the day we are both professionals regardless and we are there to develop the pupils.

During the course of their teacher training, trainee teachers are provided with advice about applying for and securing their first teaching position. Physical education is different from other subjects as there is often a covert message that men should not consider applying for posts that refer specifically to 'girls physical education' and women should not consider applying for positions referring to 'boys physical education'. Likewise, there may be an assumption among newly qualified teachers of physical education that single-sex schools are automatically seeking to appoint a same-sex teacher of physical education. Ben's comments suggested that his experience of training in a secondary school for girls had increased his subject knowledge as a newly qualified teacher and encouraged him to consider applying for teaching positions in secondary schools for girls. As a result of these experiences, Ben was far more prepared to consider his employment options as a specialist teacher of physical education as opposed to a teacher of 'boy's physical education'.

> I would now have no hesitation in applying for a 'teacher of girls PE' job. I feel confident with how to motivate girls in different ways to boys and I also feel confident in the activities that girls predominantly take part in. I think that this has increased my employability by adding a different string to my bow that not many male PE teachers can say they have experienced. I am 100% glad I took this opportunity and it has changed me as a teacher for the better. Not only can I motivate boys with an occasional banter, but now I have experience in trying to motivate teenage girls that don't usually take part in PE.

Ben's comments were further elaborated upon during the post-placement interview. When asked whether there was any reason why a male trainee teacher of physical education should not train to teach physical education in a secondary school for girls, Ben provided the following response:

> Absolutely not! I can't see anything wrong with it whatsoever. Because at the end of the day you're professional. You're doing your job. You're there to teach them physical education. Whether it's males teaching females it's not a problem, females teaching males or teaching mixed (sex) I don't see why it should be a problem at all. They are still pupils, they still need to learn and you're still there to teach them.

The experiences of training to teach physical education in a secondary school for girls undoubtedly presented many challenges for Ben but he had been prepared and mentored to deal with many of the issues outside of the pedagogical context. Previous research (Flintoff 1998) has suggested that being mentored by a physical education teacher of the opposite sex is problematic (in a mixed-sex secondary school), particularly for female trainee teachers but also for some men. At the secondary school for girls, there was no evidence to suggest that this had been the case, as Ben had been mentored and trained effectively by his female mentor, illustrated by his mentor comments in his final report of his teaching competencies.

Conclusion

Ben's narrative accounts provided a sense of empathy of the challenges for men training to teach physical education in an opposite-sex school. The physical support of female pupils, the need for sensitivity in dealing with issues of female body development, subject knowledge deficiencies outside of traditional masculine gendered boundaries and issues of changing room management were all salient issues. It was evident, however, that his professional competence and credibility was far more important to his female pupils than any issues associated with being male. Despite the rhetorical claims that much has been achieved in addressing sex-role stereotyping within physical education initial teacher training, gender issues still persist. As a postscript to this study, email correspondence received from a university colleague demonstrated that some of the gatekeepers[15] within secondary schools still regard the sex of the trainee teacher of physical education as a particularly salient issue.

> Unfortunately (school A) want a break from students (trainee physical education teachers) so I have relocated (male student's name) to (school B) for his 1st placement – to be mentored by (mentor's name). He is now down to go to (school C) for his 2nd placement as (school D) ONLY wanted a female!
>
> *(Email correspondence received 18 July 2011)*

> I am so sorry! But his 2nd placement school has changed again! Apparently (school C) only want a female student – therefore he is now going to (school E) for his 2nd placement – and he is still going to (school B) for his first placement. Hopefully this will be the last change!
>
> *(Email correspondence received 20 July 2011)*

Moreover, some secondary schools may be particularly resistant to receiving applications for permanent physical education teaching posts from newly qualified male teachers, as exemplified by an email received from a newly qualified male trainee teacher of physical education:

> I applied for a job this morning at (name of the school) in (name of the county). It did mention a female teacher on the school website but I thought I would apply anyway and this is the reply I got (from the head teacher's personal assistant)!
>
> We are looking for a female PE teacher for this post, so you may need to reconsider your application!?
>
> Regards.
>
> *(Email correspondence received 11 February 2013)*

It could be that female teachers are more suited to teaching physical education to girls in same-sex schools or even in mixed-sex secondary schools compared with males or that secondary schools themselves perceive that a gender-balance within a physical education department is desirable and important. Commenting on the overall effectiveness of physical education in secondary schools and the quality of leadership and management, the UK Inspectorate for Education, Children's Services and Skills (Ofsted 2013a) highlighted that distinctive (hierarchical gender-specific) roles within physical education departments still exist and can be an extremely productive strategy in raising standards of teaching, even though it was not clear as to whether these roles were assigned to male or female teachers respectively.

> The head of department, ably supported by the head of girls' PE, has strategically moulded a team of high calibre PE professionals with complementary skills, who share a common ethos and work together extremely well.
>
> *(Ofsted 2013a: 57)*

Clearly, more research is required to understand the challenges for males training to teach physical education in secondary schools for girls. Interpreting prevalent themes and offering a voice to the trainee teacher is critical. Analysing the perceptions of mentors may also provide a greater awareness of some of the logistical challenges of training male trainee teachers of physical education in opposite-sex schools and add an additional layer of understanding to the pertinent issues for secondary schools for girls. Undoubtedly, Ben had gained valuable professional experiences through subject knowledge enhancement outside of traditional male-gendered boundaries even though his masculine sporting ethos had not deviated too far and his gendered habitus had remained relatively intact. Nonetheless, Ben's experiences could be viewed as providing newly qualified male teachers of physical education with increased confidence in undertaking the types of teaching roles for which they have usually been dissuaded from applying for secondary schools for girls. Equally, it may help to convince teacher educators (and trainee physical education teachers themselves) that the sex of the trainee teacher of physical education is not necessarily a prerequisite for training to teach physical education in either a secondary school for girls or a secondary school for boys nor should it be the basis upon which to advertise for and appoint teachers of secondary school physical education.

So what next? The following chapter highlights the trials and tribulations of becoming a newly qualified teacher of physical education.

Notes

1　Hannah Frankel, 'My best teacher – Bradley Wiggins', *Times Educational Supplement*, 2 July 2010. Available online at www.tes.co.uk/article.aspx?storycode=6049352 (accessed 26 September 2014).

2　University of Brighton School of Sport and Service Management, 'Does Sex Matter – opposite-sex teaching in physical education' 25 June 2013. Available online at www.youtube.com/watch?v=ng1d_iPI6hA&list=PL9036FECA22DB89CD&index=4 (accessed 26 September 2014).

3　'Single-sex or co-educational schools for girls and boys?' *BBC News*, 6 February 2012. Available online at www.bbc.co.uk/news/uk-politics-16855727 (accessed 26 September 2014).

4　A primary school in the United Kingdom is an educational institution in which children start their statutory period of compulsory education at the age of 5 and finish at the age of 11. An infant school will have a nursery and teach children up to the age of 7 years (key stage one). A junior school teaches children aged 7–11 years (key stage two). A primary school includes nursery, infant and junior classes. The term 'primary school' is sometimes used to mean infant school and junior school combined as both provide primary education.

5 In England and Wales, a governor is an elected voluntary member of a school's governing body, which has overall responsibility for staffing matters and may delegate these to a governor subcommittee responsible for staffing, although there is an expectation that the head teacher will lead the process of making staff appointments in consultation with subject-specific leaders in secondary schools. Schools may give preference to a woman over a man or vice versa where a person's sex is a genuine occupational qualification, such as preserving privacy and decency in girls' or boys' changing rooms while they are in use.

6 A partnership training agreement is an agreement between schools and universities with respect to initial teacher training and standards for qualifying to teach.

7 Flintoff and Scraton (2005: 165–67) discuss how male physicality is linked directly to physical education and sport and how masculinity is always defined hierarchically in relation to femininity where one set of attributes and associated activities (men's) are viewed as more important than the other's (women's).

8 Laker *et al.* (2003: 75) have shown how gendered behaviour can be promoted as accepted practice (in physical education) through a hidden hegemonic (physical education) curriculum. In this respect, predominant powers control distribution and integration of knowledge. Thus, the (physical education) curriculum becomes a vehicle for reinforcing and emphasising the position and status of men and women within the subject.

9 A physical education technician is not a qualified teacher but an administrative member of the department responsible for setting up equipment and the general day-to-day running of the department.

10 A virtual learning environment allows for web-based access to a social space where students and teachers can interact through threaded discussions. It can also include students and teacher 'meeting' online. Students can keep a virtual online diary and may answer questions or pose questions. They can use the tools available through the application to ask or answer questions.

11 Banter is a term that refers to conversations that are primarily masculine and widely perceived within male discourse as witty and informal as opposed to serious and formal. It is also experienced by many as offensive and abusive.

12 A 'crush' otherwise known as 'limerence' is an involuntary state of mind which results from an attraction to another person combined with an overwhelming desire to have their feelings reciprocated. This can occur amongst pupils in schools with respect to their teachers.

13 Green (2008: 208) refers to the 'habitus' of physical education teachers as the internalisation of attitudes, behaviours, customs, values and beliefs that make up the subculture(s) of physical education teaching and how these become part and parcel of physical education teachers personalities or 'habituses' – their 'second nature'.

14 Lawson (1986) refers to acculturation as the first stage of a physical education teacher's socialisation into the teaching profession. This is primarily based upon childhood and adolescent sporting and PE experiences and the predispositions these are said to engender (Cited in Green 2008: 208).

15 A gatekeeper' provides access to a group that a researcher wishes to study. In a school setting it might be a head teacher, a senior manager or mentor.

7

BECOMING A PHYSICAL EDUCATION TEACHER

My geography teacher David Jackson was in large part the inspiration for me to join the local athletics club. He understood what I wanted to do because he ran cross-country for Derbyshire schools. He wasn't a PE teacher, but he was an accomplished sportsman. He encouraged me to play all sorts of sports in the early days. He understood that it's good for children to do that before they start specialising.

Lord Sebastian Coe[1]

The first section of this chapter highlights the challenges of entering the physical education teaching profession for the first time and the induction process that newly qualified teachers (NQTs) are likely to experience. First-year teachers typically experience a range of both 'highs' and 'lows' throughout the school year and sometimes both, even during the same working day. The high points experienced by NQTs tend to be associated with positive relationships with pupils and colleagues; their perceptions of professional autonomy and their experiences of achievement and change. The 'lows' experienced by NQTs are often related to the demands of the role or their reported workload and challenging relationships with pupils, with pupils' parents and with colleagues in their schools (Hobson *et al.* 2007). Attrition rates from teaching after just three years in the profession can be as high as 30 per cent.[2] This could be attributed to the fact that those who decide to leave the profession do so because of a sense of frustration and experiences of low expectations of pupils. A teacher's first school is central in the process of them becoming the practitioner they want to be. It is where they decide if they are suited to the school and the teaching profession and yet schools frequently induct NQTs into 'the system' that they must fit into. Too often, good teachers leave because they care too much to stay.[3] The first section of this chapter offers some practical advice for newly qualified physical education teachers seeking their first teaching post and embarking on their first year in teaching and meeting the requirements for all new teachers through the induction programme for NQTs. This section also draws upon vignettes of NQTs, as well as highlighting the requirements of the 'induction year' for NQTs. The aim of this chapter is to highlight the experiences and support that an NQT can expect in their first year of teaching physical education that go beyond that which can be easily found on the internet:[4]

Working as a PE teacher

Once qualified as a PE teacher you will need to apply for jobs in schools that are accepting applications from newly qualified teachers. These schools will often have extra help in place so that new teachers can be guided and mentored at the start of their careers. The starting salary for a new teacher outside of London is £21,588. Teachers in London have starting salaries of between £22,000 and £27,000 depending on location. Typically, a secondary school PE teacher can expect to teach from about 8.30am through to about 3.30pm with breaks. In addition to this they may be expected to help at after-school clubs and they will have to undertake a certain amount of planning in their own time. Teachers in state schools usually have approximately 13 weeks holiday across the year at the set school holiday times.

Skills and personality

The profile of a PE teacher can vary greatly, however, there are a number of personality traits or skills that are useful to have in this career. A good teacher will be reasonably confident, making them able to control a crowd and speak well to a class. Good organisation skills are key along with the ability to handle paperwork.

Becoming an NQT will involve a process of applying and being interviewed for a vacant teaching position within a physical education department. Securing that first post will be at the forefront of graduating teachers' priorities and choosing the right school will be critical. Rather than randomly applying for a job out of desperation, it is as important for NQTs to select the right school, just as it is for a school to be sure that have selected the right candidate for them. Typically, a school will place an advertisement for a vacant position, either online or through the print media, identifying the principal roles and responsibilities, such as the example below:[5]

We are seeking enthusiastic, committed and energetic PE teachers to work across various schools in the area. We have a number of excellent opportunities for all Secondary Qualified PE teachers including NQTs. All we ask is that you hold a UK recognised qualification, we can obtain references from your previous employers and have or are able to undergo and enhanced DBS disclosure. These positions will enable the right candidate to work in flexible conditions across both long term and short-term assignments to suit your requirements. All applicants will be expected to teach PE across key stages 3 and 4 and work with pupils of varying abilities.

Some schools may choose to specifically advertise for and subsequently appoint a male or female physical education teacher although this could be regarded as somewhat dubious practice. Under the Equalities Act 2010, it is unlawful for schools to advertise for candidates on the basis of their sexual orientation, marital status, race or ethnicity. Yet research has shown that biological sex is often an explicit requirement in the wording of advertisements for many physical education posts within secondary schools in England and has the potential to exclude male or female teachers from applying for such positions (Stidder 2002, 2005). While not strictly against the law, it does seem to flout the spirit in which sex discrimination legislation has been written. If you need any convincing of this then you might just wish to read the text below:

> The PE department are looking to appoint a vibrant, dynamic and motivated female PE teacher, The nature of the department means that we are specifically looking for a female NQT PE teacher, who would enhance an already good department with her enthusiasm, knowledge and commitment. We would like any interested applicants to contact us for an informal discussion which could be a visit, over the telephone, email or Skype.

Between January and April 2014, advertisements such as this were not uncommon in the pages of the *Times Educational Supplement* (TES), with many schools still insisting on using the terms 'male teacher' and 'female teacher' of physical education. Nutt and Clarke (2002: 161) argue that, through their recruitment strategies for NQTs of physical education, schools sustain a 'hidden curriculum' in that the division of labour among teaching staff ensures that particular activities in physical education are offered to pupils. The issues facing prospective school employers are clearly unrelated to professional competence but are more to do with the management of pupil changing before and after lessons. My own research has confirmed that secondary schools restrict employment opportunities for male and female teachers through the vocabulary used in national advertisements and thus perpetuate gender divisions within physical education, which is often contrary to the views expressed by those entering the physical education profession (Stidder 2002, 2005). Typically, an advertisement for a vacant physical education post might read 'Teacher of PE and girls' games' or Teacher of boys' PE', thus giving the impression that only women or men need apply. Despite attempts to eradicate some of the most obvious forms of sexism within the physical education profession, it has become apparent that the secondary school is unique, as it is the only stage of compulsory schooling where the arrangements for staffing in physical education lessons is often predetermined by the biological composition of the class. This is arguably reflected in the attitudes and actions of some secondary schools that send very clear messages to potential applicants regarding sex roles.

Once shortlisted for a teaching post, the interview process can be testing time for most candidates. This will involve a tour of the school, a meeting with key staff, teaching a physical education lesson, an interview conducted by a pupil forum and a formal interview with the senior management team at the school. Here are some standard questions that applicants can expect to be asked:

- How do you think your lesson went?
- What do you consider to be your strengths and weaknesses?
- Why do you want this job?
- What attracted you to this school?
- What makes an outstanding lesson? Give me an example of when you have taught an outstanding lesson?
- Where do you see yourself in five years? Do you know your potential career development path?
- Give an example of difficult behaviour? How did you resolve it?
- What do you think you can bring to the department?
- What is the role of a form tutor?
- School information management system? How does this help?
- How would you include ICT in PE?
- By law has there has to be a child protection question. Think of a safeguarding example.
- If I were to Google you today what would I find?
- How can teachers minimise the risk when using electronic communication and social networking?

Once a full-time post has been secured, schools have an obligation to provide an induction programme and support mechanism for the NQT. But, as Green has pointed out, the process is never easy:

> The workplace, especially early on in teachers' careers, is important in supporting or restricting their practices as they find themselves constrained not only by the dominant values and beliefs of their colleagues, departments and schools, but also by practical matters to do with facilities and equipment. This helps to explain why the impact of teacher education tends to be 'washed out' relatively soon after teachers begin teaching properly.
>
> *(Green 2008: 214)*

When I qualified as a physical education teacher in 1986, the induction period was known as 'probation' and for the first year of my teaching career I was known as a 'probationary teacher'. Green (2008; 215) refers to this as a period of occupational socialisation or a process characterised by consecutive generations of physical education teachers absorbing newcomers into what amounts to very similar physical education department networks. Nutt and Clarke (2002) commented that the part a teacher's occupational socialisation plays in the process of professional identification is compelling much of which comes through a teacher's own school socialisation, pre-service education and induction as a newly qualified teacher. But, as Nutt and Clarke (2002) have stipulated: 'Since the structure of teacher preparation clearly has a powerful impact upon teachers' professional perspectives, their induction into what counts as legitimate forms of knowledge and the nature of learning, ought to be subjected to more in-depth critical scrutiny' (Nutt and Clarke 2002: 161).

The 'probationary year' was supposed to protect new entrants to teaching from being exploited and prevent them from being assigned to overly difficult or challenging pupils. It was also a protective mechanism against dubious timetabling arrangements so that NQTs only taught subjects in which they were trained and qualified to teach. Being a new kid on the block, one might expect there to be challenges ahead to complete the apprenticeship and for the first term to be particularly challenging in establishing effective working relationships with staff and pupils.

In September 1986, I began my teaching career. I was informed on the first day that I would have to teach six social studies classes a week. I had never been trained to teach social studies and more to the point I did not even know what it was. I certainly did not know or have a sound knowledge and understanding of how the United Kingdom was governed, its political system and how citizens participate actively in its democratic systems of government. Nor did I have a sound knowledge and understanding of the role of law and the justice system in UK society and how laws were shaped and enforced. What on earth did that have to do with being a physical education teacher? Needless to say, I had to learn fast and stay one step ahead of the pupils. My timetable of physical education teaching included a very challenging year nine boy's class on a Friday afternoon, affectionately known as 'the graveyard shift'. Don't smile until Christmas' were the common words of advice issued to probationary teachers. Set your boundaries and ground rules in place. Be consistent. Do not have favourites. Rule with an iron fist. Read them the riot act went without saying. Sure enough, that is how my teaching career began. At the time, I considered it to be my initiation and a chance to prove myself and just got on with it. Not once did I question whether I was being taken advantage of. As an NQT I risked my credibility unless I taught the way I was obliged to teach and did the things I was told to do. I ended up saying 'yes' to everything and fell into a trap where there was an expectation that I would do everything associated with boys physical education. Thankfully, these types of experiences for NQTs are rare, as they are protected from exploitation in the workplace by induction procedures in the first year of their careers and their progress is monitored in a more systematic way. For example, NQTs can expect a reduced teaching timetable and are not expected to teach any other subject other than the subject they have been trained to teach. Induction tutors provide regular constructive feedback and opportunities for continued professional development. Pastoral responsibilities are usually delayed for NQTs until they have become familiar with the systems in place.

Green (2003) observed that some newly qualified physical education teachers replicated traditional approaches to conventional forms of practice for no reason other than convenience, despite having mixed views about the appropriateness of what was being offered and provided for pupils. These teachers worked alongside experienced professionals and 'were at the mercy' of their school's senior management when it came to curriculum decisions. The power relations that existed between younger (inexperienced) teachers and their older (more experienced) colleagues acted as a device to constrain any decisions regarding innovation and change to established patterns of organisation, staffing or delivery. The findings from Green's study suggest that the influence of NQTs, who are often viewed as being at the cutting edge of pedagogy and practice, has little or no impact on existing practice in schools, owing to the power relations that exist between younger and older teachers and sometimes perceived to be a threat. In other words, NQTs are likely to work in conditions where established patterns of provision are going to be hard to break and the maintenance of a status quo is consequently sustained. I can certainly vouch for that, as I spent the early part of my career conforming to orthodox and conservative methods of teaching that existing staff are most familiar with. But, as Green (2008: 215) has cogently argued, new arrivals to the physical education teaching profession are never completely identical to their predecessors and their adjustment is never total so what happens in the name of physical education is bound to change over time.

Much of what I taught in the early stages of my career tended to reflect traditional methods of teaching physical education and the legacy of the single-sex teacher training colleges of the 1960s and 1970s. Lessons tended to be teacher-centred, with lengthy units of work taught in single-sex groups. I sensed that some young people were disenchanted with what was on offer in physical education lessons. The majority of pupils were not part of the select chosen few; the curriculum was narrow in content and focused on a few traditional sports, leading to an elitist system that failed to encourage participation by the less able. However, I also observed what I regarded at the time as 'risky' or what others might describe as innovative practice. Teachers were prepared to confront the status quo and breathe new life into a department by offering pupils different pathways and options suited to their individual needs. Teaching was inclusive, units of work were shorter, some groups were mixed-sex. There was high recognition and status for physical education. An NQT of physical education was seen as a innovative, creative and cutting-edge specialist who knew and understood the features of effective pedagogy and teaching, had a vast repertoire of skills and had the ability to integrate cross-curricular themes, problem solving and decision-making skills into their lessons in a safe and purposeful environment. NQTs, however, are rarely encouraged to experiment with their teaching, despite their best attempts to explore alternative ways of teaching physical education. It is not until they become more established as a teacher that they have the confidence to do so. Green (2008) explains that newly qualified physical education teachers learn, accept and implement customary strategies as they are junior members of staff and keen to fit in with and become established among their colleagues. These types of experiences, therefore, are actually the rule rather than the exception.

> Newcomers to the physical education profession are frequently obliged to adapt their behaviours – and subsequently their views – upon joining their new colleagues, departments and schools, since all the surrounding positions are still occupied by the same teachers as before and they generally want things to carry on as before.
>
> *(Green 2008: 214)*

Yet, all NQTs of physical education must not forget that one of the major developments in the profession has been the unprecedented rate at which examination courses in physical education have increased, bringing unmitigated success in terms of status and credibility (Green 2008: 93). Accredited courses in physical education did not exist at the secondary school that I attended and the situation was no different at the local sixth form college, although the number of post-16 physical education courses have grown at an unprecedented rate since the late 1980s. Increasingly, NQTs of physical education are expected to teach examination courses such as GCSE, BTEC and 'A' level to pupils aged 14–18 and, as such, spend as much time in the classroom as they do on the playing field. Golder (2010) has highlighted the fact that many of these qualifications in physical education have been introduced as part of a 14–18 curriculum, as all young people in the UK are required to stay in education or training until 18 years of age from 2015. This has only served to reflect the evolving nature of physical education as a subject and of the UK Coalition Government's attention to raising academic standards but also highlighting the need for more newly qualified physical education teachers who have been trained to teach physical education theory, as well as well practical physical education.

There is recognition that the continued growth of accredited physical education courses is a reflection of the value that teachers place on accredited forms of learning (see Chapter 11). This is part of a process referred to by Green (2008: 88) as the 'academicisation' of physical education that has been apparent for over a quarter of a century, whereby there is increasing emphasis on the theoretical study of physical activity and sport in both absolute and relative terms (that is, in relation to, and sometimes at the expense of, practical activities). Green (2008) has shown how the increase in the numbers of pupils studying accredited forms of physical education has surpassed virtually all other subjects. In this respect, Ofsted (2013a) found that most secondary schools offer accredited physical education courses in order to broaden the choices open to pupils, as many schools prefer a more vocational approach to physical education, where pupils are assessed as performers, leaders or officials through accredited courses. Today, the ability to teach accredited forms of physical education is an expectation of all physical education teachers (see Chapter 11 for further discussion).

A typical job description for an NQT of physical education will require them to teach pupils according to their educational needs, including the setting and marking of work to be carried out by the pupil in school and elsewhere. Teachers are required to assess, record and report on the attendance, progress, development and attainment of pupils and to keep records. It is now commonplace for all teachers, including physical education teachers, to ensure that information and communications technology, literacy, numeracy and the school subject specialism(s) are reflected in the teaching and learning experience of pupils. Newly appointed staff will be required to take part in staff development programmes by participating in arrangements for further training and professional development and engage actively in the NQT review process. In addition, the role will include the need to communicate effectively with the parents of pupils and to communicate and cooperate with external agencies outside the formal school setting. This will involve taking part in parents' evenings, review days and liaison events with partner schools. It is important to note that, to play a full part in the life of a school, an NQT needs to support the school's distinctive mission and ethos and encourage pupils to follow this example. This might involve supporting the school in meeting its legal requirements for worship, to promote actively the school's corporate policies, to comply with the school's health and safety policy and undertake risk assessments as appropriate as well as assist in the promotion and delivery of a range of extra-curricular teams and competitions.

Since 2012, revised professional standards for teachers (Department for Education 2013a) have been introduced. These apply to both trainees and NQTs. The standards for induction have to be achieved by the end of the newly qualified year and are an entitlement for all newly qualified teachers which support a continuing portfolio. All NQTs are judged on how well they develop professional and constructive relationships and work within the law and frameworks. During their first year of teaching, all NQTs are expected to develop their professional knowledge and understanding (pedagogical practice, promoting children and young people's development and wellbeing), as well as their professional skills (planning and assessment, teaching). To enable NQTs to meet the teachers' standards and to ensure a smooth transition during their first year, they should not be given a job description that makes unreasonable demands. They should not teach outside the age range for which they have been trained, nor should they teach any subject other than the subject that they have been trained to teach. As an NQT, you should not be expected to deal with, on a day-to-day basis, acute or especially demanding discipline problems or teach classes other than those for which you are regularly responsible. You should not be involved in additional non-teaching responsibilities without the provision of appropriate preparation and support (form tutor) or be involved in planning, teaching and assessment processes other than those in which other teachers are in the school are engaged. You should not be teaching more than 90 per cent of the timetable of other main-scale teachers in the school without responsibility points. The additional 10 per cent of non-contact time is for activities that form part of the induction support programme (Department for Education 2013b). All NQTs should receive a schedule for formal assessment meetings, a timetable of lessons and support arrangements, entitlements to pay during sickness absences, maternity and paternity leave, arrangement for salary payments, provisions for pensions and other entitlements. Guidance for school health and safety and equal opportunity policy, information of other school policies including cover (you are not expected to cover for absent colleagues), a list of duties (after school, break times) and child protection training must also be provided.

To put into context the demands of the first year of teaching, a series of vignettes and reflections from NQTs of physical education are included below. These are reflective accounts of their first year of teaching during the academic year 2013–14.

Vignette 1

Your first year as a physical education teacher is 'a whirlwind year'. No longer is your hand held while you tread new waters in teaching and learning and dip in and out of schemes of work. This is for real! As the first day of school starts right up until that last summer's day, you have an onus to deliver outstanding lessons to students of varying backgrounds and abilities, to challenge and accelerate the learning of those students and to be accountable for that progress made, and that's just curricular duties. There is also pastoral duties, running a tutor group maybe? Just a small task . . . The NQT year is a whirlwind experience with many 'first time' scenarios; your first parents day, your first big mistake, your first angry parent, your first cohorts exam grades, your first encounter with the staff room (who sits where), your first scheme of work (yes one you actually wrote yourself), your first staff party but most importantly the first and hopefully not the last time you hear a student say 'now I get it'! Words of advice: do something that scares you every day and try something new every week.

Vignette 2

My advice I would give to those who are about to start their NQT year is to grab every opportunity that comes your way. If you are offered professional development courses then take them, get stuck in and help out with all the clubs and fixtures to build upon relationships with the pupils and show the initiative to observe other teachers from different departments whenever you can. Don't worry if you feel overwhelmed as I know I did when I first started at my new school, but I had so much support and because I wasn't afraid to learn and reflect on my practice, I gained a lot from my NQT year. It can be stressful at times, especially since there are several observations that need to be undertaken, but this happens within schools anyway, just not as often. You just need to take them with a pinch of salt and realise that they are only there to highlight your strengths and to improve your lessons. Build up a good relationship with your mentor and you will relax more within your observations. Lastly learn to say 'no' at times. When you first start at a school you want to make a good impression, but this doesn't mean saying 'yes' to everything you are asked to do, otherwise your workload becomes unmanageable and unrealistic.

Vignette 3

Becoming qualified and finally teaching my first lesson felt like learning to ride a bike and finally your dad lets go of the seat, allowing you to find out what it is like to ride freely but also what it feels like to crash without a cushion. People are still looking over you and helping you back up, but you must try the pedals, try your speed and learn to balance your workload. The first day of completing a full day felt like my mind was exhausted of its life. Not only do you now have to think about teaching, but little Jimmy in your form has a problem with someone in the higher years calling him names, or the weather causes you to cancel your wonderfully planned lesson, to be replaced by 70 kids in a space big enough for one of those lovely lessons. However, as time goes on, things that just did not click before, such as the warm up or how you progress a task, begins to seem slightly easier. The kids learn your ways not just your surname, and may actually begin to like you. As time goes on, you may even take a breath and have a look around and think, this is a pretty good place to be for 80 per cent of your day.

Vignette 4

I have had a very different NQT experience to what other people are having. My NQT job is in a new free school that only opened up in September 2013. The school has nine teaching staff and 75 year seven pupils, meaning there is a very unique feel to the school. Due to the low amount of students and only having one year, my teaching timetable is light compared to what it would normally be in an NQT year. I also teach all the geography at the school; something which I was apprehensive about when accepting the job. However, after being really well supported, my classroom teaching has improved dramatically and puts me in a good position ready for teaching examination PE in the years to come. I am also the only PE teacher in the school. This means I have the responsibility to create the key stage three curriculum, write schemes of work and resources, and being responsible for every student's progress in PE. While ideally I would have liked to be teaching a lot more PE, this experience has given me the freedom to create a curriculum that I think engages and appeals to everyone in the school, as well time to create resources and detailed schemes of work. I have also had some experience of what it would be like to be in a head of department role. Finally, I have really enjoyed the pastoral side of being a teacher. While this is something that you only experience partly when on your teaching placements, you then find it takes up a lot of your time at school. As a form tutor you are constantly making sure students are happy and safe at school, making regular contact with parents/carers and passing on concerns to senior leadership team. I have also been very fortunate to be offered the role of head of year seven from September. this is a great opportunity to develop my leadership skills, as well as a privilege to be heavily involved in the lives of the students in our school community. Overall, while there are some down sides to working in a start-up free school, I have had an extremely positive NQT year and have been very fortunate to build up a PE department and curriculum from the start.

Vignette 5

My NQT year has offered me lots of experiences. Having applied for a PE job, I was asked to teach science in my NQT year too – I agreed. Teaching two subjects gives me a wider skill set and provides me with different teaching experiences too. In your NQT year it is all about gaining a wide range of experiences to equip you for different situations and demands. A position for PSHCE coordinator arose at the academy in the first term and I applied for this role as I believe in the holistic education of students. Myself and another NQT are both head of PSHCE at the academy and this role has helped me develop rapport with staff around the school. Building positive working relationships with staff in your NQT year is vital. As an NQT it is important that you start as you mean to go on- set yourself and your students high standards, although you may be able to reduce the amount of times you have to reinforce these standards as your class learns how your lessons are expected to run, they are nevertheless still in place. Continue to observe other teachers, learning from other practitioners is not just for trainee teachers, it is just as useful to sit and watch other lessons being taught when you are in your NQT year.

These reflections from newly qualified physical education teachers indicate that being adaptable to different circumstances and learning from other teachers is as much a part of the induction process as the induction requirements themselves. Being professional and thick-skinned counts for a great deal in the first year of teaching. Once the induction period has been completed and the teachers' standards have been met, an NQT becomes the real thing – a fully qualified teacher of physical education. The next section of this chapter aims to provide advice for teachers entering their first year as a fully qualified teacher and reveals some of the challenges and rewards that this can bring.

Once qualified and having completed the induction year, teaching is rather like driving a car without an instructor sat next to the driver in the passenger seat or like driving without either an 'L' or 'P' plate for the initial period. It is when the physical education teacher comes of age. This section discusses the role and the type of experiences qualified teachers can expect. Case studies of physical education teachers have illustrated the challenges and rewards that come from being a physical education teacher (Armour and Jones 1998). This period of time has been referred to as the professional socialisation of physical education teachers through continued professional development (Green 2008), otherwise known as all types of professional learning undertaken by teachers beyond the initial point of training (Armour and Yelling 2004: 96) and usually focused on traditional content knowledge, new content knowledge and preparing for future promotion such a becoming a curriculum leader.

Once established as a fully qualified physical education teacher, it is the time when teachers become 'locked', 'entrenched' even 'stuck' or 'trapped' into the educational system (Armour and Jones 1998: 127) and, for some, it is hard to envisage any realistic alternative because to leave is a major disinvestment and is therefore a reluctant step to take. Teachers can become disillusioned, despondent, jaded, disinterested, demotivated, lethargic and resentful. For others, however, it is the time of realisation that the role of being a physical education teacher is the fulfilment of a calling into the profession and they genuinely begin to enjoy their job. During the formative years of my career, I experienced what Green (2008: 214) has described as 'a marked disjuncture' between what is taught at initial teacher training institutions and what is actually practised in the gymnasium or on the sports field. Retrospectively, many of my physical education lessons focused mainly on skill acquisition within a very traditional curriculum. These were typically through the teaching of sex-segregated and sex-stereotyped team games using a limited range of largely didactic command-style pedagogic approaches. Boys were taken through a series of exercises designed to help them manoeuvre an object through a defended territory to an agreed target within set parameters over a prescribed period of time. These lessons were predominantly skills-based as a prerequisite for playing regulation team games. On many occasions, I taught boys in parallel lines passing a ball to each other repetitiously before moving on to other types of drills that required precise organisation in perfectly symmetrical, angular grid squares measuring exactly ten metres by ten metres, usually finishing with an adult version of a particular team game. Was it physical literacy or physical performance that I was trying to promote?

During the 1980s, my former university lecturer Bob Chappell used to challenge my thinking by asking whether the role of the physical education teacher in schools was to produce elite athletes. Nearly 30 years on, he concludes that physical education teachers are highly trained physical educators, not sports coaches, who use physical activity to develop pupils' understanding of wider educational issues and provide the foundations of physical literacy, as well as educating young people to lead active healthy lifestyles (Chappell 2013: 37). I wish I had listened harder to his words of wisdom during those lectures, as my professional development was compromised to a point where I now feel as if I was complicit in the sportisation of my own subject specialism. While much of the rhetoric and associated theory that informed educational practice within schools often recognised the significance of biological sex and the benefits of mixed-ability groupings, with regards to physical education, very little changed. Consequently, I continued to provide pre-adolescent and post-pubescent boys with a diet of competitive, physically vigorous and aggressive invasion games that remained within the confines of acceptable male heterosexuality, without questioning the concept of what it meant to be 'physically educated'. It is perhaps unsurprising that most of my own early teaching experiences were often determined by pre-established routines which, on reflection, limited both my professional development and understanding of issues related to participation in physical education in schools. I became essentially a teacher of boy's games rather than a physical education teacher. As a result, my own personal experiences of teaching physical education involved me teaching groups of boys how to become fitter, stronger and competitive young men, predominantly through playing territorial warlike games and performance-related activities. This was what they wanted; this was what was good for them and this was what would eventually help them get a (manual or military) job.

Being a physical education teacher involves professional responsibility for planning, teaching and assessment of physical education lessons. It is the time that formal observations cease to happen in the sense of being assessed for qualified teacher status (QTS) and should give teachers a feeling of empowerment to experiment with their teaching. The reality, however, can be somewhat different. A day in the life of physical education teacher may involve the 'perfectly planned' lesson that has been mentally rehearsed and thoroughly researched being changed at a moment's notice because of inclement weather and indoor space being occupied by examination desks. At times, it can feel as if you are a second-class citizen. The science laboratories, the art studio or the computer suite are the operational headquarters for science, design and information technology but are never taken out of action because of public examinations. So why is physical education any different? All of a sudden, there is a realisation that the reduced timetable and levels of support no longer exist. Just like everyone else, the physical education teacher has a role to perform at the same level of intensity. In the early stages of my career, I wanted to use a range and variety of teaching styles to cater for differences among pupils but I never felt completely confident in doing so. Pupil compliance and control was the priority and teacher-led command styles of teaching were the most effective means of managing my physical education lessons.

There will be highs and lows throughout the academic year and, at times, a feeling of despondency. Motivation and enthusiasm are critical, otherwise it is likely that experiences such as those described by Gary Boothroyd might be commonplace:

> It is the morning after a week's half term holiday and it's a decidedly 'dodgy' November morning. Heavy rain is on the horizon and I have a five-period day of lessons ahead of me: hockey, swimming, swimming, badminton and football. Year nine, year eight, year eight, year ten, year eleven, followed by a year seven football match after school, which I foolishly arranged before we broke up for the holiday. It did not seem such a bad idea with a week's holiday to come, but from my position now on a bleak Monday morning, I feel I could well do without it.
>
> (Boothroyd 2004: 35)

These types of recollections may ring true among some physical education teachers and can exacerbate feelings of work-related stress. During my own teaching career, there were times where I felt under pressure in counteracting difficulties faced during the working day. Having supply (substitute) teachers without any expertise or subject knowledge of physical education deputising for absence colleagues was frustrating, particularly when they were employed for a long-term absence. So what did I do? I joined the two classes together and took the physical education lesson myself while the supply teacher stood to the side. There were constant battles and playing of mind games to prevent the indoor space for physical education lessons from being hijacked for examinations and protecting the time available for physical education lessons per week. Devious plans had to be implemented. One teacher I spoke to remarked that, at her particular school, she had heard a rumour that the head teacher had plans to reduce the time for physical education from two hours a week to 90 minutes. A pre-emptive strike took place, whereby an appointment was made to explain to the head teacher why the time should be increased to three hours per week. The outcome was that the time for physical education remained at two hours per week. Experiences such as those described can be mentally draining, particularly when they are combined with the practicalities of teaching. The reality of the teaching profession is that you will be faced with many compromising dilemmas and scenarios. Imagine you are in the following situations. What would you do?

Scenario 1: You have just managed to get a very difficult GCSE PE theory group to settle down for the first lesson of the day in a classroom. As they begin to work, one pupil turns up 10 minutes late and all the other pupils are distracted and start talking again. This group is behind with their course work and you cannot afford to keep wasting valuable class time. You think this pupil may have turned up late on purpose. You also think this person is a lazy pupil and not interested in taking your subject. You ask this pupil to get their homework out but they have forgotten to bring their book again. This is the third time this month that this pupil has failed to hand in homework. Then you ask the pupil to get out their pen and start filling in the worksheet that you gave the group. This pupil is taking up a lot of your time in what is a very demanding group.

Scenario 2: You scan the playing field to see if the pupils are on task and notice that one pupil is flicking mud at another pupil. You ask the pupil to stop it. Later in the lesson you notice that the same pupil is distracting other pupils by doing exactly the same. At the end of the lesson you ask to see the pupil. The pupil says the reason for this was because they didn't understand the task but you wonder why, if this was the case, they didn't say anything earlier in the lesson. You give the pupil a detention after school the next day. The pupil says that they cannot attend the detention tomorrow and asks if they can do the detention another time. You are pressed for time but there are a few occasions when you could meet the pupil's request.

There are no definitive answers to these situations other than being professional in your approach. But they do highlight how the school environment and the pressure that teachers face on a daily basis can wear individuals down. At this point, I wish to draw attention to the experiences of physical education teachers in order to inform readers of the challenges and rewards that teaching can present. Below is a reflective account of a four-year teaching career from a physical education teacher at a school that had recently been awarded academy status.

Vignette 6

> I've missed more than 9000 shots in my career. I've lost almost 300 games; 26 times, I've been trusted to take the game winning shot and missed. I've failed over and over and over again in my life. And that is why I succeed.
>
> *(Michael Jordan, legendary Chicago Bulls basketball player)*

When I trained to be a PE teacher I always thought my main job would be to teach students across a wide range of physical activities to increase their overall physical literacy. In many ways, the quote above resonates with how I felt this learning would take place through a variety of learning environments designed to allow students to fail in a 'safe' environment and become comfortable in acknowledging their weaknesses and how to get better. I believe that this would in turn create more reflective students who could achieve highly because of this ability. Indeed, a year eight student said to me recently that they see failure as a first attempt in learning. I liked this saying and feel that if students grasp it then success is the inevitable outcome. What I discovered in practice is that, at all costs, the external examinations at the end of student's secondary education are all that matters to those in positions of power. How a student develops inter- and intrapersonal skills, self-esteem, how to work in a team, how to deal with winning and losing (success and failure in many examples) are paid lip service at best by knowing that it is vitally important to a child's development but not at the expense of being labelled a 'failing' school because they have not made government targets within exam results. I believe this is a juxtaposition that most teachers in all subjects face as their transition from a utopian, whole-child-centred school that is creating well-rounded individuals gives way to the realisation that students are not allowed to fail, safely or otherwise, and they have very quickly learned that if teachers' pay is directly affected by their output they can sit tight and wait to be inevitably spoon fed the necessary answers to succeed in the all important exams.

In all of this rapid change to our current curriculum it is almost ironic that the area of the PE curriculum I enjoy teaching most is 'Developing a mental determination to succeed'. I try to build all of my lessons on it across all activity areas in an attempt to prepare them for life outside of education. So, it is with great shame I see it is omitted from the National Curriculum 2014.

In previous chapters of this book, I drew attention to the fact that subject experts do not necessarily make great teachers. It is pedagogical knowledge, coupled with subject expertise, which makes great teachers. Practice without theory can be a dangerous thing. The question is, where is this knowledge acquired? On the job? Through academic study? Systematic training at universities? A combination of all three? Adoniou (2014: 21) suggests that, when done well, a university is the crucible of innovation and change in education. It gives young teachers the confidence to do the kind of teaching they want to do. In schools, newly qualified and early practitioner teachers may feel that they are constantly wearing an educational strait-jacket because school leaders, senior staff, colleagues and parents prevent them from doing anything outside the norm. They are terrified of taking any risks. This reminds me of the 1989 film, *Dead Poets Society*, starring the late Robin Williams as the inspirational English teacher, John Keating, at the conservative and aristocratic Welton Academy in Vermont. In one memorable scene, he takes his students outside of the classroom to focus on the concept of '*carpe diem*' (seize the day) and asks them to march in unconventional ways in order to look at the world from a different perspective and to challenge the notion of uniformity. Eventually he is fired.

Becoming a fully fledged physical education teacher requires resilience and hard work. There are no short cuts in developing effective working relationships with pupils and staff and, at times, there may be feelings of being undermined. In contrast, there are also high expectations of teachers entering their subject specialist profession. On one hand, an NQT has to fit in with existing practice and, on the other, an NQT has be aware of innovation and change. Kirk (2013: 220) notes, physical education teachers lack a perspective on their field; they are, effectively, trapped in the present tense. Time moves on and so does education.

This has prompted Green (2008) to ask whether the profession is experiencing a significant occupational shift where physical education teachers remain in the classroom, sports coaches are on the field, health and fitness instructors are in the gymnasium, dance teachers are in the studio, outdoor education instructors are on the mountain or lake. The most effective physical education teachers are those who are prepared to experiment with new ideas, to trial alternative approaches to teaching and to adapt to changing circumstances. The most effective teachers do not, however, run before they can walk. There is a danger that a teacher's early drive and enthusiasm inevitably becomes worn out and they become beaten by the system (Armour and Jones 1998: 130), even before they can begin to make a difference to pupils in schools. If there is one piece of advice that I could offer beginner teachers of physical education it would be to pace yourself. A word to the wise – do not feel guilty if you say 'no'. Take one day at a time. Don't dance before you can walk. Don't sing before you can talk. Once established in the teaching profession the logical progression would seem to be into middle management. The next chapter illustrates the experiences of holding a middle management position in a school such as being a curriculum leader for physical education.

Notes

1   Vicky Shiel, 'My Best Teacher – Sebastian Coe', *Times Educational Supplement*, 19 June 2009. Available online at www.tes.co.uk/article.aspx?storycode=6015782 (accessed 26 September 2014).
2   Misty Adoniou (2014) 'Leaving because they care too much to stay', *TES Scotland*, 13 February 2014. Available online at www.tes.co.uk/article.aspx?storycode=6403351 (accessed 26 September 2014).
3   'Becoming a PE teacher', *Qualifications to be a Teacher*, 2014. Available online at http://qualificationstobeateacher.co.uk/becoming-a-pe-teacher (accessed 26 September 2014).
4   Adoniou (ibid.).
5   Protocol Education; see www.protocol-education.com/PE10441681/pe-specialists (accessed 26 September 2014).

8

BECOMING A CURRICULUM LEADER FOR PHYSICAL EDUCATION

> It was one of the school sports teachers who really had an impact on me. Ian Smith taught maths as well but I just had him for rugby. He gave me a real understanding of the game and why we play it, and why the team and the concept of a team is the single most element. Mr Smith was a very quietly mannered teacher. He never shouted. It's clever, really; he was so softly spoken that we all had to be quiet to hear what he was saying. That's how he kept us focused.
>
> *Lewis Moody, England rugby international*[1]

This chapter discusses the process of becoming a curriculum leader for physical education (head of department). Not so long ago, I may have written two chapters within one, in so far as being head of girl's physical education and head of boys' physical education. I say this because there has been a long tradition of physical education departments within schools being divided according to sex. Typically, the head of boys' physical education would manage the boys' changing rooms, the boys' physical education curriculum, the male physical education teachers and exclusively teach the boys, while the head of girl's physical education would do exactly the same for the girls and never the twain shall meet. This has been a practice unique to physical education compared with how other curriculum subjects were organised and managed. It is well known that there are divisions within subject disciplines but in physical education these are usually aligned with sex. It is inconceivable to imagine other subjects to have the same arrangements as physical education: head of boys' science? head of girls' English? I don't think so. In one school that I visited, the boys' and girls' physical education departments were on separate campuses and only met as a department once a month.

There has been some notable advancement in this aspect of physical education, such as the use of gender-neutral language in the description of job titles. My research has shown that schools have in the past actively promoted sex-role stereo-typing in their advertising for vacant physical education management posts in their schools through discreet and subtle inference that the post is only open to a male or female teacher respectively (Stidder 2002, 2005). In the past, I have even found examples of advertisements for in-service training courses related to 'preparing to become head of girls' physical education' (Stidder 2002). Thankfully, those days are almost over. For example, a trawl through the job advertisements in the *Times Educational Supplement* for the first three months of 2014 showed that there were no requests for 'heads of boys' PE' or for 'heads of girls' PE' but for 'curriculum leaders', 'directors of learning' or 'heads of faculty'. In 2002, my analysis of job advertisements for managerial positions in physical education showed that 43 per cent of posts advertised were gender specific. In 2014, I could find no evidence of sex-role stereotyping in advertising for managerial positions in physical education. It would seem that the physical education profession has come a long way in making significant progress with respect to sex-role stereotyping.

In this chapter, advice is provided in terms of expectations, roles and responsi-bilities of middle managers, such as curriculum leaders, related to managing staff, curriculum design and accountability, which requires leadership and vision. As you will see from the reflective accounts of current curriculum leaders for physical education later in this chapter, much of the role requires planning schemes of work for pupils with diverse learning needs; monitoring standards of achievement using data; budgeting and resourcing; health and safety issues such as writing risk assessments. It is not for the faint-hearted and, for some individuals, it might be a case of biting off more than they can chew. One of the key roles of a curriculum leader is, in consultation with other department members and ideally the pupils themselves, to design a curriculum that will have universal appeal to all pupils. These are critical decisions but, all too often, these are made without the voice of the pupil. MacPhail (2010) has alluded to some of the reasons why pupils are rarely consulted about curriculum decisions:

> There may be a tendency to underestimate the extent to which pupils care and are perceptive about their educational progress. Pupils enjoy, are motivated by, and strengthen their self-esteem and respect by being consulted about their school experiences and welcome the opportunity to share their ideas that may help them to learn more effectively. This can convey to pupils that they are legitimate members of the schooling system, and acknowledge that a worthwhile school experience relies on the pupils and teachers' informing each other's learning. That is, the teacher's practice of teaching is integrated with and through pupil consultation and subsequent participation.
>
> *(MacPhail 2010: 228)*

So how does a curriculum leader for physical education provide a broad and balanced physical education curriculum? What activities might appeal to a greater number of pupils? Certainly, research suggests that an overemphasis on traditional team games is not the answer and the provision of a more diverse physical education curriculum could be in the interest of more pupils. Studies (Griggs 2008; Stidder and Binney 2011) have shown that listening to the pupils' voices can inform the design of the physical education curriculum and help to reach and appeal to a much broader population of pupils within a school. Ultimately, this should be the aim of every curriculum leader for physical education. Within the physical education curriculum, schemes of work are continually reviewed and updated. Curriculum leaders oversee formative and summative assessment procedures, including those that are used for internal purposes for examination courses. These should include a range of teaching and learning styles that provide a rich experience for pupils and to incorporate a variety of assessment methods at key points to enable accurate judgements on pupil progress. There is usually a requirement for curriculum leaders to develop departmental strategies for the pupils' spiritual, moral, social and cultural development, including citizenship.

Typically, a curriculum leader for physical education will be line-managed by an assistant head teacher and will provide leadership and management to a team of physical education teachers, which enhances the quality of teaching and learning of physical education in the school. The role may seem glamorous and even exciting but there are two sides to every coin and it can be exacerbated by internal politics and hidden agendas. Green (2003: 124) noted that many curriculum leaders for physical education often felt that their head teachers 'interfered' directly or indirectly, which constrained their capacity to act effectively in the school where they operated. One of the outcomes of such interference was the necessity for curriculum leaders to exploit 'sport' in what they deemed to be in the best interests of their schools in terms of recruiting more pupils through proactive marketing of sport, particularly through their provision of what they termed 'extra-curricular physical education'. Green (2003) also found that curriculum leaders were perceived to be the focal point to activating change but junior members of the department often felt constrained in expressing their views because of the hierarchal line-management relationship they had with their respective curriculum leaders. One of the difficulties of line managing other members of a physical education department is trying to get 'older' teachers to change their ways in line with changes to government policy. Green (2003) found this particularly difficult for male teachers who were perceived by female teachers to be able to 'talk a good game' during formal government inspections in the guise of Ofsted but would revert to their usual practices of 'knocking hell' with the boys and having a game of football or rugby. This was particularly difficult for more established male physical education teachers of the media-type portrayed in chapter two of this book – namely Messer's Sugden, Woodcock, Baxter and Digby. In Armour and Jones' (1998) study, there were distinct tensions within one physical education department between male and female teachers. The situation was exacerbated in circumstances where male and female physical education departments had been combined into a joint department. The fracturing of male and female staff relationships within physical education departments may have been an unintended consequence of merging two departments which have traditionally operated separately and autonomously into one in an attempt to gain greater gender equality

The expectations of a curriculum leader reveals the extent to which the roles and responsibilities of a curriculum leader have been extended compared with those of being a classroom teacher. The key phrases that schools tend to include in their job descriptions for curriculum leaders are consistent when reading a range of job descriptions for middle management positions. Curriculum leaders of physical education should inspire department members by personal example and hard work. They should effectively manage the human resources at the department's disposal, including teaching, non teaching and support staff and create a vision, sense of purpose and pride in the department. Curriculum leaders for physical education will be responsible for continuously improving the quality of teaching and learning in the department and maintaining discipline in the department including supporting staff during lessons when appropriate. They play a major role as a middle manager in the development of all aspects of the school, including its policies and their implementation and help to create an effective team by promoting collective approaches to problem solving and curricular/department development. Curriculum leaders chair and produce the agenda for effective department meetings and ensure minutes are made, kept secure and others informed as appropriate. It is the responsibility of a curriculum leader to implement school assessment and target setting policies and make effective use of data to monitor and evaluate the achievement and attainment of pupils in the subject and play a role in the provision of extra curricular activities.[2]

Being a lead practitioner in a team of physical education teachers often requires the curriculum leader to develop departmental strategies and procedures (using national and school guidelines) for teaching and learning for pupils with special educational needs and to work with learning support teachers to ensure pupils are set subject specific targets. Specific duties will require curriculum leaders to consult, produce and regularly review the physical education department handbook, which should state the agreed procedures, practices and aspirations of the department, such as aims and objectives for physical education, assessment, recording and reporting, pupil inclusion (special educational needs and disabilities, gifted and talented pupils, those with English as an additional language, gender differentiation, etc.) and the development of citizenship. Moreover, the exhaustive list includes curriculum leaders forging appropriate and mutually beneficial links with local sports facilities and coaches, inviting specialist coaches to the school both to enhance the pupil/teacher skill base and provide encouragement for pupils in their sporting development, managing the department's contribution to the school prospectus and website and managing the department's contribution to the school newsletter and including a regular article of sporting interest. If that was not enough, curriculum leaders have other responsibilities such as managing the department budget efficiently and to obtain best value for money, maintaining an inventory of all stock items and being responsible for maintenance, upkeep and replacement of sport equipment. Some curriculum leaders despair at the administration that comes with role as shown in Armour and Jones' (1998) study. Some physical education departments appoint physical education technicians for the very purpose of administration so that a curriculum leader can concentrate on their pupils and their subject. You may well ask where is the time to teach physical education? Time was always my biggest enemy but if things did not get done because of time then I always thought that I was managing myself poorly.

In order to put the role of a curriculum leader for physical education into perspective a series of vignettes and reflective accounts from current secondary school curriculum leaders of physical education in post in 2014 are included below.

Vignette 7

I have been teaching PE since 2001. After two years I became an assistant director of learning for PE and now as a director of learning (DoL) for PE. I have, since secondary school, wanted to work as a PE teacher as I have always had a real passion for sport and always had positive role models throughout my life and education enthusing me to want to continue to be part of encouraging young people to gain lifelong experiences through the medium of sport and education. I have seen many changes with regards to teaching and the role of PE DoL over the 13 years I have been teaching which highlights the importance of adaptability for anyone wanting to pursue a career in education. The term 'accountability' I believe has been the pinnacle focus for all DoL's leading departments and the leadership/management is vital knowing that everything that happens as a result in your subject area stops with the DoL which is accountable for all results across all key stages. Education nowadays is massively a 'results driven game' but I believe as a PE DoL it is still our responsibility to provide students with the right courses and experiences through PE to enable them to leave school having achieved something from the PE lessons regardless of the impact that has on local or national results tables. This ranges from your A* grade GCSE PE students looking to go on and study A-level PE and hopefully a degree in PE or sport to students who simply leave school wanting to continue with some form of physical activity or sport involvement from playing for a local team, joining a gym or having a leadership role within a sporting context. Unfortunately, due to the current government constraints on head teachers and wanting to single out specific subjects as higher importance we could have PE devalued in some schools and is the role of the PE DoL to fight to keep the subject on the curriculum and allow students to gain qualifications from PE.

Vignette 8

If I take time to think about it, for me, being a head of PE has to be the best job going. Sport is a major factor in my life and can, if used well, bring out the best in people across the world. Combine that with working with children and seeing them become good citizens justifies my view of this career. Good security, reasonably good pay, and working indoors. After a few years of learning the trade, there comes a time when decision making about what you do comes to the fore and you want to have a real impact on education within your subject. I speak to so many friends and acquaintances whose abiding memory of PE from their schooldays is negative. From the stereotypical bully, the questionable morals and the less than academic, to the soft touch, the woolly liberal and anti-competition lazy bones. If there is one thing I want to do, it's to change these images and have as many young people as possible leave school with memories of PE which are happy and respectful. A head of PE can influence this far more than anyone else. By ensuring that all students' experience of PE is positive, that parents are impressed by the education that their children receive, that colleagues around the school learn to respect the work that PE teachers do, that head teachers and senior colleagues collectively place PE high on the schools list of priorities and by creating a positive image in the community, not just through the most able pupils achieving success but also through all pupils engaging in physical activity in a positive way. As a head of PE, you learn skills over and above those of a teaching practitioner. Managing data, managing resources, managing colleagues, long-term planning and appreciating wider aspects of education as well as keeping colleagues up to date become key to your day-to-day work. Occasionally taking up opportunities to innovate and influence the direction of education has proved to be rewarding. It's not always stress free and you have to take the rough with the smooth. Best summed up however and to paraphrase a long standing soccer manager... 'I have to say that overall, we played very well'.

Vignette 9

Have you got what it takes to be an outstanding curriculum leader? Making the decision to progress your career is not one to be taken lightly. However, the rewards are incredible and the sense of achievement fantastic; when you can take a look back at a year's results and various successes and think, 'That's my team, we did that'. Not only is the role of head of department even more time consuming than regular teaching; it requires you to have your eye on several balls at the same time. After all, you have a team to consider now and senior management to report to! You can already work effectively as part of a team, but can you guide, direct, motivate and even inspire your colleagues? You will need to not only manage your team; you will have to lead them. So, as well as looking after your students and your team; what about you? After all, you'll be so busy, planning, preparing, training others, analysing results, writing reports, conducting observations and appraisals; and let's not forget about your day job – teaching – there is the chance you'll forget about your own development. You need to have a plan and dedicate time to doing your own thing too, as we are never too old or too experienced to learn. Middle management is not for everyone and, sometimes, it can feel as though you're being pulled in several different directions. It can be quite a lonely place too; but with the right prioritisation of tasks and careful communication, a balance can be achieved.

Vignette 10

I became a head of PE as this was always a goal of mine. I wanted to be able to shape the curriculum and extracurricular programme in line with what both staff and pupils wanted and to do this I had to be in charge. I saw the opportunity of becoming a head of department a challenging but exciting position of responsibility that I thoroughly enjoy. The added bonus of man-managing a team of real characters has always been something that has interested me and I am currently relishing the challenges that this brings to the role. New heads of PE need to be aware of time management!!!! You can become so easily consumed by the volume of work that it completely takes over your life. Now I am three years into the post, I have developed a traffic light system in my 'in tray' which allows me to prioritise work that comes in whether it be on a daily basis or longer term. This has been ground breaking in helping me manage my time/workload. The other real challenge that I have found is that you need to be able to change your style of management to each individual that you manage. This is not easy and is something which takes considerable time and thought about how you can do this effectively. My main roles are to lead the PE department. I am also head of KS four and head of examination PE. I am the line manager for all the PE staff and I manage staff, budget, curriculum and DEF (department evaluation form) as well as cover staff.

Vignette 11

I have been teaching physical education for ten years and have had different roles and responsibilities both within the faculty but also across the whole school, ranging from healthy schools coordinator, head of KS4, school governor and member on the Big Parks Project board. I started my head of faculty role in a shared capacity, which I found very difficult and restrictive until I finally took on the role alone and have been doing so for the last five years. Being a head of faculty is one that poses various challenges in the first few years and it takes time to learn the role and understand how to be an effective middle leader. There are a number of things you need to consider and understand in order to be an effective leader. Firstly, understanding what your role within school is, being aware that you are the engine for change across the school driving the vision created by senior leaders into reality. You may or may not have been part of that decision/vision making process and you may agree or disagree with that vision, but ultimately you need to see the bigger picture, share your views but accept your role is to make the school better. Creating professional breathing space between you and your team will allow you to operate effectively and in bringing about any change. This can make you feel isolated but it is important to be able to understand and empathise with your team and their concerns without undermining your senior leaders. Being a leader is all about relationships, working with everyone in a positive way. It is ultimately about having positive worthwhile relationships which will allow you to create a shared vision for your entire team to buy into. Without your team on board nothing will be achieved and the pupils in your school will lose out. Your role is to be aware of all the current trends and political shifts, understand and filter what is worth knowing and changing, protecting what is already in existence while at the same time create a highly effective change culture which allow pedagogy to adapt and grow.

Vignette 12

Becoming a curriculum leader (head of department) for physical education rather than pursuing a pastoral middle leaders position was a decision I made based on wanting to be able to influence curriculum design and the way PE is delivered within my school. My passion for my subject has grown with every year that I've witnessed the profound and sometimes immeasurable positive impacts that it can have on so many areas of young people's lives. The sad reality is that the high level of holistic development that PE can provide is not always mirrored with the respect and admiration it deserves as a subject. The beauty of being a head of PE is that you're obligated to consider what is best for the students, to protect them, and your subject from poor directives and unfortunate circumstances. As the representative for PE you are sometimes invited to be part of the decision-making process at the highest level, and if you're lucky enough to have strong leadership at the top of the school (and I consider myself very lucky) and work hard enough, you're professional judgement throughout these important consultations will hopefully be taken on board. Those moments where you can affect significant change by either driving your own ideas forwards, or providing oppositional arguments against what you believe will have negative repercussions on your subject and students (or 'little wins for PE' as I like to celebrate them as) are what keep me coming back.

All of these vignettes are success stories of physical education teachers who have achieved leadership positions within schools and are currently aspiring to make a difference to the way in which physical education is managed and presented to pupils. They are a reflection of the way in which the teacher training process equips them for the demands of being a curriculum leader. These reflective accounts of curriculum leaders in physical education help to contextualise the complexities of the role. The next section of this book discusses the concept of moving on to different roles in the teaching profession. Before doing so, the opening chapter of Section Three aims to explore the nature, purpose and importance of reflective practice in physical education.

Notes

1   Tom Cullen, 'Mr Smith and Mrs Craig by Lewis Moody', *Times Educational Supplement Magazine*, 10 January 2014: 37.
2   'Brockhill Park Performing Arts College – Job Description: Subject Leader for Religious Education'. Available online at www.google.co.uk/url?sa=t&rct=j&q= &esrc=s&source=web&cd=2&ved=0CCYQFjAB&url=http%3A%2F%2Fwww.tes.co. uk%2FUpload%2FAttachments%2FTES%2F3011618%2FSL%2520RE%2520sept.doc x&ei=kKsuVMnFCcrtaJXVgagJ&usg=AFQjCNGwBJfl3nm2eS78zoJ9j98Dn6r71Q& bvm=bv.76802529,d.d2s (accessed 3 October 2014).

SECTION THREE

Moving on

9
BEING A REFLECTIVE PHYSICAL EDUCATION TEACHER

Mr Davies' real influence on me was on the rugby pitch. He was enthusiastic. He encouraged us to keep going, keep improving, no matter how many times we lost. His most profound influence came from three principles that he drummed into us from the beginning. One: that everyone on the team was equal – there was no special treatment and no stars. Two: that when we turned up for training on a Monday night we had to show a bit of attitude, show we wanted to be there. Three: that he wanted us, as individuals and as a team, to be as successful as we could be and to play to our full potential. His tips helped me to become an international rugby player. But he also gave me lessons in life. I still live by those principles today.

Sean Fitzpatrick, New Zealand All Blacks Rugby Player[1]

This chapter discusses the value of reflective practice for professional development. The professional and occupational socialisation of teachers is discussed citing Laker (2000) and his assertion that the training, work-related experience and teaching within a particular curriculum model reinforce and constitute a particular view of what to teach, how to teach and who to teach. A series of autobiographical life stories and lesson observations are included, which draw upon critical self-reflection as the basis for understanding professional identity and what constitutes good professional practice. Armour and Jones (1998: 136) state that we must look back to see ahead. This is exactly my intention in writing this particular chapter.

High-quality physical education has been defined by Department for Education and Skills (2002: 2) as giving young people the skills, understanding, desire and commitment to continue to improve and achieve in physical education through a range of sport and health-enhancing physical activities in line with their abilities. Hardman (2011) alludes to high-quality teacher training as being a prerequisite for high-quality education but this must be relevant to contemporary education and requires teachers to be reflective lifelong learners. High-quality teaching is therefore dependent on and defined by informed and reflective practitioners attuned to ideals and values fostering true learning experiences in a dynamically changing world (Hardman 2011: 192).Those who resist change are guilty of putting up a defence mechanism triggered by their own insecurities of their own incompetence in responding to curricular developments and societal changes invoked by demands for appropriate, innovative approaches to teaching (Hardman 2011:192). Cale (2010: 3) states that in order to become an informed and reflective practitioner, aspiring physical education teachers need to understand themselves, including their values, beliefs and philosophies, and be able to reflect on how these influence their teaching. Fernández-Balboa (1997) believes that teachers cannot be expected to know, understand and teach pupils unless they know and understand themselves first. Laker *et al.* (2003: 76) suggest that an increased understanding of ways in which teachers perceive their professional identity and their subject specialism can contribute to the facilitation of the development of the reflective practitioner and potentially enhance the professional and personal growth of both the pre-service teacher and his or her future students.

The work of Schon (1983) and Moon (1999) draw attention to reflective practice and self-reflexivity as a means of improving professional development. In respect of professional development in a physical education context, Zwozdiak-Myers (2013: 148) suggests that reflective practitioners gain a degree of autonomy needed to make professional judgements in response to both major educational trends and their own unique situations. Hayes and Burdsey (2012: 137) state that teachers should be self-reflexive so that they understand the complex dynamics of discrimination in schools. This can eschew stereotyping and combat all forms of racist practice, for example. To ignore the value of self-reflexive practice is to be culpable for perpetuating a culture of inequality in school physical education and sport. Brown (2005: 19) maintains that critical self-reflection can reconstruct existing knowledge that challenges stereotypical understandings and practices in physical education. However, in Brown's analogy of a computer system, this takes time to 'wipe', 'input' and 'store' new information so that a multi-layered, multi-dimensional habitus can be contextualised, rather like a hologram, as opposed to a hard drive on a computer.

While the importance of being a reflective practitioner is recognised as a quality of being a good physical education teacher, many who enter the profession simply become technicians rather than reflective practitioners. One may ask then, what is the point in populating the physical education profession with reflective practitioners when such an avowed goal is simply unattainable. As Green (2008) states: 'Reflexivity in physical education is just a naive aspiration as trainee teachers focus on their practically based skills and competencies and seldom contemplate broader philosophical concerns' (Green 2008: 224).

Does this mean that teacher educators should reject the development of reflective professionals or should they aspire to make teacher education part of a reflective and critical framework within which teacher's attitudes can continue to evolve? In seeking to understand my own professional identity, I have attempted to construct a culmination of secondary school experiences gained as a pupil, trainee teacher, qualified teacher and teacher educator within the field of physical education. In a previous publication (Stidder 2012a), I drew upon my own experiences to illustrate ways in which physical education lessons at school could be an alienating experience for some pupils and how reflexive practice can help to critically evaluate and improve professional practice. I now wish to elaborate on those experiences and highlight how these have shaped my own professional thinking and given me a greater understanding of ways in which physical education can develop young people holistically but at the same time shatter their personalities, as depicted by journalist Sophie Warnes:

> Being slightly deaf, I found that my life was made easier by altering the way I go about things. I always tried to position myself so that I was in the right room at the right time, or near enough to the corridor that I could hear my name. Sometimes I got it wrong, and I remember once not hearing my name and thinking it was a bit strange. I was approached by the [PE] teacher who screamed 'are you deaf or something?!' at me – I had to explain, in front of thirty-or-so wide-eyed girls that um, yes, I *was* deaf and that it's actually in my file and I thought all the teachers knew this automatically so that I didn't have to go through this humiliation in every single subject. They [PE teachers] thought I was being difficult; I thought they may as well have been robots for all the empathy and understanding they demonstrated.[2]

The promotion of reflexivity is actively encouraged for those aspiring to become teachers and considered to be central to research, as well as to pedagogical processes and practices. Zwozdiak-Myers (2013), for example, suggests that teachers who ask searching questions about educational practices arising from professional concerns and contexts are open to new ideas which exemplify and underpin the concept of the teacher as a reflective practitioner in the first instance and then as an extended professional and researcher. Pollard (2008) has shown that high-quality teaching relies on reflective teaching to develop and maintain subject expertise among trainee teachers, newly qualified teachers (NQTs) and experienced practitioners. Tindall and Enright (2013) suggest that one of the principal ways of gaining self-knowledge is to engage in reflective practice so that they understand why they teach, what they teach, who they teach and how they teach. O'Sullivan et al. (2010: 54) use the metaphors of a mirror and a collage to explain that reflective practice is about looking at oneself as a practitioner and developing one's professional identity through picturing the many parts involved in the process. From a research perspective, it is a form of critical self-reflection that requires the articulation of values, beliefs, investments and life experiences and the potential influence of these on the collection and interpretation of data and in communicating research findings (Hastie and Hay 2012: 82). O'Sullivan et al. (2010: 62) suggest that reflection is a habit of mind to be cultivated and is central to professional growth as a teacher. It develops and refines teaching knowledge and capacities and ultimately aims to maximise the learning experiences of pupils. Likewise, reflexivity involves analysis, assessment and improvement of professional practice and requires self-appraisal through the questioning of aims and actions, monitoring practice and outcomes while considering alternatives through critical self-reflection both 'in action' and 'on action' (Schon 1983; Pollard and Tan 1987; Hayes *et al.* 2001). In this context, reflexivity can be a valuable pedagogical tool which can play an important part in the professional behaviours of teachers and considered to be essential for professional development (Luttenburg and Bergen 2008).

Reflexivity has been the subject upon which some qualitative researchers have based their understanding of physical education. For example, Armour and Jones (1998: 10) have stated that physical education teachers have many identities and roles and while we understand and learn a great deal about teachers and professionally related issues through listening to their life stories, it is important to analyse our own backgrounds and position in relation to the research process. In this respect, reflexivity can help physical education teachers to help each new generation of physical education teachers learn from the last so that knowledge can continually build and inspire in exactly the same way as advancements in medical science for example. As Armour and Jones (1998: 136) have stated: 'If we are not drawing upon wisdom from the past, we are in effect, constantly re-inventing a slightly wobbly wheel'.

Fernandez-Balboa and Brubaker (2012: 30) invite researchers to join them on a journey of self-discovery and to engage in their own (self) inquiry using memory, knowledge and intuition to establish their own position as a researcher so that research can be approached in purposeful and satisfying ways. In order to understand my professional journey, I have attempted to evaluate various factors that have influenced my professional thinking and how these factors have been responsible for my own perceptions and actions as a teacher of physical education and have attempted to understand more about the ways in which my own experiences as a physical education teacher can inform future practice. I have, therefore, attempted to assess my professional development and to provide an account of the experiences, which has given me the impetus to write this particular chapter. In this respect, I have assessed the process of my own 'occupational socialisation'. Consequently, I now have a greater awareness of what Brown and Rich (2002: 80) refer to as 'the gendered physical education teacher identity' and how my prior experiences of sport and physical education in schools have led to me accepting standardised (gendered) beliefs and values associated with the teaching of physical education in schools. In other words, my 'rite of passage' in becoming a male teacher of (boys) physical education.

Zwozdiak-Myers (2013) highlights three types of reflective discourse. These range from descriptive, reflective conversations based upon concrete experiences of physical education teachers to comparative, reflective conversations based upon beliefs, assumptions, theories, values and conceptions of physical education. In addition, critical reflective conversations, whereby physical education teachers have their judgements about what is 'most reasonable' and 'relatively certain' based upon the evaluation of available data, are all part of the process. O'Sullivan *et al.* (2010: 62) refer to a timeline of reflection. For the NQT, this will focus on surviving the lesson, managing pupils, keeping within time constraints and teaching content. The timeline for reflection shifts over time, where a reflective teacher now focuses on understanding pupils, the appropriateness of tasks, aligning learning needs and interests and assessing leaning objectives. The process of self-reflection enables teachers to critique current practices, challenge existing values, create and deliver relevant and meaningful physical activity experiences for the current generation of children and young people. In short, the future of the physical education profession is dependent on critically reflective professional enquirers.

My main recollections of physical education, when I was a pupil at school, were largely based upon gender and social class. The relationship between physical education, gender and social class is not new, although at the time that I attended secondary school research into physical education and these aspects of social inequality were just emerging. As a male pupil, many of my experiences of physical education in schools were different to those of my female peer group, which led to me to believe and accept that there was a strong rationale and justification for different programmes of activities, sex-segregated groups and same-sex staffing arrangements. As a trainee teacher over a period of four years in the 1980s, physical education in secondary schools reflected important pedagogical debates of the time, associated with policies that addressed social equalities, and sex-role stereo-typing (Sherlock 1977; Graydon 1980; Leaman 1984, Evans 1986). By the late 1970s, most of the selective single-sex grammar schools had been dissolved. One of the outcomes of research was the potential benefits of mixed-sex and mixed-ability physical education classes within secondary schools (Turvey and Laws 1988). As a result, some of my training experiences were with coeducational classes, albeit a limited number and often restricted to the new intake of 11-year-old pupils. These experiences, coupled with teaching activities that I had not previously learned, predictably and inevitably challenged my professional competencies and view about the nature and purpose of physical education.

In 1990, I was given the opportunity to teach physical education in North America, when I accepted a Fulbright Scholarship. My experiences of teaching physical education required me to teach girls and boys exclusively in mixed-sex groups. This was a requirement of federal legislation, known as Title IX, the only piece of substantive legislation that has dealt with gender and education, which was passed by the United States Congress in 1972.[3] Title IX required all schools receiving federal funds to ensure that all physical education classes were taught in coeducational groups. The growth of coeducational physical education at the high-school level of education in North America and then later in the UK secondary sector was ostensibly aimed at reducing gender inequalities for girls. The teaching experiences in North America provided me with an insight into the potential benefit that coeducational physical education could provide girls and boys in ensuring equality of opportunity and access to the physical education curriculum.

It also made me more aware of the impact of federal legislation and the mandatory requirement to provide coeducational physical education upon the daily practices of many physical education teachers and reinforced the need to differentiate the planning and teaching of physical education lessons for boys and girls. Equally, the teaching experiences in North America challenged my own views and dispelled many of the myths and prejudices associated with girls physical education that I had witnessed during a relatively short teaching career in England. I had noticed that girls were extremely proficient in competitive team games and were more than capable of running the same distances as boys in track and field athletic events. My observations in North America were that many more girls were actively more involved in physical education and particularly in school sport compared with girls in the UK. Parents and teachers would often attribute this to Title IX. Planning for a class of 30 pupils in a mixed-sex setting, however, required careful thought and had to be effectively controlled to avoid the dominance of boys.

As a result of my experiences in North America, I was far more prepared to question the ways in which pupils experienced their physical education lessons. The 1990s were potentially exciting times for physical education teachers as a national curriculum for physical education (NCPE) was due for implementation into state-funded schools at the start of September 1991, which promised to provide equal access and opportunity to the physical education curriculum for all pupils. This period of time was an opportunity for physical education teachers to redefine the way in which boys and girls experienced their physical education lessons in schools. Many of my own experiences of teaching physical education during the 1990s led to a postgraduate study which assessed the merits of single-sex and mixed-sex physical education in England (Stidder 1998). The study revealed that the grouping arrangements for physical education held particular importance for adolescent girls but, despite the fact that pupils were ambivalent to the sex of the teacher, physical education teachers often preferred to teach physical education to same-sex classes and to teach physical education in a same-sex school. In a mixed-sex secondary school where pupils were taught physical education in single-sex groups, female teachers were particularly resistant to teaching parallel boys' classes, even in activities where they had particularly high levels of expertise. Female physical education teachers would attribute their reluctance to teach boys to issues associated with classroom management and control as well as concerns that 'boys would not take them seriously'. In contrast, male colleagues expressed reservations about teaching girls for reasons associated with physical contact and lower levels of enthusiasm.

What I had observed in England was very different to my own professional experiences of teaching physical education in North America. Consequently, many of these issues led to a doctoral study that compared the impact of educational policy in North America and the UK and its impact upon the teaching of physical education to girls (Stidder 2009a). During the course of my doctoral research, a series of lesson observations took place and field notes were recorded. In one mixed-sex physical education lesson at a North American high school, 38 pupils took part in a basketball lesson which was taught by an experienced male physical education teacher and highlighted the way in which mixed-sex groupings in physical education could have an adverse effect on girls in particular:

> Basic cardiovascular warm up was followed by paired work in which students took part in a series of passing drills. Girls worked with girls within eight pairs and a group of three. Likewise, boys worked together in eight pairs with one group of three. Class then divided in half and practised lay-up and rebounds into two lines at opposite ends of the court. One ball was used for each of the groups of 19 students. Teacher then called the first ten names off the register to form two teams of five. These pupils played a full-court basketball game with the girls and less competent players having little or no involvement and the dominant male players commanding much of the action. In the meantime, 28 students sat on the side of the court waiting their turn. This was first lesson of the new semester. The four games that took place lasted anything from 2– 5 minutes with the last group having no more than 2 minutes of court time. At the end of the class the teacher explained that he would be implementing a rota for future lessons in which a percentage of the class would not be required to 'suit up' for class as there was, in his opinion, too many students in one class. Students were given the option to bring homework to the PE class or to spectate. Students were dismissed to change and left the gym while the teacher went to his office – When asked if he had any responsibility for changing supervision, he did not see this as part of his role.
>
> *(Stidder 2009a)*

In another North America high school, the popularity of individual activities that focused on health and body management, such as yoga, were particularly favoured among some pupils. This particular form of exercise focused on a holistic approach to the body, mind and spirit, which was rationalised as enabling students to cope with the challenges of daily life. These pupils took part in 'Hatha' yoga classes at the beginning of the day, in which they performed exercises involving stretching and flexing, breathing techniques, relaxation and meditation:

> Observed a health and wellness class in the dance studio. This was a mixed group (15 girls and 4 boys) taught by a female teacher. The class took part in yoga and was something that the teacher had learned in India. Students were shown a variety of body positions with the emphasis on meditation and relaxation. Students had chosen to take this class instead of regular PE for which they gained PE credits. There was a calming and peaceful atmosphere as the students continued with their activity in dimmed lighting and with soft background music. Lights were off and candles lit. Soft pipe music was played in the background. Students engaged in a series of stretching exercises in total silence. The teacher later explained that yoga prepares students for focused concentration for the day ahead.
>
> *(Stidder 2009a)*

In contrast to this, pupils at an English secondary school were subjected to what most children might regard as an off-putting experience:

> Year 9 mixed-sex football lesson. Weather is poor with mild rain falling and strong wind. 20 pupils of which 8 are girls and 12 are boys. Most boys and girls dressed in school PE kit – half a dozen girls have coats on and training shoes (no football boots). The warm-up activity is a jog from the changing rooms to the school playing field. Pupils are asked to get into pairs and pass a ball between each other over 5 metres from a stationary position. Girls work with girls and boys work with boys. Pupils continue for five minutes and then move to a dribbling practice running with the ball to a line 5 metres away and back to the starting position before changing with their partner. There are no demonstrations of the required technique. Pupils then divided into two teams of 10 and play a game using the junior football pitch that is pre-marked. One team are in red tops and play against the remaining 10 who are in blue school rugby jerseys. Boys tend to dominate the game with very few girls actively involved. The teacher finishes the lesson saying that the kids have had enough and that it's too cold and wet to continue.
>
> *(Stidder 2009a)*

And yet, at one of the English secondary schools observations of physical education lessons suggested that girls and boys preferred to work in parallel groups rather than mixed-sex groups. This point was emphasised during a particular lesson observation of a sport leader's session run by the physical education department for year ten pupils:

> Year 10 junior sports leaders lesson 15 pupils: seven boys and eight girls. Pupils dressed casually in a range of different sports attire. Lesson focuses on communication through the teaching of hockey. Pupils split into four groups and each pupil is asked to teach a passing skill to the rest of the group. Pupils work in self-selecting groups (one group of three boys, one group of four boys, two groups of four girls). The teacher moves from group to group offering feedback. Pupils then play two games (3 v 3 boys with one referee), (3 v 3 girls with one referee and one time keeper). Teacher finishes the lesson with a short evaluation.
>
> *(Stidder 2009a)*

The way in which boys and girls participated together was noticeable in a particular practical lesson at an English secondary school where there was full cooperation and integration between boys and girls:

> Year 11 GCSE Netball lesson. 16 pupils. 12 girls and 4 boys. Short cardio-vascular warm up followed by a 7 v 7 game. Two pupils take it turn to umpire. Pupils rotate their playing positions every 5 minutes. Teacher

observes and assesses pupil performance as part of the syllabus criteria.

(Stidder 2009a)

In other lessons, participation rates were high and girls worked enthusiastically and were extremely responsive towards the teacher:

> Dance studio. 22 girls. No non-participants. Girls dressed in t-shirts and jogging bottoms. Teacher plays a video of a choreographed sequence of movements. Teacher explains key terms and movements. Girls practice sequences of movement in groups of four with music in the background. Teacher moves from each group and offers feedback. Girls link movements and devise a choreographed dance. Each group then performs to the other groups. Teacher finishes the lesson with a plenary session. Girls are highly motivated and enthusiastic throughout.
>
> *(Stidder 2009a)*

> 24 girls, 2 non-participants. Lesson takes place indoors. Each pupil has a basketball and dribbles the ball within predetermined boundaries practicing a range of turns and technical skills. Pupils divided into pairs and asked to perform their favourite skill and for their partner to copy them. Teacher selects a couple of examples for demonstration. Pupils move to groups of 5 or 6 and take part in a 4 v 1 or 5 v 1 possession game with the defending player changing every minute. Pupils then play an end zone game (6 v 6 and 5 v 5). Teachers concludes the lesson with a plenary session.
>
> *(Stidder 2009a)*

Despite the pessimism of some researchers (Kirk 2013), much of what I have subsequently observed in schools has indicated that significant progress has been made to the teaching and learning of physical education. As my career has developed in higher education, I have visited trainee physical education teachers during their school-based teaching practices. In some schools, I have witnessed lessons that were inclusive and pupil-centred, such as an athletics lesson where a mixed-sex group of 11-year-old pupils worked as a team to beat the men's and women's world record for long jump in the fewest number of standing jumps and attempt the fewest number of throws to beat the existing world record for discus. In another lesson, mixed groups of boys and girls were required to produce the fastest relay team by dividing up the distance of 400 metres and allocating different stages over shorter and longer distances. There have been occasions where trainees have taught running, jumping and throwing circuits in a sports hall when the weather has been poor. These lessons were highly organised, using adapted and modified equipment such as foam javelins and quoits. Pupils worked in mixed-sex groups to time and record a series of individual tasks such as a multiple-speed bounce, a 5-metre sprint, a standing two-footed jump, a vertical leap and a hop, step and jump.

During one visit to a secondary school, I observed a series of orienteering lessons with 11- and 12-year-old pupils designed to promote literacy, numeracy and information and communications technology. Pupils worked in mixed-sex groups within the confines of the school grounds using decision-making and problem-solving skills to navigate their way around an orienteering course using a map and compass to collect letters at numbered control points. Pupils were then divided into pairs. Each pair was given six different numbers on their map to visit and collect letters. The lesson then progressed to a timed event where pupils worked in groups of three and competed in an 'odds and evens' relay. One pupil collected letters at specified odd-numbered controls at the same time as their partner collected letters at a given even-numbered controls. The third pupil stayed at base until the first pupil returned with the answer and handed over. This was a continuous task where pupils were active throughout. Teams were then asked to make up the longest word with the vowels and consonants collected and add up the numbers they been to. The lesson finished with a timed orienteering event where the controls further away from the start were worth more points than those nearer to the start. Pupils had to decide their route using the scale of the map and decide how long it was likely to take them to complete the course within the time limit set. Points were deducted for every minute that the pupils were late. In other lessons I have observed, the teaching of cross-curricular themes using technology whereby pupils took photographs of orienteering control points on their mobile phones as evidence of completing a course. This was developed by using 'QR codes'[4] at particular locations on a map, which were scanned by pupils using their mobile phones.[5] In other lessons, 11-year-old pupils worked collaboratively to solve a series of problems through joint decision making and activities designed to promote teamwork, communication, trust, respect and personal responsibility.[6]

In another school, I took great delight in observing a mixed-sex class of year seven pupils engaged in dance activities. The theme was South African dance (gumboot dancing using rhythms of 8- and 16-beat motifs). There were excellent questions at the beginning regarding the origins and history of gumboot dancing, where miners slapped their gumboots as a means of communication. Resources such as music, worksheets and poems were included. Pupils were divided into individual tribes and had to research the name of their tribe. Each tribe were allocated a dance master. Key words such as 'slap', 'stamp' and 'clap' were emphasised. Differentiated learning outcomes were included and referenced to the NCPE level descriptors (four, five and six). A range of different teaching styles were employed and each pupil was involved in peer assessment and self-assessment. The positioning and mobility throughout the lesson was exemplary and there were several opportunities for diagnostic and corrective feedback to pupils regarding their performance. Pupil activity levels throughout were extremely high. There were high-order questions ensuring a pupil-centred focus in a safe and purposeful learning environment. Organisation and management of learning were exceptionally good. Interaction with pupils was extremely positive and showed evidence of effective teaching and learning. The trainee teacher demonstrated very good subject knowledge of this particular aspect of physical education. The activities and tasks were progressive, age appropriate and relevant to the learning objectives.

These are just few examples of the innovative approaches to teaching and learning through physical education that I have witnessed. Much of what I have observed in schools should be celebrated. Where physical education lessons have been of high quality, they have been taught by high-quality trainees who motivate and inspire young people irrespective of the activity and the class organisation. They have enthusiasm, passion and drive for their subject and a desire to promote the benefits of being physically active and physically educated. But, let us not forget that high-quality trainees are dependent on high-quality training. So where to go next? The following chapter considers the natural evolution of becoming and being a physical education teacher. That is, the passing on of subject knowledge and pedagogical skills to future recruits to the profession and being a mentor.

Notes

1   David Harrison, 'Mr Davies by Sean Fitzpatrick', *TES Magazine*, 21 June 2013: 24–5.
2   Sophie Warnes, 'For some children, PE lessons are far from enjoyable', Independent BLOGS, 10 August 2012. Available online at http://blogs.independent.co.uk/2012/08/10/for-some-children-pe-lessons-are-far-from-enjoyable (accessed 26 September 2014).
3   United States Congress, 20 USC 1681a, (1988) Title IX, Education Amendments of 1972, Public Law 92–318.
4   Quick response codes are two-dimensional barcodes, whereby a machine-readable optical label contains information about the item to which it is attached. It is scanned using a smartphone, which converts the code to a website URL and links directly to the relevant information.
5   University of Brighton, School of Sport and Service Management, 'Orienteering day', *YouTube*, 16 April 2013. Available online at www.youtube.com/watch?v=3cbcTapT4Pw&list=PL9036FECA22DB89CD&index=9 (accessed 26 September 2014).
6   University of Brighton, School of Sport and Service Management, 'Outdoor and adventures team building day', *YouTube*, 24 July 2013. Available online at www.youtube.com/watch?v=gb9HnSr3cZE&index=7&list=PL9036FECA22DB89CD (accessed 26 September 2014).

10

BEING A MENTOR IN PHYSICAL EDUCATION

Mr Musselwhite ran the school football team when I was about eight or nine. His enthusiasm rubbed off on us. You can't take football if you're not really into it, and Mr Musselwhite was really into football. You remember your teachers when you're that age. He was slightly built and I just remember he had a moustache. I was centre forward and the tactics were 'Hit the ball over the top and Roger will get to it'. He made us a team and it was my first experience of somebody treating us as a team, rather than a group of individuals knocking the football around. I was really happy at school up to 11. Then I went to the grammar school and I struggled academically. I was saved by sport. My life was about sport. I was lucky that we had good playing fields and a good PE department. I did all right in my O-levels and A-levels but really it was all about sport.

Roger Black, 400-m silver medallist 1996 Atlanta Olympic Games and member of the gold medal-winning 4 x 400-m team in the 1991 World Championships[1]

Becoming a trainee teacher of physical education involves an element of school-based experience under the mentorship of an experienced teacher, who provides guidance and support in meeting predetermined UK government standards for qualifying teach. During the period of school-based training, sometimes known as teaching practice, mentors make formative and summative judgements about the trainee teacher with respect to their progress in meeting the standards for qualifying to teach (Department for Education 2013a). Brown (2005: 24) suggests that the process of becoming a physical education teacher is 'an ideal practical apprenticeship model for the identification and transference of traditionally gendered forms of practice'. Trainee teachers of physical education are encouraged to watch, listen and copy the practices of more experienced physical education teachers and incorporate them into their own pedagogy. As trainees are required to comply with UK 'state' requirements to gain certification, they are more likely to reproduce rather than to challenge certain practices that are considered to be legitimate, otherwise they run the risk of failing their qualification. To challenge establish patterns of delivery and organisation in physical education provides a compromising dilemma for those who advocate innovation and change within the physical education profession. Trainees may risk the loss of their qualification unless they accept already established views (Mawer 1996).

My early recollections of my university training were of education studies lectures alongside practical physical education sessions in a range of activities including games, educational gymnastics as opposed to Olympic-style gymnastics, athletics and swimming. At certain points in the year, we were placed in different secondary schools for school-based training under the mentorship of an experienced teacher. This is where I learned my 'craft' and the science of pedagogy. It was my chance to put theory into practice and to experiment with teaching and learning styles, to build up my subject knowledge content, improve my organisational skills and reflect upon my performance. The challenge was to impress the person who ultimately would make subjective judgements about my teaching – namely, my mentor. Looking back at these experiences, the influence of those who trained me shaped my pedagogical practices but rarely did I theorise or reflect upon them. I was in survival mode and simply preoccupied with getting through my teaching practice rather than exploring innovatory approaches to my teaching and overcoming 'the pedagogy of necessity' (Tinning 1988). I made short-term adjustments to the immediate demands of my training to achieve my primary goal of 'qualifying' as a teacher of physical education (Green 2008: 212) and, retrospectively, my views and practices at the time were neither 'shaken nor stirred' by my training (Evans et al. 1996: 169). These types of experiences are not uncommon among trainee teachers. Research has shown that my early recollections of becoming a physical education teacher are part of five broad stages of professional development. Cale (2010: 9) summarises the work of Furlong and Maynard (1995) and explains that trainees' idealism fades when faced with the reality of the situation and they become concerned with their own personal survival by trying to 'fit in', to manage and control their classes and become established as a teacher.

This chapter explains the role of the mentor in school-based initial teacher training and the importance of supporting trainee teachers with their professional development. It discusses effective models of mentoring of trainee teachers in school-based settings, where the role of the teacher acting as the mentor has become an increasingly important aspect of partnership training schemes between schools and universities. Mentoring is regarded as a core professional development activity for all members of the teaching profession. The bedrock of successful mentoring programmes is the forging of school–university partnerships and is widely advocated internationally as a key feature of teacher education and training (Armour et al. 2013: 213). Mentors primarily have a practical role, whereby knowledge is passed on about the day-to-day demands of teaching physical education and undoubtedly occupy a strategic role (Nutt and Clarke 2002: 158). They play a substantial part in the socialisation of trainee teachers, especially when they are older, more established and more set in their ways (Green 2008: 212). Indeed, the mentor is a key person with whom the trainee teacher has the most daily contact with during their school-based training. Using Stroot's (2002) analogy of participation in sport, mentoring could therefore be seen as a 'one-way' process, with the trainee teacher passively absorbing the information provided by the mentor modelling the behaviours, attitudes and norms of being a physical education teacher. The influence of significant others (mentors for example) shapes the socialisation of trainees into teaching physical education, suggesting that that trainee and mentor are a product of society – a lump of clay to be moulded by outside factors (Stroot 2002: 132). While much has been written about mentoring in a generic sense, few texts other than Mawer's (1996) edited collection and Chambers (2015) forthcoming text has specifically addressed the issues for physical education teachers, trainees and partnerships in school-based training. The introduction of more school-based and employment and training routes into teaching has meant that the role of the mentor has become increasingly more prominent within initial teacher training but the priorities remain the same. Trainee and new teachers need support and mentoring to protect them from conservative elements within their respective schools otherwise the practices and perspectives acquired during their university-based training are likely to fade (Capel 2005).

During the 1980s, part of my training as a teacher was based in a number of secondary schools. I was mentored by established teachers who, by virtue of teaching in a successful department, embodied 'good' practice. Green (2008: 211) describes a mentor as a 'wise' tutor who functions as both trainer and counsellor in providing peer assistance and peer review. Little did I know at the time that the mentors who trained me would be so influential on my practice as a teacher in the future. They provided advice and guidance on subject knowledge and teaching styles rather than on broader philosophical dimensions of physical education. Retrospectively, the mentors who trained me made me realise how important the place of mentoring is within the training process in alleviating anxieties and concern among trainee teachers, as well addressing specific training needs. I have also realised that good mentoring is reciprocal and not hierarchical, based as it is upon mutual respect between the novice teacher and the expert teacher. However, this was not always the case, as I had observed some questionable practices in action. In one secondary school during the 1980s, pupils were streamed into ability groups according to the time they achieved in a three-mile cross-country run. In another school, pupils were graded A to E according to their attitude in physical education lessons and 1 to 5 according to the numbers of successful penalties or free throws scored out of five attempts. Parents would receive an annual statement of their child's progress in physical education on that basis. Those of average ability would receive a grade of 'C3' accompanied by three words: 'satisfactory progress made'. One teacher had said that this was typically a standard phrase used for those children for whom he could not put a face to a name. This reminded me of

Boothroyd's (2004:246) recollections of his own school reports in the 1960s, where his physical education teacher simply wrote 'good at games'.

While university-based training provides trainees with many foundation skills and helps to prepare them in applying these skills during school-based placements, partnership training has the leading role in producing the next generation of physical education professionals who are confident and able to teach across the NCPE activity range in a variety of different contexts. School-led training will require further development and awareness among those involved in initial teacher education, to provide trainees with the capabilities of responding to the demands that contemporary education presents. Previous research (Stidder and Hayes 2006) suggests that teacher training practices in schools have improved and are having a positive impact on the preparation of new recruits. The development of partnership training schemes suggests that partnership training in schools has responded to many of the challenges that contemporary physical education has presented. The development of partnership training schemes is encouraging and has provided many more opportunities for the professional development of trainee teachers but will require further development as revised standards for qualified teacher status are introduced within initial teacher education and partnership training.

Irrespective of the training route into teaching mentioned in earlier chapters of this book, all training routes into teaching share one common denominator – the mentor. Armour *et al.* (2013: 214) believe that there is an implicit assumption that mentoring is understood, primarily, as being only of benefit to the novice trainee and is indicative of a traditional mentoring model. But, they argue, if mentors view the role as reciprocal and of benefit to them, then a multidirectional model would seem to be the most effective process in which both mentor and mentee can engage. In a sense, mentoring is about the role of the journeyman and the apprentice. For Hardy (1996: 71), mentoring is about deliberately helping trainees to understand the rationale behind decisions made in physical education settings, which requires structured opportunities and time for the trainee to reflect upon the outcomes of such experiences. Tait (1996: 87) believes that mentoring involves the facilitation of learning, the development of ideas, the transformation of knowledge, the encouragement of critical reflection, with regards to pedagogy and conceptual issues. However, the role must be clearly defined rather than leaving it to chance. Training and understanding is fundamentally important. As teachers of physical education gain more experience during the course of their careers, it is likely that they will take on the role of mentoring a trainee teacher. It is likely that they will already have a range of responsibilities in schools but, as Rossi has stated,

> the demon that conspires to thwart the professional development of trainees is time, a commodity in extremely short supply in school. With prospective mentors often in middle-management roles, spending time with a student teacher is often invasive in the day-to-day route activities in which teachers are involved.
>
> *(Rossi 1996: 189)*

Teachers become mentors for a multitude of reasons. Some see it as an integral part of being a professional while others see it as a way of preparing future recruits to become 'agents of change'. However, without dedicated time, effective training and preparation for the role, mentoring a trainee teacher can be more of a hindrance than a help during a busy day. Being a mentor requires a commitment to the role and a desire to pass on knowledge to others who have the same career intentions. There must also be a commitment from the school in which the training takes place to ensure that both parties have the opportunities to reflect and review the progress of the trainee.

For over ten years I mentored trainee teachers and became acutely aware of their overwhelming desire to belong and providing a sense of belonging was critical. Apart from subject knowledge enhancement and pedagogical competence, being made to feel part of the subject department and being referred to as a member of staff as opposed to 'the trainee teacher' was top on their list of important factors to being on placement. During the time when I was mentoring trainee physical education teachers, I approached the role as a 'critical friend' and always tried to provide constructive advice on how to improve teaching and learning. The daily social interactions between the trainee teacher and me was part of a reiterative process whereby the formal and informal routines and rituals of physical education were replicated and re-enacted. I was fortunate enough to have a mentor like this when I was training to teach. Rather than being thrown into the deep end, I was lowered into the shallow end. In one particular lesson, he would use a stopwatch to record the number of minutes I would speak. Each time I spoke, he would start the watch and when I had finished he would stop the watch. At the end of the one-hour lesson, he asked me to estimate the total amount of time I had been speaking for during the 60-minute lesson. I was shocked to discover that I had spoken for 25 minutes of the total teaching time. Needless to say, I became a very child-centred teacher of physical education after that particular experience. I was also grateful for the opportunity to teach outside of my comfort zone and to experience teaching activities such as trampolining and swimming rather than simply playing to my strengths. By the time I had completed my teacher training, I believed that I was a well-rounded and competent teacher of physical education who could offer breadth, depth and balance of experience to young people in schools.

Mentoring, however, is not about producing clones or carbon copies of the mentors, even though trainees are influenced by their mentors to the realities of teaching and the preferred pedagogical practices of their mentors (Green 2008: 211). Because trainee teachers are in greater proximity to their mentors on a daily basis, they inevitably see their mentors as more realistic representatives of what they aspire to be and therefore emulate what their mentors do. The net result is that custom and practice tends to be reinforced rather than challenged. It is about the trainee teacher gathering ideas and building up their repertoire of skills and then adding their own personality to the delivery of the material to the pupils. But it is also about giving them the confidence to organise and manage a class effectively including a range of strategies to cope with situations that invariably arise during a lesson.

Mentors should have a clear understanding of the responsibilities and roles of the induction tutor – it is the trainees' entitlement. Mentors should have the specific knowledge, skills and understanding of training, mentoring and coaching NQTs through their initial year in teaching. Outstanding mentors are confident in their understanding of the characteristics of high-quality learning and teaching, as well as being open-minded and receptive to new ideas and innovative approaches and experienced observers of teaching. They are genuinely committed to supporting the development of others and provide constructive feedback and engage in positive dialogue with the NQT. In the schools that I have visited, the very best mentors monitor the trainee's progress against the standards for qualifying to teach. The process involves mentors providing constructive feedback on lesson planning and teaching. Each time a trainee teaches a class, the mentor reviews the lesson plan, provides initial feedback, observes the lesson and provides verbal and written comments during a debriefing session. Each week, the mentor and trainee meet to discuss progress and to set targets and actions for the following week. Midway through the training period, an interim report is written and the placement ends with a formal report in line with the standards for qualifying to teach.

So what do mentors look for in a trainee teacher of physical education? What is the difference between being good or being outstanding? Box 10.1 outlines some questions describing features of an outstanding trainee teacher. These questions can be used to help 'demystify' what the outstanding means in the context of teacher education for both trainers and trainees and relate specifically to the UK standards for qualifying to teach. Mentors can use the following questions in observations and discussions to support trainees' development towards becoming an outstanding teacher. Mentors can use the questions to interrogate their plans and evaluate their teaching against each of the teachers' standards for qualifying to teach.

BOX 10.1 Questions describing features of an outstanding trainee teacher

Teaching standards 1 and 7: learning environment
- Does the trainee motivate/inspire the pupils to enjoy the subject?
- Has the trainee explained the relevance/value of the subject?
- Are all the pupils engaged?

Teaching standard 3: curriculum knowledge
- Does the trainee introduce some important concepts and make some connections within the subject?

- Does the trainee use subject specific language effectively?
- Does the trainee help pupils to develop a range of skills in using and applying their subject knowledge?
- Does the trainee give pupils opportunities to carry out investigations in the subject and use analysis to identify causal relationships?
- Does the trainee have a high level of confidence of their subject knowledge and their understanding of effective learning in the subject?

Teaching standards 4 and 5: planning and teaching
- Does the teaching enable pupils to make connections between topics and see the 'big picture'?
- Does the trainee use a wide range of teaching strategies to stimulate all pupils' active participation in their learning?
- Does the trainee use innovative and imaginative resources, including practical activities and, where appropriate, the outdoor environment?
- Does the trainee encourage independence, allowing time for thinking and discussion?
- Are the barriers to learning and potential misconceptions anticipated and overcome, with any errors providing points for discussion?
- Does the trainee recognise and address any literacy challenges the subject may raise?
- Is the teaching rooted in the development of all pupils' conceptual understanding of important concepts and progression within the lesson and over time?

Teaching standards 2 and 6: learning outcomes and assessment
- Does the trainee give time for pupils to work independently and take the initiative?
- Does the trainee encourage pupils to think for themselves and be willing to try when faced with challenges?
- Does the trainee encourage pupils to learn from mistakes and false starts?
- Does the trainee assess pupils' understanding through questioning, listening and observing?
- Does the trainee communicate high expectations, enthusiasm and passion about the subject to the pupils?
- Does the trainee monitor and record the impact of their teaching on pupils' progress over time and adjust their teaching at individual, group or class level accordingly?

(Adapted from Ofsted, *Promoting Improvement in Initial Teacher Education (ITE): Primary mathematics*. Ref. 20130016. Manchester: Ofsted, November 2013).

This leads me to ask what makes an outstanding mentor? In my role as a teacher educator, I have observed a number of mentors working collaboratively with trainee teachers and have seen the way in which feedback is provided by the mentor to the trainee following a physical education lesson. During one particular joint observation, the mentor used the trainee's lesson plan to write annotated notes. This provided the basis for discussion during the debriefing and for more detailed written feedback. The mentor used prompt questions such as 'what was good about that lesson?', 'What did they pupils learn?' and 'If you could repeat the lesson again what would you do differently?'. At another school, the mentor used an iPad to film the trainee during their lesson and then asked the trainee to review the footage and write a self-evaluation for discussion at their weekly review. But what do trainee teachers think are the qualities of an outstanding mentor? Below are two trainee perspectives from trainee physical education teachers.

Vignette 13

A great mentor to me is someone who wants to support a trainee to become his or her best. They've been a PE trainee themselves so understand how daunting it can feel, therefore show support by scaffolding your learning just like that of their pupils. They're approachable, organised and get to know you, giving you personal stepping-stones to aid you in becoming the best PE teacher you can be with realistic challenges. They are great role models and can show you what an outstanding lesson looks like. They let you know they're on your side with lots of hints and tips to encourage you on your placement journey. They big you up when you do great to build your confidence. They guide you and pose constructive questions to help you find your way in making progress. They empathise when you've had a bad day or a bad lesson by handing you a tissue, making you laugh and rebuilding your spirit. They understand the learning experience is not just one way and together the mentor and trainee can learn lots from each other in developing both of their teaching practice.

Vignette 14

Throughout your teaching placement you will have a mentor who will act as your support. I have been extremely fortunate to have worked with not only two fantastic mentors but two fantastic PE departments on both of my placements. They have been supportive throughout, allowing me the opportunity to experiment with different ideas in a variety of lessons, as well as giving important guidance and constructive feedback. Self-reflection is, of course, important after lessons, however feedback from others gives a great insight and different perspective to help you improve.

Likewise, becoming a mentor has led me to ask why mentors choose to take on the responsibility of nurturing and training a trainee teacher. Below is an anecdotal account of one particular experienced mentor and their experiences of the role.

Vignette 15

Your years at university, training to be a PE teacher can, for many, be the happiest, most stress free years you have. Your weeks spent on teaching practice are often regarded as the most hard working and they are without doubt where you learn what it's really like to be a PE teacher. I was fortunate during my own training to learn from three fantastic and very different mentors, not forgetting the head of PE in my first full-time post. It's time to give something back. To pass on what you know to a new generation. Being a mentor is something that has in itself been highly rewarding. Not in any material terms but to see people who often become friends flourish in the teaching profession is certainly something to be proud of if you have in some way contributed to that success. It isn't always easy and in all honesty, when reflecting on one or two trainees, a case might be made for locking shut the gateway to the profession. However, knowing that those trainees are now teachers, one a head of year and the other a mentor herself, justifies having faith that they could progress. All the others have gone on to achieve success as teachers and now leaders in the profession. It's great to think that while undoubtedly success for them is deserved and self-generated, your mentorship during the five months or so that you got to know them has helped them in some way.

The penultimate chapter of this book aims to provide details about other potential career pathways a physical education teacher might wish to pursue. It highlights the natural evolution of physical education teachers into more varied roles within education. Readers will see that there are many opportunities and directions for physical education teachers to expand their repertoire of skills and contribute to the wider context of teaching in secondary schools.

Note

1   'My best teacher – Roger Black', *Times Educational Supplement*, 11 September 2009. Available online at www.tes.co.uk/teaching-resource/My-best-teacher-Roger-Black-6022725 (accessed 26 September 2014).

11

THE WIDER ROLE OF BEING A PHYSICAL EDUCATION TEACHER

The PE teacher who made a real difference to me was Nicky Dawes from Oakwood secondary. All the PE staff at Oakwood were good, but Miss Dawes was the one I really got on with. She gave everything to the job, and I suppose I identified with her. She was always encouraging me to play sports. When I went to Reigate College at 16, there was a guy called Paul Walker who was very encouraging towards girls' football. He was brilliant. He was probably the reason I got an A in my PE A-level, because he was a fantastic teacher. Some teachers didn't have time for girls' football but he used to coach the girls' team and encouraged us as much as the boys. At that point I was playing for the college team and for Horsham Ladies in the Southern League. The college team made it to a cup final and within about 10 minutes I had scored a hat trick. Mr Walker took me off and said: 'I want to give the other girls a chance to play, because you will go on to win other things'. I was upset because I wanted to play, but I respected him too because I understood that he wanted the others to feel part of it.

Faye White, captain of Arsenal and England Ladies football teams (1997–2012)[1]

Any physical education teacher will tell you that they wear many professional hats. Quite often, they wear more than one hat at a time and this not only causes a great deal of role conflict but creates compromising dilemmas. Many physical education teachers spend their time multi-tasking as their roles have become increasingly more diverse. In this penultimate chapter, the wider role of becoming a physical education teacher is discussed. It addresses issues such as the physical education teacher's pastoral responsibility, being a health educator, the teaching of accredited courses in physical education across the 14–18 age range and being a sports coach. This chapter also highlights alternative career pathways for physical education teachers within the education system, such as becoming a pastoral leader and a senior manager. Armour and Jones (1998: 130) have observed that as physical education teachers progress through their careers they are increasingly faced with decisions which could effectively relocate them in administrative roles as opposed to their teaching roles. For many physical education teachers, a career paradox emerges which puts them in a 'no-win' situation. Promotion to middle and senior management positions is often what drives physical education teachers away from their subject in an attempt to gain greater professional status, recognition and credibility and it is often the price to pay for divorcing themselves from their pupils and their subject. Irrespective of the routes into management, one thing that is certain is that the pastoral care of pupils will be a requirement that all schools will have of all teachers.

Being a form tutor

When I began my teaching career, I was informed on my first day that I would be the form tutor of a year eight class with a reputation for having some of the more challenging pupils, even though I had not received any formal training in the area of social work. Things are different today, with specific training for trainee teachers and newly qualified teachers with respect to the pastoral role that teachers are often expected to assume. During my time in North America, I observed 'home room' teachers checking on pupil attendance in the morning by performing a 'roll call' and then reciting 'the pledge of allegiance' but I had little to do with the pastoral care of pupils, which was the responsibility of in-house counsellors. In most schools in the UK, becoming a form tutor involves teachers working within a pastoral system, which means that they have to become a form tutor to an assigned group of pupils. This involves the promotion of the general progress and wellbeing of individual pupils and of the form tutor group as a whole. Form tutors liaise with a pastoral leader (many of whom are physical education teachers) to ensure the implementation of the school's pastoral system. They register pupil attendance, usually twice a day, accompany them to assemblies, encourage their full attendance at all lessons and their participation in other aspects of school life. Form tutors evaluate and monitor the progress of pupils and keep up-to-date pupil records, as well as contributing to the preparation of action plans, progress files and other reports. They alert the appropriate staff to problems experienced by pupils and make recommendations as to how these may be resolved. The role requires form tutors to communicate with parents and with persons or bodies outside the school concerned with the welfare of individual's, after consultation with the appropriate staff. Form tutors contribute to personal, social, health and cultural education, according to school policy. They are also required to apply the behaviour management systems so that effective learning can take place.

Being a health educator

It would be very difficult to argue against the fact that health promotion and lifelong participation in physical activity is an avowed goal not just for the physical education profession but for all professionals involved in the health and wellbeing of all young people. On 27 March 2014, Britain's Chief Medical Officer, Dame Sally Davies, stated in her annual report that being overweight was considered to be normal and that one-third of children were overweight or obese.[2] This represented double the number in the 1990s. Testimony to this was the fact that retailers were using larger sized mannequins in their window displays creating a false dichotomy among parents and children. Meanwhile, Dame Sally Davies suggested that sugar had become 'the new salt' and spoke of a new 'sugar tax' being introduced to British society. And yet, many young people often misinterpret the value of physical activity because of mixed messages given to them by teachers, health professionals and even the media. This often causes confusion. Is it true that if there is no pain then there is no gain? This leads to other associated questions that have particular importance for all young people in terms of developing a positive attitude towards leading a healthy active lifestyle. Is sport just another word for physical education? Are competitive team games the best way to improve general health and wellbeing? What do physical fitness tests in schools actually measure? Is exercising to exhaustion as with the multi-stage (or bleep) test actually beneficial to a young person's developing body? Being a health educator poses a number of other critical questions regarding opportunities for all pupils to engage in purposeful physical and health education programmes. But are physical education teachers best equipped to tackle the obesity epidemic among young people?

The perceived lack of physical fitness among young people begs the question as to why physical education has continued to be delivered using a limited range of teaching approaches, the most prevalent of which are formal, didactic and teacher-centred (Kirk 2010) through a set of traditional sex-stereotyped team games and often taught using inadequate resources and facilities? It is for these reasons that some schools fall short in promoting lifelong healthy, active lifestyles for pupils because the actual day-to-day content of the physical education curriculum has remained relatively unchanged, which has particular consequences for future participation, such as an increase in sedentary lifestyles. A key role of a physical education teacher is to think of imaginative ways of engaging all pupils in health promoting physical activities that could potentially provide an incentive to pursue the types of physical activities further and thus contribute to the health and wellbeing of each individual pupil. Stidder and Griggs (2012) have discussed the health benefits of providing an alternative physical education curriculum, particularly in light of the rising obesity levels among young people in schools. Ofsted (2009) reported that alternative and creative approaches to physical education are paying off but schools and teachers need to be more ambitious to improve worrying levels of health and fitness among school-aged children. The rate of obesity in young people continues to rise. For example, nine of ten adults and two-thirds of children could be obese by 2050.[3] Research into children's health has considered 'alternative' and innovative ways of engaging pupils into activities that will help to improve feelings of health, fitness and wellbeing and address healthy weight management (Stidder and Binney 2011). Health-related exercise activities might include aerobic dancing, yoga, tae bo, pilates, tai chi and boxercise. Rather than dismissing the advent of technology and, in particular, the increased popularity of computer games such as the Nintendo Wii Fit®, teachers might consider ways of embracing these types of games into the physical education curriculum. Many young people in schools are alienated from participating in physical education lessons when there is an excessive emphasis by teachers on circuit training and cross-country running, as well as pointless fitness tests, which are both fruitless and counterproductive in helping young people to understand the nature and purpose of such activities (Harris and Cale 2006). The interests of young people have moved on and changed since health-related fitness regimes were introduced into schools. Lifestyle activities have become more and more prominent among young people (Wheaton 2013) and it would seem that physical education teachers in schools have missed a trick by failing to acknowledge the popularity of activities such as skateboarding.

Being a sports coach

Traditionally, being a physical education teacher has meant being a sports coach as well. Debates, however, have raised the issue of whether physical education teachers should assume that coaching sport and team games, in particular, to elite squads of pupils should in fact be part and parcel of their role as educators (Stidder and Hayes 2012). It has also bought into question whether physical education teachers might not necessarily be the best or the most appropriate people to deliver a programme with a heavy sporting orientation for a privileged few. Green (2008: 72) has observed that where growth in extracurricular physical education has occurred, the main reason appears to be increased involvement of external sports coaches, specialists and sports organisations, rather than physical education teachers, which might be a sign that physical education teachers prioritise other contractual duties at the expense of their involvement in what successive governments have referred to as 'school sport'. The increased political pressures on physical education teachers to raise academic standards with the rise of accredited awards in physical education may be symptomatic of the increase in the numbers of external coaches now assuming this role, leading to the voluntary redundancy of physical education teachers as 'sports coaches'. The rise in the number of sports coaches in schools has been 'on the cards' for a considerable number of years. I have noticed that physical education teachers have almost second-guessed their futures by using professional development opportunities to improve their teaching of academic physical education rather than building up a repertoire of sport coaching-orientated qualifications.

In the past, the extracurricular coaching responsibilities that physical education teachers often assumed constituted a significant part of the role which typically involved the provision and organisation of activities that took place outside of the formal curriculum. In some schools, these activities can take place before the school day begins, in the form of breakfast clubs or lunchtime practices, or after the school day, when prearranged competitive games take place against other schools. During the halcyon days of the 1970s and 1980s, inter-school sporting fixtures also took place at weekends, before the combined effects of an industrial dispute between teaching unions and the government stopped a number of extracurricular activities from taking place. Some of these duties involve physical education teachers coaching school teams and making 'fixtures' and are, perhaps unsurprisingly, related to sport and traditionally sex-segregated and gender-stereotyped team games. These teams tend to reflect they way in which physical education lessons are organised in that they are arranged in single-sex groups and taught by same-sex teachers. In the UK, the responsibility for girls' teams lies with female physical education staff and vice-versa for the boys' teams, and it is not unusual for schools to include this when advertising for teachers of physical education. Typically the boys' teams play football (soccer), rugby, basketball and cricket, whereas the girls' teams play netball, (field) hockey and rounders, and this is often used in promotional material within school brochures.

When I began my teaching career, I was a naive twenty-something entering a school where routines and practices were already established and deeply rooted. It never occurred to me to question why things were done or how they were done. For a number of years, I accepted, even bought into, the idea that teaching physical education was about performance, competition and winning trophies. If I had had a pound for every game I refereed or umpired I would be a rich man by now. At the time, I merely regarded myself as a 'foot soldier' who was there to deliver whatever I was told to teach and how to teach it. There were days when the actual teaching of physical education got in the way of other priorities with which I was involved. It sometimes felt that teaching physical education was just inconvenient. This is not a new phenomenon within the physical education profession, particularly for male physical education teachers. This was recognised as particularly problematic in that competition in the form of team games was taking over the professional lives of physical education teachers at the expense of teaching curricular physical education. Donovan (1997: 17) expressed his concerns as a practising physical education teacher in a state-funded school where extracurricular sports fixtures and competitions accounted for a considerable amount of his time and energy and led to disproportionate amounts of time being devoted to the elite athletes. The role conflict that Donovan (1997) experienced was simply a reality of everyday life within a physical education department. But does it have to be that way? I am now acutely aware that I was a 'buy one get one free' type of physical education teacher, who spent more time preparing school sports teams and arranging fixtures than I did planning my formal lessons. Not only did I arrange the fixtures, pick the teams, referee the home matches, drive the mini bus, write the match reports and wash the kits, I was also expected to teach high-quality inclusive physical education lessons. Organising representative school teams was not in my job description and nobody ever stopped to tell me that this was counterproductive to high-quality physical education teaching and learning. Neither was I ever discouraged from running school teams. There were times when I felt that my professional and personal life was dominated by the undue pressure to 'get results' and to have something to shout about, even though there were some high points associated with these experiences. In essence, I was a victim of what Green (2008: 213) refers to as a 'coaching orientation', in that I was unable to manage my dual role, either in theory or in practice. Just as Green describes, I had to assimilate what I had experienced during my initial teacher training through a prism of my own sporting presupposition and preoccupation, which meant that my behaviour was inclined towards a blend of more deeply seated values, beliefs and attitudes within the context that I operated. As Green (2003) has shown in other cases, it was more to do with my circumstances and the constraints within my particular school setting. I was part of a self-replicating group who had been influenced by experiences gained in teacher training and from being mentored during teaching practice whereby my normative behaviour was reinforced by the expectations of fellow male physical education teachers and the tradition of the school.

As my teaching career in schools came to end towards the end of the 1990s, Donovan (1997) claimed that there were a sizeable number of British (male) physical education teachers who were more committed to school sport than curricular physical education. These teachers had been caught up in a vicious circle – damned if they did and damned if they didn't. This led me to ask a question of myself. Was I the director of elite performance or was I a teacher of physical education? For many, the role conflict and tension between coaching and teaching may have been caused by a false perception that producing winning teams would help them gain promotion in their respective schools. On reflection, my career as a teacher of physical education may have become more like those of other former physical education teachers turned football coaches, such as former Dutch football managers Louis Van Gaal, Rinus Michels and Guus Hiddink, all of whom taught physical education before becoming successful international coaches and managers. I suppose that was an option but in the same way that the late Tony Benn (Labour Member of Parliament for over 30 years) left the House of Commons to concentrate more on politics, I left the teaching profession to focus more on education.

During my time in North America at the beginning of the 1990s, what struck me most was that physical education and school sport within the respective schooling systems differed significantly. The separation of curriculum physical education and high school athletics (competitive sport) for example, was in direct contrast to the place of sport within the physical education curriculum at my UK institution. The intramural athletic programme (extracurricular sport) provided opportunities for pupils with superior athletic ability to develop and fully use this talent through organised competition with pupils of similar ability from other schools. The school sports teams were orientated towards highly organised inter-scholastic competition and viewed as totally separate from the formal physical education curriculum and delivered by specialist salaried coaches, who were employed to take on this responsibility throughout the year or season under the management of a school athletic director. Physical education teachers were occasionally employed on a separate contract to undertake these responsibilities, such as my role as a throwing coach for the school's track and field athletics team. These teams were usually reserved for elite performers, often in single-sex teams, and had performance-related outcomes associated with them. In comparison, the extracurricular school sport in the UK was organised voluntarily by (mainly same-sex) physical education teachers (and sometimes by non-physical education specialist teachers) who had a keen interest in a particular sport. Specialist coaching experience and qualifications were often a stipulated requirement within job advertisements for physical education teachers. Nearly 25 years on since my time in North America, this was finally acknowledged as a major issue in the current provision of physical education and sport in UK state-funded schools:

> In secondary schools, the PE teacher carries out the role that, in independent schools, is carried out by a director of sport. They are not only teaching physical education; they are trying to provide after-school sporting opportunities, hire, fire and employ coaches, and organise the competition. In independent schools that is done by a separate role, called the director of sport, and that allows the PE department to teach the curriculum and the director of sport to manage the out-of-school opportunity. That does not happen in our state schools.
>
> (House of Lords Select Committee on Olympic and Paralympic Legacy 2013: 38)

The role of physical education teachers in the provision of inter-scholastic sport within the school in North America was, therefore, peripheral while in the UK the roles and responsibilities of physical education teachers in the provision of school sport were central. While federal rules and regulations influence and govern the delivery of physical education in high schools the interpretations of federal policy is not the same in each of the states of the United States. It is often the state policy rather than the federal (national) policy that has greater impact on educational institutions. The workload demands today on the contemporary physical education teacher in the UK and the public accountability that goes with it means that physical education teachers are literally bursting at the seams with respect to coping with the demands that schools place upon them within the time that they allocate to carry out the role. Simply trying to fit in extracurricular responsibilities, for which physical education teachers receive no additional time or financial reward, is perhaps impractical and just unfeasible in the twenty-first century and is a prime example of how history has stalked physical education not necessarily to its advantage (Capel and Whitehead 2013: 236). The days of 'goodwill' may be over and it might be time to hand over the reins to external sport coaches.

Being a 14–18 physical education teacher

Attempts to establish the academic credentials of physical education have existed in debates among physical education professionals for well over 20 years but it has become standard practice for physical education teachers to teach theoretical principals through physical activities as part of accredited programmes of physical education in schools. Physical education teachers have campaigned for greater theoretical justifications for their subject and other more laudable and educationally valued goals than merely playing sport in the upper years of secondary education (Green 2008: 231). The study of sport, rather than the practice of sport, has in some cases provided the basis of all programmes of physical education for pupils after the age of 14 in an attempt to bolster the place of physical education on the academic curriculum (Stidder and Wallis 2003, 2012), leading some academics to comment that this has left the subject on the horns of the recreational and academic debate (Green 2008: 10). One of the hallmarks of the intellectual development of physical education has been the growth of accredited courses and the process been described as 'rapid', dramatic' and even 'unprecedented' (Green 2003). It is safe to say that a proportion of the work that physical education teachers do will be with pupils aged 14–18 in the classroom as well as the gymnasium.

The contemporary physical education teacher now has a very different repertoire of skills, which requires them to teach more and more in a classroom-based setting as the numbers of pupils aged between 14 and 18 who are taking public examinations in physical education continues to rise. Some physical education teachers may see the increase of accredited awards in physical education as adding 'educational gloss' to the subject and, in the process, a way of gaining increased academic and professional status. Others have said that, in some cases, the educational worthiness of examination physical education and justification for its place on the curriculum were merely afterthoughts and considered to be 'additional goods' to bolster the physical education curriculum (Green 2003: 142). Previous research (Stidder and Wallis 2012) has shown that externally accredited courses in physical education for 14–18 year old pupils in the UK have continued to gain support among teachers at an unprecedented rate. While the numbers of pupils who take the GCSE examination course in physical education has remained relatively stable between 2010 and 2014, the introduction of other accredited types of courses in physical education and dance have added to the range of accredited courses in physical education available to pupils.

There is now a vast range and an eclectic mix of accredited awards available for pupils aged 14–18, such as GCSE, BTEC, Sports Leaders Awards, Duke of Edinburgh Awards, A-level and level three national vocational diplomas in supporting the delivery of physical education and school sport (Qualifications and Credit Framework). Golder (2010) has highlighted the fact that many of these qualifications in physical education have been introduced as part of a 14–18 curriculum, as all young people in the UK are required to stay in education or training until 18 years of age from 2015. This has only served to reflect the evolving nature of being a physical education teacher and the UK Coalition Government's attention to raising academic standards. Physical education teachers can now expect to teach accredited awards in physical education to pupils aged 14–18 as part of their contemporary role. Indeed, many job advertisements specify and insist that the teaching of examination physical education is a prerequisite. My own experiences of physical education lessons in the latter part of my compulsory schooling were purely recreational. At the beginning of my penultimate year of secondary school, I was provided with 'options' with regard to the types of physical activities I wished to pursue during the one-hour lesson devoted to physical education each week. These choices of activities usually meant that the boys played five-a-side football while the girls played netball. I did not learn how to swim at school nor was I provided any opportunities to try new or different activities. If I was lucky, my physical education teacher would take the lesson, otherwise they were usually supervised by other non-specialist teachers from other departments. Accredited courses in physical education did not exist at the secondary schools I attended and the situation was no different at the local sixth-form college.

Curriculum developments and trends in physical education have shown, however, that non-examination or 'core' programmes of physical education after the age of 14 are fast becoming the exception rather than the rule in secondary schools, with more schools than ever providing accredited forms of physical education and dance in place of 'core' programmes (Ofsted 2009). My own research suggests that, with more schools moving towards compulsory accredited programmes of physical education, the skill set required of a contemporary physical education teacher is completely different to that of only ten years ago (Stidder and Wallis 2012). There is increasing recognition that the continued growth of accredited physical education courses is a reflection of the value that teachers place on accredited forms of learning (Ofsted 2009). This is part of the process referred by Green (2008: 88) as the 'academicisation' of physical education, which has been apparent for over a quarter of a century, whereby there is increasing emphasis on the theoretical study of physical activity and sport in both absolute and relative terms (that is, in relation to, and sometimes at the expense of, practical activities). Green (2008) has shown how the increase in the numbers of 14–16-year-old pupils taking GCSE and 16–18-year-old students studying advanced-level physical education has surpassed virtually all other subjects. Within a 13-year period schools have witnessed a growth rate of 221 per cent at GCSE and 2863 per cent at A level. Green (2008) has referred to this growth as an 'explosion' which represents a step change in the way in which physical education is organised at key stage four and post-sixteen. Similarly, there has been a steady increase in the numbers of pupils following alternative forms of traditional 'core' physical education, such as leadership awards, which now account for over 140,000 young people aged 14–19, through Sports Leaders UK.[4] In this respect, Ofsted (2009) found that most secondary schools offer 14–16-year-old pupils GCSE physical education and other accredited physical education awards, to broaden the choices open to pupils, as many schools prefer a more vocational approach to physical education where pupils are assessed as performers, leaders or officials through accredited courses.

Much of the impetus for the increased numbers of pupils taking an accredited award in physical education has been the result of increasing concerns among physical education teachers that pupils who only take 'core' non-accredited physical education receive less than one hour per week of physical education (40 minutes of activity) and there is little connection in the way physical education is organised in key stage three and what is offered in key stage four 'core' physical education (Ofsted 2009). There is an overwhelming educational rationale, therefore, for teaching compulsory accredited awards in physical education compared with 'core' non-accredited programmes, particularly when the use of non-specialist staff in 'core' physical education lessons at key stage four, especially in games teaching, is sometimes unsatisfactory, as pupils tend to be supervised rather than effectively taught (Ofsted 2009). At the Greensward Academy in Essex, the physical education department has attempted to tackle the issue of post-14 physical education by moving to wholesale GCSE physical education for all pupils in years 9, 10 and 11. Over 600 pupils follow a three-year programme consisting of two practical one-hour lessons and one 60-minute theory lesson over a two-week timetable. All physical education teachers teach this course, which has become standard practice with respect to their professional role and responsibility, while pupils have accepted this as a natural progression after the first two years of their secondary schooling. Likewise, the Queen's School in Hertfordshire has introduced compulsory accredited physical education courses for all pupils in years 10 and 11. In 2014, 214 pupils were entered for GCSE physical education and 50 pupils took a BTEC award in sport.

With the first cohort of pupils due to stay in full-time education until 18 years old from 2015, the teaching of physical education to pupils aged 16–18 will pose a number of dilemmas. What do you do with a class of 30 pupils over the age of 16 who have only ever experienced 'core' or non-accredited forms of physical education? What will the key stage five physical education curriculum consist of? Certainly, in the context of post-16 education, the retention of non-accredited version of physical education may not sit too well among other academic subjects. While teachers may have more professional freedom to make informed choices on behalf of their pupils, they will also face greater accountability and academic rigour in the design of post-16 physical education programmes. To those physical education teachers seeking greater status and recognition in the profession, the introduction of more accredited courses in physical education after the age of 16 might not necessarily be a bad thing, as shown by Branson (2014) in her description of how one post-16 provider has anticipated these changes of events by restructuring the timetable and offering sporting pathways that are unique to each individual student. On a final note, it is perfectly feasible that a physical education teacher could potentially teach their specialist subject without ever setting foot inside a gymnasium. It could be that they just specialise in the teaching of theoretical physical education. For other physical education teachers, a combination of teaching theory and practical to pupils aged 14 and over might be more appealing. There is almost no escaping the fact, though, that the teaching of accredited awards in physical education is an integral part of being a physical education teacher, particularly when you consider that just under 100,000 of all

16-year-olds took the GCSE physical education course in 2012 while just over 1700 of 18-year-olds took an advanced-level qualification in physical education (Department for Education 2013b).

Being a pastoral leader

In many schools that I have visited, it is not uncommon for at least one member of the physical education department to be a pastoral leader for a particular year group of pupils. In some schools, they are referred to as heads of year, progress managers, achievement managers or directors of learning. This role typically comes with a teaching and learning responsibility, for which there is an additional salary payment. Irrespective of the title, teachers who become pastoral leaders are responsible for pupil's emotional wellbeing and academic achievement. Pastoral leaders look after the welfare of pupils and monitor attendance. The role can be full time and non-teaching, while in some schools the role is aligned with teaching duties, especially when it comes under the job title of head of year. Typically, the main responsibilities of a pastoral leader are to be the first point of contact and liaison between families and other children's agencies, such as social services or child health; to be friendly, helpful and welcoming to parents and others visiting or making contact with the school; to provide a good role model for students; to develop a relationship with students which is professional, firm, fair, caring and friendly; to maintain an appropriate and professional distance with students in more informal situations or when dealing with sixth form students; to implement behaviour policy and deal with student behaviour issues.[5]

The Department for Education and Skills (2005: 22) stated that:

> We believe it is important for schools to have effective pastoral support systems. We recognise that in primary and special schools this is the responsibility of the head teacher and often their deputy. Secondary schools use pastoral support teams. Dealing with the pastoral needs of pupils can requires the school to use external agencies, such as those services provided by the local authority, police, health, social services and other agencies.
>
> *(Department for Education and Skills 2005: 22)*

Physical education teachers do make great pastoral leaders. I know. I have met plenty of them. But the question for physical education teachers is whether they are prepared to sacrifice their teaching role in favour of a pastoral role. For me, I was never tempted to go in this direction. I was never trained to do this job.

Being a senior leader

Becoming a senior leader is a professional career move that some physical education aspire to and eventually achieve. Some physical education teachers get to the point where they think that they cannot be a physical education teacher forever. In an article in the *Guardian* newspaper, a 62-year-old head teacher at a large secondary academy school who began his career as a physical education teacher explained why so many physical education teachers go into senior leadership positions in schools and why they are so good at it:

> You can't be a PE teacher forever. Or, if you do carry on, it may restrict your career progression as you get older. I realised that I needed to think about my career path. I started teaching in 1974. Early on, I become a head of house for the school. That was the first opportunity I had to consider career development. After five years in the role, I was in a position where I could apply for an internal deputy headship. Senior positions gave me a platform. Once I'd got the first job as deputy head, I was able to go on and apply for other positions elsewhere. After building up my experience and portfolio, I eventually became head. I didn't start teaching with the idea of being a head teacher – even when I was a deputy. But I was driven by aspiration and the desire to be successful. It was about looking at the opportunities that present themselves and taking them at the crucial times. I've always been into coaching. As a PE teacher, you already have some natural leadership qualities. Many PE teachers find themselves going into senior positions in challenging schools because those are often the sorts of schools they can most make a difference in. There's certainly a need for a strong presence.[6]

The National Professional Qualification for Headship (NPQH) is a qualification for individuals who have aspirations to become a head teacher or principal and are 12–18 months from applying for headship posts and ready to take up a headship as soon as they graduate. The programme is no longer mandatory but evaluation evidence from trainee heads who have completed the NPQH demonstrates that the programme remains a high-quality leadership development programme which has direct impact on the individual, the school in which they work and their pupils.

Typically, individuals spend time at a school in a different context for a minimum of nine days and complete three essential and two elective modules. Each module requires up to 50 hours of blended learning, typically consisting of workplace learning (about 20 hours) practical activities, face-to-face activity, including peer and facilitated learning, reading and reflection online learning. The final assessment process enables them to demonstrate their leadership in practice through the successful completion of school improvement work undertaken in their own and other school settings, as well as their capacity to perform well in presenting, at interview and in making decisions in test environments. It is competency based, testing the key competencies that are required for successful headship. The final assessment comprises three tasks, one in their own school, one in their placement school and a case study.[7]

Being a university lecturer

I suppose that in a chapter of this type it would be remiss of me not to include a brief synopsis about becoming and being a university lecturer of physical education. I have heard that those who can't do teach and those who can't teach work in universities. That is just a myth. I have now spent more time as a university lecturer than I did as a school teacher. In 1998, I was seconded to the University of Brighton after completing a Master's degree in education. Ten years after I had left university to become a teacher, my return to studying had 'whetted' my appetite to continue with research and also to contribute to the training of the next generation of physical education teachers. Part of my role includes engagement with scholarly activity, such as writing this book and peer-reviewed journal articles. Becoming a physical education lecturer was somewhat of a culture shock compared with teaching in schools. Despite the lower salary and fewer holidays at the time I entered higher education, it was an opportunity to make a difference to the training of physical education teachers. Since 2004, I have been the pathway leader for the PGCE physical education course. Today, I also manage the School Direct physical education training route and the Troops to Teachers initiative for physical education trainee teachers. This involves teaching, and quality assurance. I visit trainee physical education teachers on a regular basis while they are experiencing periods of school-based training and carry out joint observations of trainees with their respective mentors and provide feedback as part of the university and school partnership.

Summary

The career pathways that physical education teachers might follow are varied and diverse and require a unique skill set to carry out a multitude of roles. Green (2008: 232) predicted that in the near future the twin processes of 'sportisation' and 'academicisation' appeared set to dominate physical education which academics, head teachers and physical education teachers appear happy to endorse as both processes appear to be gathering pace. But a word of warning should be taken from Nutt and Clarke (2002: 162) in that teachers of examination physical education must begin to reconcile the tensions that inevitably arise between the multiplicity of role definitions and identify the actual role they are expected to fulfil with respect to the statutory entitlement of all young people to an equitable physical education experience. Armour and Jones (1998) showed this to be the case with 'Arnold', a 36-year-old head of physical education who had little enthusiasm for physical education, preferring to devote enormous amounts of time to careers and pastoral issues, leaving him with little energy for teaching his subject specialism. The final chapter of this book brings to a close the lifecycle of the physical education teacher and reflects upon the journey that has been travelled.

Notes

1   Richard Lea-Hair, 'My Best Teacher', *Times Educational Supplement*, 21 May 2004: 6. Available online at www.tes.co.uk/teaching-resource/My-best-teacher-394942 (accessed 26 September 2014).

2   Classed as having a body mass index above 25; Nick Triggle, 'Overweight seen as the norm says chief medical officer', *BBC News*, 27 March 2014. Available online at www.bbc.co.uk/news/health-26765078 (accessed 27 September 2014).

3   Sarah Knapton, '9 out of 10 adults will be obese by 2050', *Telegraph*, 9 November 2008. Available online at www.telegraph.co.uk/health/3411540/Nine-out-of-10-adults-will-be-overweight-by-2050.html (accessed 27 September 2014).

4   See www.sportsleaders.org (accessed 3 October 2014); Sports Leaders UK aims to get communities more active and healthy by providing recognised vocational sports leadership qualifications. Originally founded over 30 years ago, Sports Leaders UK was set up to support people across the UK who would like to give back to their local community. It now assists over 140,000 young people a year to give them the skills, advice and confidence to provide sporting opportunities to their neighbourhood.

5   'Becoming a Pastoral Manager', *TES Connect*, 10 September 2014. Available online at www.tes.co.uk/article.aspx?storyCode=6281162 (accessed 27 September 2014).

6   Martin Williams, 'Making the Switch: How I Moved From Sixth Form to Primary Teaching', *Guardian*, 11 October 2013. Available online at www.theguardian.com/education/2013/oct/11/sixth-form-primary-teaching (accessed 27 September 2014).

7   'Guidance: National Professional Qualification for Headship (NPQH)', *gov.uk*, updated 22 August 2014. Available online at www.gov.uk/national-professional-qualification-for-headship-npqh (accessed 27 September 2014).

12

THE TWENTY-FIRST CENTURY PHYSICAL EDUCATION TEACHER

> When you look at elite sportsmen there are invariably many moments in their lives that get them to the top. But for me, this was perhaps the most significant of those moments: Two teachers giving me permission to believe I could do it. I understood at the time the significance of what Mr Garrett and Mr Jordan were doing. I allowed them to help me. They persuaded me to cast off the cynicism and self-doubt.
>
> *Duncan Goodhew MBE, 100-m breaststroke gold medallist at the 1980 Moscow Olympics*[1]

The first section of this book provided the contextual information required to become a physical education teacher. Section two considered the lifecycle of the physical education teacher from 'cradle to grave'. Section three highlighted the natural evolution from becoming a physical education teacher to being a reflective practitioner, mentor and senior manager. This final chapter attempts to put together all the pieces of a very large jigsaw puzzle from early childhood through to adult maturity. In writing this book, I have realised that there is certainly more to becoming a physical education teacher than meets the eye. It would not be an over exaggeration to say that becoming a physical education teacher has undergone major transplant surgery and that the twenty-first century physical education teacher has a very different role compared with their twentieth-century counterpart. Readers will have noted that it is a complex business, even for teachers of physical education, let alone trainee teachers, to understand who they are and what they are trying to achieve in the name of their specialist subject. As my career has developed, I have realised that my initial teacher training was only the start of my professional development as a teacher. Becoming a physical education teacher is a lifelong process, which involves the development of a personal understanding of the teaching and learning process, understanding wider issues in the profession generally and the subject specifically, as well as understanding of oneself (Capel and Whitehead 2013: xii). The process takes place incrementally over time. After all, it has taken me 30 years to write this particular book.

The twenty-first century physical education teacher has to accept that pupils today are very different learners compared with pupils at the turn of the century. Frapwell and Hawman (2014: 6) have referred to the twenty-first century climate of physical education as a 'game-changing zeitgeist' since the introduction of new and emerging technologies into physical education lessons. The invention of the X-Box®, Nintendo Wii® and other gaming consoles has gradually taken over the lives of young people. Taking part in regular physical activity may not necessarily appeal to most of them. Children are highly influenced by other external forces and are bombarded with daily messages about what their priorities should be in life. Secondary school pupils, especially, can be easily persuaded that to succeed in life there are far more important things than being active. Slezak *et al.* (2013) talk of a 'physical education revolution' in a world of technology and instant gratification, where young people know the price of everything but the value of nothing. Likewise, senior managers in schools might know the costs involved in running a successful physical education department but few may recognise the real value and impact that physical education has on a child. Physical education teachers have had to adapt and change the way they teach to meet the needs of pupils in schools. The speed at which technology, for example, has transformed the landscape in which physical education teachers teach and pupils learn is unprecedented, particularly with the advent and use of tablet devices. If we consider the question of what a pencil, calculator and mobile phone all have in common and then consider the answer is that they have all been banned in schools at some point in history, it perhaps puts into perspective the world in which we now live. It is not inconceivable to think that we are on the cusp of some dramatic changes and may even see the first paperless school in the very near future unless it already exists. So what does this all mean for the twenty-first century teacher of physical education? In one school where all pupils lease an iPad®, I observed a trainee teacher incorporate technology into the teaching of physical education. The following extract may help to visualise the lesson.

> Year 7 gymnastics – accurate replication of actions, phrases and sequences. Pupil success is judged on their ability to repeat actions, phrases and sequences of movements as accurately as possible. The learning objectives and intended outcomes were shared with the pupils at the beginning of the lesson along with the expected levels of attainment using a digital whiteboard. The introductory tasks were very good. There was much evidence of self-assessment through a traffic light system and the task cards produced were of high quality. There was very good use of peer assessment and video analysis as all pupil's were able to use their individual iPad to capture still images, record moving images, use slow motion and freeze framing. A range of different teaching styles were employed and each pupil

used their iPad effectively for peer assessment particularly using the slow pro application. This aspect of the lesson was innovative, creative and forward thinking. The positioning and mobility throughout the lesson was exemplary and diagnostic and corrective feedback to pupils regarding their performance of different body shapes was provided to pupils. The rock, paper, scissors exercise was vey inventive. Pupils were able to demonstrate to others and non-participants were actively engaged also using iPads. Pupil activity levels throughout were extremely high. A very effective plenary session concluded the lessons with interactive questions being asked using the teacher's iPad.

In another school, a trainee teacher had incorporated the use of technology to effectively manage the behaviour of the pupils in her class.

> Year 8 badminton – outwitting opponents: this includes activities in which the concept of success is to overcome an opponent in a face-to-face competition where each opponent can directly affect the other's performance and the key is to outwit the opponent(s). For example: net/divided court games (such as badminton, volleyball). Courts were set up in advance with task cards and assessment levels placed on each court. A very good introduction to the lesson took place with learning objectives shared with the class. Pupils worked on task throughout the lesson and were very active and receptive. Some pupils worked with shorter handle rackets. This was a large class of 32 pupils. Behaviour management strategies were in place via an online app (Class Dojo) that monitored pupil behaviour. This was recorded onto an iPad and shown in real time on two large screens in the sports hall. Pupil progress was regularly checked against levels of attainment and peer assessment. Pupils worked in pre-selected groups according to levels of ability and challenged through achievable tasks. Pupils rotated as scorers, officials and performers. The higher ability group performed to an exceedingly high standard. There was much evidence of teacher facilitation of learning with positioning and mobility dynamic throughout. The lesson was highly organised with pupils constantly on task. There was both physical activity and education taking place with cross-curricular links. A very good plenary session concluded the lesson.

To highlight this even further another snapshot example of an outstanding physical education lesson is presented below.

> Year 8 dance – exploring and communicating ideas, concepts and emotions. This includes activities in which success is judged on the degree to which the performer makes contact with the audience and communicates their ideas, feelings and emotions. The theme was 'secret agents'. Dance charades were used as a starter activity. This was very imaginative. Learning objectives were locked inside briefcases and pupils had to break the code in order to

share these with the whole group. Using a countdown on an iPad ensured they were focused quickly. The use of an iPad to bring up the name of a pupil inside a golden star was an excellent way of engaging all pupils. This was high-quality teaching of physical education with many cross-curricular themes and links such as literacy through making the shape of words such as SPY. Pupils made excellent progress with respect to musicality and dance dynamics. The use of the lighting system and orange neon skipping ropes pulled across the width of the studio to make a spider's web to simulate laser beams was an excellent idea to exemplify the movements of as secret agent!! The start middle and end freeze frames allowed them to construct a story to their dance and the use of the story boards helped them to achieve this. Cameras were an excellent resources with this. The contact and lift work brought their performances to life. A range of different teaching styles were employed and each pupil was involved in peer assessment and self-assessment. The choice of music was very appropriate – James Bond theme tune. Pupils were engaged in the learning throughout both in a practical context and a very effective plenary session at the end of the lesson. The positioning and mobility throughout the lesson was exemplary and there were several opportunities where diagnostic and corrective feedback to pupils regarding their performance. Assessment strategies were clearly in place. Pupil activity levels throughout were extremely high. There were high-order questions ensuring a pupil-centred focus in a safe and purposeful learning environment. Organisation and management of learning were exceptionally good. Interaction with pupils was extremely positive and showed evidence of effective teaching and learning. The trainee teacher demonstrated very good subject knowledge of this particular aspect of physical education. The activities and tasks were progressive, age appropriate and relevant to the learning objectives.

In another school, the trainee teacher demonstrated the capacity to teach in a classroom as opposed to a gymnasium. During a year ten BTEC lesson the trainee teacher focused on developing pupils understanding of the muscular and skeletal system.

There was much evidence to suggest that the trainee had high expectations of his pupils and his enthusiasm for his subject provided a stimulating environment for pupils to learn (in this case in the classroom as opposed to the gymnasium or sports hall). Pupils were actively engaged in learning and responded with enthusiasm through question and answers sessions and whole class discussion. The trainee showed a very secure command of his subject knowledge related to the theme and structured the lesson in a very effective way taking into account different learning needs as well as the logistics of time. He had produced some very innovative resources to support his teaching and the learning of his pupils. The starter activity was appropriate through shared learning intentions. The use of the 'paper' skeleton provided a visual stimulus for the pupils linked to the names of bones (cranium, ulna, and radius). This was followed with an adapted game related to the whodunit detective game 'Cluedo' demonstrating creativity in his teaching and engaging the pupils in the learning process. The use of mobile phones for internet access provided an added dimension to his teaching and the pupils learning. His personal and professional conduct was outstanding.

The way in which pupils are taught physical education is dependent on those who teach them. This is equally dependent on the way in which physical education teachers are prepared for the challenges of working within contemporary education. What is certain is that being highly trained and qualified is critical whether the training is school led or university led. All children are entitled to be taught by a qualified teacher. There have to be checks and balances in place. As long as there is rigour and robustness supported by academic, pedagogical and professional training then we can forget the old adage that 'a little knowledge is a dangerous thing'. Academic qualifications and training play an important part in becoming a physical education teacher but the need to have qualifications to teach has been largely ignored at a political level. I would like to believe that initial teacher training will play a major part in developing future teachers of physical education, which will provide them with the skill set to introduce fresh alternative approaches to the teaching and learning of physical education in schools through a more diverse health-related curriculum that might make a small, but nonetheless, significant contribution to the health and wellbeing of every pupil in schools. But the twenty-first century physical education teacher will need time to administer the state-sponsored war on obesity (Monaghan 2014). Rather than contributing to the de-professionalisation of physical education, the use of sports coaches and other external specialists that is being witnessed in schools may be a blessing in disguise for overstretched and overworked physical education teachers. Is it too much to expect one single physical education teacher to teach academic physical education, sport, health, swimming, dance and outdoor education? Sport coaches could be part of the solution to pupil inactivity rather than be part of the problem. Sir Michael Wilshaw accused head teachers in state-funded schools of being lukewarm about competitive sport, with many not taking it seriously enough, regarding it with suspicion and as an optional extra (Ofsted 2014: 2). Perhaps head teachers are concerned that poorly trained coaches of sport, who have little understanding of pedagogy, could potentially marginalise pupils who are disaffected and unmotivated and could be deterred from physical education altogether when they perceive it to be a substitute for competitive sport. Equally, there is a danger that adopting a sport-based approach to physical education simply provides an infrastructure for budding 2016 Olympians at the expense of all other pupils, including those with disabilities, who often feel left out of physical education lessons altogether, for which there is no excuse in law and should be no reason in practice. The answer might be that all maintained schools and academies give separate responsibility for teaching physical education and coaching sport, which would give physical education teachers and sport coaches the time to do both well (Ofsted 2014). Appointing a director of sport, a full-time, salaried, non-teaching position with responsibility for organising teams, coaches, referees, transport and facilities similar to the North American model that I experienced would indicate that the politicians are willing to actually 'put their money where their mouths are'.

The provision of competitive school sport is something that may entice many parents when considering their child's secondary education. As Green (2008) has shown us, schools have become part of an educational marketplace where parents are the 'customers' and pupils are the 'consumers'. Physical education teachers have become suppliers of a package of quality-controlled consumable items that are supposed to provide worthwhile experiences. Ofsted (2014) recommended that all maintained schools and academies should offer a range of sports but promote a few to excel. These schools should provide enough time in the physical education curriculum and sport enrichment programmes to attain high standards in these sports. Schools should use expert coaches to work alongside teachers to coach more able pupils and school teams, and head teachers should hold them to account for the success achieved by pupils. This is all well and good but, like anything in life, you only get what you pay for. But is this what all pupils in state schools actually want? Has anyone ever bothered to ask them? If the customer is always right, then one might ask why their voice has been muted for so long and why service providers have been so resistant to change. Pupils are frequently seen but are seldom heard. On 18 March 2014, the BBC reported that a 14-year-old schoolboy had been excluded for two days from his secondary school in Blackpool for leading a walk-out with 40 other pupils in protest against a lack of mathematics homework.[2] I ask myself whether pupils would do the same because of a lack of curriculum time devoted to physical education or because of the lack of variety in the physical education curriculum. Some may say that I am playing devil's advocate but others might think that I have a point. All too often, pupils are ignored when it comes to curriculum decisions simply because their views about the nature of physical education are not shared by those who either deliver or are on the receiving end of physical education (Green 2008: 7). 'Choice' and 'voice' are frequently rejected in favour of a teacher-led curriculum typically focused on competitive skill-based games rather than a 'made to measure' programme suited to a broader population of pupils. Physical education teachers have never kept sport at an arms length, insisting instead on keeping the 'sacred cows' of traditional team sports despite the views of a different generation of young people. In a 12-month study of 3000 pupils, the Youth Sports Trust (2014) found that in cases where girls were allowed to design the content of their physical education classes participation rates in physical education lessons doubled.[3] Teachers of physical education who are prepared to accept a pupil-centred and pupil-led curriculum that provides for alternatives are more likely to open up new possibilities to shape the physical education curriculum into one that will meet the needs of a greater number of pupils (Theodoulides 2012: 47). The problem is that politicians base their judgements on the measurable, the observable and the quantifiable, such as trophies, medals and results, whereas physical education teachers base their judgements on the social, physical, emotional and educational development of their pupils through the process of teaching and learning. Physical education teachers will need to decide for themselves what takes priority and accept that they cannot do both jobs well. Despite the political rhetoric related to inclusion and providing breadth of experience to pupils in schools, it has become increasingly evident during the course of writing this book that history is repeating itself. A return to more competitive school sport for pupils has gathered momentum as a major area of policy development (Ofsted 2014) and some might say that we have begun to witness the re-militarisation of physical education through the Ministry of Defence and Department for Education-sponsored 'Troops to Teachers' programme. Prime Minister David Cameron's public pledge[4] to make competitive sport a greater part of physical education and Education Secretary Michael Gove's intention of bringing ex-soldiers into schools was perhaps testament their own school education. After all, the Duke of Wellington was reputed to have said that the battle of Waterloo was won on the playing fields of Eton. In spite of an admission that there had been a 'missed opportunity to create an Olympic legacy in schools' two years after the London Games, the subtext of Mr Gove's plans was that our classrooms were so out of control and our children were so overweight that there needed to be a crackdown on unruly behaviour in schools and more emphasis on physical training. Drastic military action was called for. According to Mr Gove, we needed more of a 'boot camp' mentality in our namby-pamby schools.[5]

On 18 November 2013, the House of Lords Select Committee on Olympic and Paralympic legacy put this statement into the public domain:

> The UK faces an epidemic of obesity and the promise of inspiring a new sporting generation was a crucial and tantalizing part of the legacy aspiration. A post-Games step change in participation across the UK and across different sports did not materialise.
> *(House of Lords Select Committee on Olympic and Paralympic Legacy 2013: 5)*

The warning signs were there to see. The National Obesity Forum recommended that while physical education in schools was part of the solution to tackle teenage obesity, due care should be taken when promoting competitive sport, as it may deter those who are not keen on it and could result in children either returning to or increasing their sedentary lives.[6] If forcing children to play more competitive sport at school had been a legal issue then the politicians and their accomplices could have been held to account for vicarious liability – being responsible for the actions of another when engaged in some form of joint or collective activity. Is it any wonder then, that stories began to emerge of children's' football coaches taking this to the extreme and the general public's reaction? On 3 December 2013, Bains and Massey reported a news item about an under-tens male football coach who had been fired by his club for being over competitive. It was hardly surprising, given the media coverage of the government's vision for more competitive sport in schools and the coach's admission that he was only running the team for the benefit of his own son. What was even more outrageous were his views of winning at all costs. In an email sent to parents he stated that:

> I am only interested in winning. I don't care about equal play time or any other communist views of sport. You are not doing your sons any favours by suggesting that the world is fair or non-competitive. Everything in life is a competition so in my view get them used to it.[7]

This just goes to show that competitive sport has its ugly side where players bend and break the rules and has the propensity to lead to acts of aggression (Theodoulides 2013), such as the recollections of BBC children's television presenter Helen Skelton while at secondary school in the 1990s:

> I loved physical education and was in every team – hockey, netball, cross-country running – even though I wasn't any good at those sports. Hockey was my favourite, but I used to take it a bit too seriously. I once got thrown off the pitch for hurling a hockey stick at someone on my team. I got annoyed because I didn't think she was trying hard enough.[8]

Even worse than this, on 26 March 2014, the BBC reported that police were investigating an incident where an 11-year-old boy suffered a deep wound to his face and received nine stitches when he was stamped on by another pupil in a football match which took place during a privately run after-school club.[9] I hope that the many sports coaches about to give school assemblies and physical education lessons to 420,000 children in over 5000 primary schools across England know exactly what they are going to say. These coaches may be interested to know that a poll by the Chance to Shine cricket charity and Marylebone Cricket Club (MCC)[10] in 2013 found that nine of ten children were struggling in a 'pressure cooker' when playing sport which was resulting in many youngsters cheating or bending the rules to win. The survey revealed that 87 per cent of children had felt under pressure to win, with 64 per cent suggesting this has led to a teammate fouling, diving or time wasting. Almost 50 per cent said they feel this pressure from other children, including teammates, while 11 per cent said they felt it from teachers, 10 per cent from coaches and 6 per cent from their parents. One in five said they put pressure on themselves. But the poll also found that many youngsters would not feel happy if their opposition cheated and got away with it, with more than 50 per cent saying it would make them angry, and 50 per cent saying it would leave them frustrated. The survey also revealed the types of unsportsmanlike behaviour that children were resorting to. Almost 33 per cent admitted that they had regularly witnessed time-wasting in games, while around 40 per cent said they had seen professional fouls and 25 per cent had seen others diving on the pitch. On 22 April 2014, a further Chance to Shine survey[11] revealed that the physical educationalists were locking horns with the sports professionals to the point where parents were more concerned about their children winning than their children themselves giving the message to their children that 'winners never quit, and quitters never win'. In contrast, over 60 per cent of pupils aged 8–16 said that they would be relieved, not bothered or happier if winning or losing was not a factor in physical education and school sport.[12]

Earlier in this final chapter, I referred to emerging news stories related to overzealous fathers who were subjecting children to the so-called benefits of 'healthy competition' in sport. During the course of writing this book, there has not been a shortage of these types of news items. In fact, it has become increasingly evident that a 'war of words' has broken out between the pro-competition lobby and the anti-competition campaign. Proponents have included teachers, parents and coaches who have all expressed different views with respect to the psychological harm that intensive competition can cause children. On 28 January 2014, Colin Dunne ranted about the demise of competition in one of the last remaining bastions of British male sport – rugby union.

> The old boys with the crumpled ears, the knackered knees and the Mike Tindall noses will be weeping into their pints. Their game, rugby, which is possibly the last area of life where you can find real men, has finally been seized by the politically correct. Surrey rugby are insisting that their 'mini rugby' teams, for children aged 6–11, must be of mixed-ability – No 'A' and 'B' squads here – and that any team that is winning too easily must be deliberately weakened by having better players moved elsewhere. There must be no overall winners in the junior league. No winners? That's right. And hence no losers either. Every game must be declared a draw. Difficult to strap your boots on with any enthusiasm for a game that has an unsatisfactory result before you even start.[13]

The politically correct party poopers, as some might describe them, would have been up in arms by the sarcastic nature of these comments notwithstanding the suggestion that competitive sports such as rugby was the last area of activity where little boys could behave like little boys used to, free from counsellors on the touchline asking them how they *feel* about being tackled. As I have stated previously, in the right hands carefully managed competition can be a very valuable educational tool but in the wrong hands it can cause irretrievable damage. Make of it what you will, and as counterintuitive as it may seem, Anna Cain claims that boxing, for example, can teach aggressive and disruptive children about the rules of life and learning from failure.[14] It can be a metaphor for teaching children that losing is part of life – you get hit, you fall down, you get back up again. The boxing academy for children aged 13–16, she refers to, teaches children about control and discipline. Part of the ethos is to reward children but also to punish them by getting them to do push-ups, write essays or confiscating precious belongings until their behaviour improves. By their own admission, the boxing academy does robust and at times confrontational work with these disruptive children.

In this respect, while there have been some notable changes in both philosophy and practice of physical education, the politicians intended to provide more opportunities for pupils to engage in competitive school sports[15] and to dismiss activities such as Indian hand dance and circus skills, revealing the level of ignorance with respect to what physical education represented in schools leading some physical educationalists to comment that:

> What many school sports events actually do is reinforce a sense of failure and frustration among those who are the first to drop out once they leave school. Who wins? Those who are already engaged in sport beyond the school gates and do not actually need school competition at all!
>
> Marchant (2013: 43)

In effect, the damage had been done. The alignment and integration of physical education and school sport has recreated the perception that they are the same thing and that physical education teachers are sports coaches in disguise. The normalisation of coaching and the widespread acceptance that physical education and sport are, to all intents and purposes, identical twins has also reaffirmed the public and media perception that physical education teachers just coach sport. It has also become evident that the teaching of physical education and school sport have become increasingly politicised and influenced by hidden agendas driven by ideological policies and visions of how children, the curriculum or schools ought to be. This begs the question, therefore, of whose interests are really at stake? Politicians? Pupils? Parents? Policy makers? Practitioners? Pedagogues?

As a former teacher of physical education, I have realised that I spread myself too thin and ended up juggling too many balls at the same time. As a result, I became a jack of all trades and a master of none. As new recruits enter the physical education teaching profession, new ideas and innovations will emerge. At the same time, these new ideas will not materialise without enthusiasm and commitment to learning as the centrepiece to teaching physical education in schools. I do not underestimate the importance of being a physical education teacher in the twenty-first century and neither should anyone else who has the privilege of being in this position. There cannot be any half measures. Pupils cannot be short-changed. Their physical education is a fundamental entitlement. For the twenty-first century physical education teacher, it is a critical time to bring the physical education curriculum into line with the changing activity preferences of pupils while at the same time provide opportunities for young people to be active and healthy. I realise that for this to happen, teacher trainers and educators will be involved in wiping the hard drives and reprogramming preservice physical education teachers who have been said to be fundamentally unresponsive during their training to any attempts to encourage them to reflect critically upon various aspects of physical education outside of competitive team sport (Green 2008: 211).

Has it simply been a case then, that initial teacher educators have been flogging a dead horse for too many years in an attempt to abandon the 'sacred cows'? In terms of taking part in physical activity and sport, one of the dangers of a school-led system of initial teacher education is that trainee teachers of physical education may remain unaware of their actions and attitudes towards sport. Secondary school physical education teachers must be sensitive to the fact that the adolescent years are particularly challenging times for many pupils, as physical and emotional changes occur which cause greater self-consciousness and higher dropout rates from physical education lessons. Equally, it is at this stage of compulsory schooling that physical education becomes a specialist subject in its own right taught by highly trained subject specialists who are extremely influential on the activity patterns of pupils, both within and outside formal secondary school settings, at a time when lifestyle choices, activity preferences and exercise habits among young people continue to change. The emotional ballast that competitive sport is supposed to entrench in young people may have actually had the complete opposite effect in a significant number of the teenage population.

The rhetoric of public policy and the reality of localised practice in schools mean that the twenty-first century physical education teacher will be a central player in the delivery of actual physical education experiences. Offering voices both to those who excel in a physical activity and those who have become disaffected, disinterested and disillusioned with school physical education is critical. Physical education in twenty-first century secondary schools requires physical education teachers who are willing to question the practices of the past and to develop relevant and appealing experiences for all young people. As I stated in the opening paragraph of this book, children are the adults of tomorrow. They will remember their schooldays in the same ways as the individuals cited at the beginning of each chapter of this book. They will have school reunions and talk about their most vivid recollections. Any physical education teacher with a conscience will want their former pupils to remember them later in life in a positive way rather than with contempt. In this respect, I am reminded by Andy Miller, a self-confessed hater of sport and his own recollections of his physical education teacher:

> On the sports field he was a track-suited tormentor with a whistle. It was this lack of enthusiasm, this covert bullying, that gradually wore me down. I was hopeless at sport, and because sport is played mostly in terms of winners and losers, members and non-members, I stayed hopeless. Wasn't it the job of the teacher to teach me how to be better at it? Or to find a way of sustaining my flagging enthusiasm, rather than leaving me to be figuratively and literally beaten down into the ground? Apparently not.
>
> *(Miller 2002: 15)*

The process of becoming a physical education teacher in the twenty-first century is now more varied and many who aspire to enter the profession are faced with a number of different pathways into the teaching profession. But the journey does not end once the teacher becomes qualified, irrespective of the chosen path and direction taken. Teachers of physical education should take the time to invest in their own lifelong learning and reflect about practice particularly in the context of a politically driven system that involves trainees, teachers, curriculum leaders and senior managers. Certainly, the demands of a school-led system of initial teacher training could remove the very backbone that university-led teacher training used to provide to trainee teachers and the continued professional development afforded to teachers throughout their careers. In effect, the writing has already been on the wall following the introduction of *The Importance of Teaching* by the Department for Education in 2010 and the normalisation of school-led initiatives and employment-based routes into teaching, leading many academics to predict the likely outcomes and consequences of trends and developments in physical education. It is clear that policy makers believe that teacher training should be more hands-on but there is a danger of neglecting theory at the expense of practice. Misty Adoniou suggests that the 'silver bullet solution' is for university and school partnerships to provide opportunities for theory to be played out, and played with, in the real world of the classroom but to be careful not to implement school-based apprenticeship models that sidestep theory altogether, as education needs transformation not replication.[16] So, does physical education initial teacher education have a future in universities or has its fate already been decided? Is the move towards school-led training to be welcomed? Is school-led teacher training a much needed facelift whereby physical education is being pulled, stretched, nipped and tucked into school-led settings? Will the days of university-led initial teacher training be something that in years to come is looked at in the same way we now view smoking in public, with more and more emphasis being placed on school-led initiatives? Whether qualifying to teach physical education in schools is through employment-based routes, school-led training, postgraduate certification or undergraduate study is difficult to say which is the most effective mode of training. It may simply be a matter of 'horses for courses'. Each individual will decide what is best for them.

Looking back at my career, it has become increasingly clear to me that the role of the physical education teacher has undergone somewhat of a step change on a par with having cosmetic surgery. The demands and expectations of the contemporary teacher of physical education are significantly different since I became a member of the profession. After 30 years in the teaching profession, I have reached the conclusion that, with the overwhelming, intense and relentless pace of change in education, if I were to return to teach physical education in secondary schools, I would not be doing the job I was trained to do, such has been the dramatic redefining of my specialist subject. But, while there have been some notable advancements in the teaching of physical education as a result of improvements in the training of teachers, there remain a number of practices that have been stubbornly resistant to any attempts to change what happens in the gymnasium or on the playing field. My opening gambit in the first few pages of this book was to claim that pupils in secondary schools are still experiencing the types of physical education that I received when I attended secondary school in the 1970s, despite the best attempts of physical education teachers to overhaul the way it is presented to pupils. In seeking an explanation for this, it is particularly useful to return to Green's (2008) analogy of physical education representing the 'meat' in the sandwich (the what) that sits between the nature and purpose of physical education (the why) and the actual delivery of the physical education curriculum (the how). In doing so, we see that gender-stereotyped competitive team sports still make up the vast majority of curriculum experiences. These are typically arranged in single-sex groups, taught by same-sex teachers, who are usually situated in separate male and female departments. Sex-segregated physical education is often justified as being educationally beneficial to pupils on the grounds that they are more receptive to these types of experiences. On the surface, it would seem that without these ingredients we might not necessarily have a physical education curriculum at all. But, with the advent of a revised national curriculum for physical education in September 2014, there are golden opportunities for schools and teachers to reinvent and redesign what has, to all intents and purposes, been a standardised fast food menu available to all pupils across the UK from Brighton to Birmingham, from Bristol to Burnley. Frapwell (2014: 19) urges schools to be creative and to develop their own menus that are not standardised to the American fast food extent but free from data-driven practices. Earlier in this book, I highlighted the fact that some physical education teachers have often justified certain types of practices in schools on the basis that they have worked for decades and there is no point in changing anything. The American statesman and former United States Secretary of State Colin Powell has often been cited when it comes to change. His words may be representative of the conservatism that still exists among some physical education teachers: 'If it ain't broke, don't fix it is the slogan of the complacent, the arrogant or the scared. It's an excuse for inaction, a call to non-arms'.

For the vast majority of readers of this book, I realise that they are heirs to the struggles that have taken place in the physical education profession to gain status and recognition. Armour and Jones (1998: 134) claimed that the issue of status is an intractable problem for physical education and a key characteristic of the lives and careers of physical education teachers. Readers will have seen that I have personally been involved in these struggles as an undergraduate student, teacher and lecturer but, in 2014, these problems persist. It has been difficult to win the hearts and minds of parents, pupils and colleagues and at times, it has felt as if I have been treading in treacle. But the advancements that have happened during my career, such as the unprecedented increase in the numbers of pupils studying examination courses in physical education, should not be underestimated. Physical education in schools now enjoys significantly more kudos as it did previously. Physical education is a core foundation subject in schools, examination courses in physical education are very popular, post-16 courses in physical education continue to rise and the study of sport and physical education related courses after the age of 18 attracts significant numbers of applicants to universities. Physical education teachers are degree-qualified, some undertake postgraduate studies in the field, physical education teachers are remunerated at the same rate as other subject teachers, and there is an established research culture and field in physical education.

But physical education teachers have been constantly swimming against the tide in trying to convince others that physical education is not sport and is as educationally worthy of other high-status academic subjects. Thirty years on, I can now reflect that I entered the physical education teaching profession with a firm educational base but this soon faded as I encountered what Armour and Jones (1998: 127) refer to as 'the status wall'. I have constantly felt the need to justify both my subject and myself as a teacher of my subject in more educational and academic terms. Indeed, my career progression has depended on it. While the 'status wall' of physical education many have been dismantled, significant parts of it remain and, as forward thinking as the changes have been, does this mean that those entering the profession in the twenty-first century should accept the way things are because they are better than before? Should they see their role as custodians of the status quo or change makers of the future? At this stage it seems fitting to hear from trainee teachers themselves who are about to the enter the world of physical teaching in September 2014.

Vignette 16

My aspiration to become a PE teacher has been present from a very young age and was inspired further by those who taught me at secondary school. They helped to continuously develop my sporting abilities and leadership skills through their own fantastic practices, leadership styles and unswerving positive attitudes. The more I developed my skills, the more I wanted to learn and have the opportunity to inspire pupils to take part in physical activity through my teaching, just as my teachers inspired me. Aspiring teachers should always seek out new opportunities that push themselves out of their comfort zone, but be prepared, mistakes will be made along the way. I was nervous about these mistakes when I started my first placement, however, one of the first lessons you will learn is that these mistakes all help to develop you as a practitioner. Even the most meticulously planned lessons may not go according to plan and some days will seem like this happens numerous times, but this is where you get the opportunity to reflect and decide where you can improve to make it work next time around. These teaching experiences pass by in a flash and the more you put into it, the more you will get out of it. Every new experience counts for something, however, one of the strongest pieces of advice I can give is to engage with a variety of staff and teaching styles through observing lessons; this is something that will certainly assist in gaining new ideas and seeing how experienced teachers adapt to the same situations you are likely to come across. Of course, organisation is key, and ensuring I keep up to date with lesson plans and evaluations while getting in the right amount of time to relax is difficult. This is down to each individual, so whereas I like to work hard during the week so I can relax at the weekend, it is understandable for others to need some time off each evening. This aspect is down to the individual, and it is important to listen to yourself and find out the best working method for you. For anyone considering being a PE teacher, I would strongly encourage you to gain as much experience as possible, both in and outside of university, but first and foremost, it is important to enjoy yourself. Creating a positive atmosphere through you enjoying the subject and activities you're teaching will inspire all pupils to get involved, as well as hopefully inspiring the next generation of PE teachers.

Vignette 17

My aspiration to become a teacher of physical education manifested as a result of the positive experiences I had while I was at school. I was inspired by my own physical education teachers who taught in a creative, fun and enthusiastic way. These past experiences helped shape me into the teacher that I wanted to be: a positive role model enthusing children to aspire and achieve to be the best that they could be. While harnessing this passion I embraced every opportunity throughout my ITT to experience teaching in different contexts and activity areas. While sometimes I felt completely out of my comfort zone, 'going the extra mile' and constantly engaging with teaching led me to develop confidence, and I soon began to understand my own strengths in pedagogy. I was told during my training to 'do something every day that scared me'. Engaging with personal challenge helps to develop resilience and self-assurance in what you are ultimately setting out to do: teach. My advice to anyone wanting to become a physical education teacher would be: have a sense of humour, being funny and being able to laugh at yourself when it all seems to be going wrong is ok, children like to see you are human! Insofar the positive memories you help children to make in physical education may help determine their attitudes and beliefs towards physical activity as they enter into adulthood. It is our job as physical educators to promote the love of our subject ensuring children know how to lead a healthy and active lifestyle.

Vignette 18

My own experiences of PE were not the best. Teachers would usually send us for a run to the fence and back for a warm up, which was then normally followed by waiting our turn and getting bored in various athletics events in the summer or just being given a ball of varying shape to play our own games in the winter. I was always a sporty kid but for all I enjoyed being active and playing sport, my school PE lessons did not engage or challenge me. Ultimately this made me decide to become a PE teacher, because I wanted pupils like me and more importantly not like me to have better PE lessons in school. While the last four years of my teacher training have been the best four years of my life, it has been a rollercoaster of an experience with various highs and lows. The highs, for me, have planted themselves more vividly in my memory than the lows. However, I can't emphasis enough that if you want to be an outstanding physical education teacher, one that inspires young people to be active, engaged, making progress and having fun within your lessons. In addition to enthusing them enough to continue being active into and throughout their adulthood, then you must be committed to making the difference. In doing so, you will be exposed to a plethora of experiences that will challenge but reward you everyday. Furthermore you will have an enjoyable and highly successful career in teaching.

Vignette 19

My top tips for making the commitment and working your way to becoming a PE teacher would be: be an opportunist. Throughout your training you will be given some of the greatest opportunities both voluntary and paid to work with young people in various settings that will support you continuing professional development. Be proactive, get involved and challenge yourself in new areas to gain new experiences and develop. Reflect – take time to think about an experience and ask yourself questions; how did that go? How could I have made it better? Then use these reflections to make improvements next time. Also listen and reflect on feedback from tutors, peers and teachers. Use peoples experience to make your practice better. Have a sense of humour – don't take yourself too seriously. Pupils like teachers who can laugh at themselves and also laugh with them. Humour can also dilute low level behaviour issues, turning a negative environment into a positive one. Be organised – researching; essay writing; presentations; practicals; lesson planning; lessons evaluations; writing up evidence for teaching standards; teaching lessons; observing lessons; after-school clubs; fixtures; continuing professional development. You name it, you'll be doing it all! Start as you mean to go on and be prepared, not only to make it easier for yourself but also be at your best for your pupils. 'Failure to prepare is preparation to fail', my lecturer told us that in my first year and it's been ringing in my ears ever since, why? Because it's true! Be a role model – pupils look up to you, so it's a great opportunity to guide them in the right direction to achieve their best. Leading by example sets a standard for your pupils to follow. If you turn up late, looking scruffy and disorganised, they will think it is okay to do the same! Stay balanced – teacher training is tough but the best teachers I've seen have a good work–social life balance. Work hard but be kind to yourself and take time out to recoup. Most importantly, be the teacher you want to be. We all have our strengths and we all have our areas for improvement, however, no two teachers are the same. We all have our own style and pupils will like you for being the greatest version of you.

On this note, it is worth remembering that the individuals that you have just heard from are the physical education teachers who will shape the future of the subject in the twenty-first century. They are the next curriculum leaders, mentors and senior managers in our schools. They will have the authority and influence to make change happen. They will have the skills and subject knowledge to perform the routine checks and fine tune the subject so that it is literally firing on all cylinders. For progress to be made, the answer might be to change the ingredients and recipe to reflect the taste, trends and fashions of the day that has greater appeal to a wider population of pupils. Perhaps a pitta or a tortilla instead of two slices of bread? But change just for change's sake is not necessarily the way forward. If we accept Green's (2008) assertion that each new generation of physical education teachers inherits a physical education world that is processual and, as such, reflects the existence of widespread continuities alongside degrees of change then the future of physical education seems a little brighter. Change happens because there is a will to change among those who have vision and passion for their subject. As the old saying goes, nothing changes if you change nothing. In 2002, who would have imagined that ten years later there would be a female curriculum leader for physical education in a large specialist sports college for boys (Rees 2012)? Who would have believed that we would see the first female commentator on a men's professional football match on the BBC's flagship sports show *Match of the Day* and that female sports presenters would be commonplace on the television screens of the UK? It may have seemed inconceivable that we would see a 26-year-old female physical education teacher (Sian Massey) officiate in English Premier League football matches and that a female football coach (Helena Costa) would be appointed as the head coach of men's professional team in the French second division.[17] Likewise, the prospect of having a female member of the English Football Association's independent board may have seemed just a pipe dream. All of this has happened in just ten years. What might happen in the next ten years? The women's FA cup final to be played at Wembley on a Saturday and broadcast live on all major television channels? Wonders may never cease!

Capel and Whitehead (2103: 238) suggest that physical education teachers need to work individually and collectively to achieve change and must be alert and responsive to changes in learners' needs and cultural attitudes. New entrants to the physical education teaching profession need to be empowered with the confidence and commitment to affect change in respect to the aims, content, curriculum organisation and teaching method. In other words, the future of the teaching profession is in their hands. Physical education teachers cannot do anything about the past but they can learn lessons from reflecting on previous practice and shape the future of their subject in accordance with contemporary issues in education and society as a whole. The current generation of physical education teachers has a professional and moral obligation to pave the way for their future successors. The next generation of physical education teachers has to be better than the last but they need to be cautious about playing the coaching game. New entrants to the physical education teaching profession must understand that physical education and sport are two separate aspects of school life and should be treated as such. The separation of curriculum physical education and competitive school sport would certainly be a move in the right direction, allowing pupils with superior athletic ability to develop and fully apply their talent through organised competition with pupils of similar ability from other schools orientated towards highly organised inter-school competition and should be viewed as totally separate from the formal physical education curriculum. The responsibility for this should be with specialist salaried coaches, who are employed to take on this responsibility throughout the year or season under the management of a director of sport. Physical education teachers might be occasionally employed on a separate contract to undertake these responsibilities just as I had experienced in North America, where I received two separate salaries, but they should also be aware that this may be a conflict of interest.

A great deal has happened since I began writing this book and has provided much of the content of this text. Shifts in government policy have been part of a long-term strategy for education in England since the election of a UK Coalition Government in 2010. Teachers, researchers and academics have had to keep pace with the relentless speed of change in initial teacher training, physical education and school sport. At the point of submitting the manuscript to this book, perhaps the most significant change of all occurred. On 15 July 2014, the man responsible for the sweeping changes to education was removed from his office as Secretary of State for Education. One of the many tributes paid to Michael Gove was that he weakened the grip of left-wing academics on the teacher training process, making it possible for outstanding schools to train teachers themselves.[18] Whether the 'left-wing academics' will ever regain their grip on the teacher training process is uncertain as a new Secretary of State for Education (Nicky Morgan) takes offices. What exactly this means for the twenty-first century physical education teacher is also difficult to predict. Will competitive school sport play a major role in the future careers of physical education teachers? Will a focus on health, academic achievement and participation in physical activity be more prominent in the job descriptions of the twenty-first century physical education teacher? Can we expect to see the twenty-first century physical education teacher coaching less sport and teaching more physical education? Will the twenty-first century physical education teacher be teaching more of the same to the more able or will there be radical reform, as suggested by Kirk (2010), whereby a paradigm shift in the thinking of new entrants to the profession becomes increasingly more evident? Most worrying is Kirk's suggestion that physical education may cease exist in the twenty-first century and become extinct within our secondary schools unless there is radical reform. Slezak *et al.* (2013) suggest that it is time to stand up and speak out about the value of physical education because if no else does, eventually physical education will disappear from the curriculum.

In concluding this book, I am reminded of the old Chinese proverb – yesterday is history, tomorrow is a mystery, today is a gift; that is why we call it the present! Can physical education teachers learn from the past? Can they enjoy the present? Can they anticipate the future? I believe they can. But those who do not learn from history are destined to repeat it. It is worth remembering that people have long memories when it comes to their schooldays and teachers are often the culprits. Moving with the times is important if the type of recollection below is to be avoided.

> My school PE days were back in the 1960s and I do recognise lots of what people are saying about PE teaching. I still remember being taught to swim by my primary school class teacher (who was no way a professional PE teacher!). He used to teach us with his pipe permanently stuck in his mouth – sometimes alight! I did learn to swim though.

Pupils will not benefit from a replica of physical education endured by their own mothers and fathers, potentially taught by the same physical education teachers in exactly the same schools. If I compare the physical education I received as a pupil with the physical education I taught as a teacher, it makes me aware of the seismic shifts that have occurred in the profession. If I compare the physical education I taught as a teacher with the physical education I have taught as a lecturer, even greater change has happened. If I compare the physical education I have taught as lecturer with what physical education might look like in the future then the scale of change is likely to exceed the rate of previous developments. But what might that look like? Can the twenty-first century physical education teacher expect to teach a more diverse, health-related physical education curriculum, which includes swimming, in fit-for-purpose facilities? Can all pupils expect to receive one hour of physical education a day in schools? Will competitive school sport be available to pupils who want it provided by those who have the time and expertise to deliver it?

There are 11-year-old pupils in secondary schools today who will be teaching physical education in 2030 or who may be writing books such as this in the future. What are they currently experiencing? Who are the people teaching them? What will they have to say 15 years from now? The important message for those becoming a physical education teacher is to be a first-class representation of yourself not a second-class imitation of someone else. To have an inner belief that she may never lift the cup at Wembley but she will never forget who gave her the dream. To have a commitment to change and confidence in the phrase that only dead fish swim with the tide. To get the message across to children that they cannot use the phrase 'I can't do that' without ending the sentence with the word 'yet'. Pupils need to believe that their fear of failure should not be greater than their desire to succeed and that anything is possible when you believe in you. For all of those involved, self-belief, confidence and courage to challenge the status quo is what counts. As a secondary school physical education teacher, look at the 11-year-old and picture the 18-year-old – what difference will you make?

As I bring this chapter and this book to an end, I ask myself one final reflective question. Are we any closer than when we started in understanding what it takes to become a physical education teacher? I hope so. Only time will tell whether this modest text has gone some way in helping the next generation of physical education teachers prepare for their future roles in secondary schools as educators of health, facilitators of leisure, providers of recreation, coaches of sport and teachers of academic physical education. What is certain is that any attempts to modernise the way in which physical education is presented to pupils in secondary schools will rely on the 'agents of change' – those who understand the purpose of their subject and are intent on becoming a physical education teacher!

Notes

1   Tom Cullen, 'Mr Garrett and Mr Jordan by Duncan Goodhew', *Times Educational Supplement*, 14 February 2014: 31. Available online at www.tes.co.uk/article.aspx?storycode=6403354 (accessed 27 September 2014).

2   'Bispham High School pupil excluded in homework protest', *BBC News*, 18 March 2014. Available online at www.bbc.co.uk/news/uk-england-lancashire-26626824 (accessed 27 September 2014).

3   'Girls Active', Youth Sport Trust; see www.youthsporttrust.org/how-we-can-help/girls-active.aspx (accessed 27 September 2014).

4   'Boris Johnson urges two hours of PE a day', *BBC News*, 9 August 2012.

5   Francis Gilbert and Adnan Sarwar, 'Should more ex-soldiers become teachers?' *Guardian*, 24 November 2010. Available online at www.theguardian.com/comment-isfree/2010/nov/24/soldiers-teachers-michael-gove (accessed 3 October 2014).

6   National Obesity Forum, *State of the Nation's Waistline – Obesity in the UK: Analysis and Expectations*. Available online at www.nationalobesityforum.org.uk/index.php/136-news_/688-state-of-the-nation-s-waistline-obesity-in-the-uk-analysis-and-expectations.html (accessed 27 September 2014).

7   Inderdeep Bains and Ray Massey, 'Tyrant of the under 10s: Football coach fired after he tells boys they're not playing for fun', Daily Mail, 3 December 2013. Available online at www.dailymail.co.uk/news/article-2517768/Tyrant-10s-Football-coach-fired-tells-boys-theyre-playing-fun.html (accessed 27 September 2014).

8   Adeline Iziren, 'Mr Connell by Helen Skelton', *Times Educational Supplement*, 24 January 2014: 37.

9   'Kent boy "has head stamped on during football"', *BBC News Kent*, 26 March 2014. Available online at www.bbc.co.uk/news/uk-england-sussex-26759122 (accessed 27 September 2014).

10 Marylebone Cricket Club and Chance to Shine, '"Pressure cooker" of school sports turning children into a win-at-all costs generation', 15 April 2013. Available online at www.chancetoshine.org/news/pressure-cooker-of-school-sports-turning-children-into-a-win-at-all-costs-generation (accessed 27 September 2014).

11 Marylebone Cricket Club and Chance to Shine, 'It's only a game? Competition in school sport under threat', 22 April 2014. Available online at www.chancetoshine.org/news/it-s-only-a-game-competition-in-school-sport-under-threat (accessed 27 September 2014).

12 'Competitive sport puts off schoolchildren – survey', BBC News, 22 April 2014. Available online at www.bbc.co.uk/news/uk-27113085 (accessed 27 September 2014).

13 Colin Dunne (2014) 'How will youngsters learn about life if we don't let them win (and lose) at games?', 27 January 2014. Available online at www.dailymail.co.uk/debate/article-2547076/How-youngsters-learn-life-dont-let-win-lose-games.html (accessed 27 September 2014).

14 Anna Cain (2014) 'Behaviour – Boxing Clever for a fighting Chance', *Times Education Supplement*, 13 February 2014. Available online at www.tes.co.uk/article.aspx?storycode=6403356 (accessed 27 September 2014).

15 Patrick Wintour, 'David Cameron defends move to scrap compulsory targets for school sport', *Guardian*, 8 August 2012. Available online at www.theguardian.com/education/2012/aug/08/cameron-scraps-targets-school-sport (accessed 27 September 2014).

16 Misty Adoniou (2014) 'Leaving because they care too much to stay', *TES Scotland*, 13 February 2014. Available online at www.tes.co.uk/article.aspx?storycode=6403351 (accessed 26 September 2014).

17 John Hooper, 'Costa becomes European football's first female professional team manager', *Guardian*, 7 May 2014. Available online at www.theguardian.com/world/2014/may/07/helena-costa-clermont-foot-football-first-female-manager (accessed 27 September 2014).

18 Toby Young, 'Cabinet Reshuffle: Has Michael Gove been eaten by the blob?, *Telegraph*, 15 July 2014. Available online at http://blogs.telegraph.co.uk/news/tobyyoung/100280038/cabinet-reshuffle-has-michael-gove-been-eaten-by-the-blob (accessed 27 September 2014).

APPENDIX 1:
SURVIVING YOUR PGCE YEAR

Term 1 (hold on tight)

By far, term one is the most difficult and longest terms of the year – if you survive this one you are almost half way through. Be prepared for going to school in the dark and leaving school in the dark. The weather will be a pain, particularly if you do not have much indoor space. Just try to have a plan B available if your lesson gets taken indoors and try to get a good idea about what the department does in bad weather. On that note, make sure you have spare kit at school to change into if you get soaked: my first placement was outside, no matter what!

There will be no time for all the good things that you used to do as an undergraduate; socials, shopping, even exercising and eating will become a luxury. That is how difficult this term will be and my advice is don't panic you are NOT ALONE. Every teacher has gone through this (although admittedly sometimes they need reminding of this). Make sure that you look after yourselves and look out for each other.

When you come back for the Thursdays and Fridays at university, you can tell a lot about how everyone is doing. If it wasn't for the support that the other students gave me to stand up to some of things my school were asking me to do I would not have made it past December. This term, you will be faced with plenty of obstacles so, if you have any difficulties, as you will most likely have, please talk to someone who you feel comfortable talking to – your mentor, your lecturers or a fellow trainee about it. Chances are you are not the only one, don't just ignore it.

Christmas break (time to relax)

You made it – congratulations, if you have got this far, the hardest part is over! This is your time to recover, so make the most of it. You must take the time to re-energise otherwise you will burn out. You will most likely have work to do over the break but set aside a certain amount of time. I went home and didn't look at any work until four days until the end and then got anything I needed to done.

Term 2 (keep it up)

January was a turning point for a lot of us. Things were becoming far more natural and planning time decreasing. You are in the closing stages of your first placement; you will have your routines, clear boundaries with your class and starting to develop working student–teacher relationships. Then, before you know it, you will be saying goodbye to your classes and even wish that you were staying! In some schools, the pupils are used to trainees coming and going but, for others, it can be quite hard and they will ply you with cards and gifts, if you are lucky ☺.

You will have some time at university during this term, between placements. It might seem keen but this is the time to start applying for jobs. This was the best decision I made in the whole year, because I managed to do all my applying and go my interview during this time. It meant that I didn't have to go through the stress whilst balancing placement! Also, the ones that advertise early normally mean that they want you to start before summer which means you get paid over that time – AMAZING! In this term, you will also start your second placement. My main piece of advice is to try your best not to compare the two, particularly not to speak about it to your new department they will have their ways and don't want to hear how your old placement did things that was better than theirs.

Term three (so close)

You are only at your second placement school for half of the summer term, so it is really important at this point to get experience in as many different summer sports as possible. It may be the only experience you get before a year's time in your new school as an NQT!

At this point in the game, you will have a good idea whether you are going to pursue a career in teaching. Even if you are thinking that it is not for you, you are so close to the end, try your best to see it through: you never know, you might change your mind. At the end of my PGCE, even though I had got myself a permanent job to start in July, I still doubted my decision to go into teaching purely because I was so stressed out during my PGCE year that I didn't want to live my life that way. BUT, have faith, back to what I said at the start of this, I was working until 10 p.m. each night and through my weekends. Whereas now I plan my lessons in my school diary for the following week in my frees on Friday and then make sure I have no work to do over the weekend. This may mean staying at school until 6 p.m. each evening but it is worth it. I now do nothing over the weekends and we are in the hardest term of the year! University is a great place to do your training; the staff will go above and beyond for you so don't forget to ask for help: the last thing anyone wants is for you to suffer in silence!

APPENDIX 2:
PAY SCALES OF TEACHERS

Head teachers

Group 1–8 is dependent on the size of school. Small primary schools for children 4–11 years of age would be group 1. Large secondary schools children for 11–18 years of age would be group 8. Head teachers are often awarded a high 'spine' point within the group number as they are the highest 'leader' in the school. The lower spine points within the range is given for other leaders such as deputy and/or assistant head teachers. The decisions about this are made by a board of governors to the school. Governors can include appointed persons from the local government offices and volunteer persons from the local community.

Leadership spine

This is a simple scale which is concerned with all persons in a school who take on a whole-school leadership responsibility; it does not include responsibility for sections or faculties within a school. It includes the pay for all head teachers, deputy head teachers and assistant head teachers. L1–5 would be for deputy head teacher in a very small school.

Advanced-skills teachers

This category is, at this time, becoming quite rare in England and will soon disappear; however, it is a scale for which a very good teacher can apply to be considered for. This teacher has to be able to prove to the head teacher that he or she can teach to a high level of skill and can coach other teachers to become also highly skilled teachers. They have to show consistent and sustained evidence of students achieving high results in their examinations and many other admirable evidence of excellent work.

Lead practitioners

This is becoming more and more common in England. It is very much similar to Advanced skills teachers but is favoured by head teachers and governors because it gives One range. Therefore each school can decide for itself according to their own finances how much salary they will offer for their most skilled teachers. The Lead practitioner teachers must be able to lead groups on improving teaching and learning in a school and they must be able to communicate good practice to all teachers throughout the year.

Excellent teacher

As with advanced-skills teachers, this category is being phased out.

Unqualified teachers

Some schools may wish to employ persons with special knowledge, skills and experience who may help to educate young people but they have not been trained to teach. This category is often used in schools that are independently financed and not part of the state system. However, it can still be used in state schools.

General teaching scales

Most teachers in England are either paid on the classroom teachers' scale and those with extra responsibilities also receive an award for teaching and learning responsibilities.

Classroom teachers

This applies to ALL teachers. There is a nine-point scale. All teachers start their employment on M1. During each year of work, teachers have to gather evidence that they are deserving of a move to the next scale up. To start with, the evidence gathering is not very difficult and all, with the exception of very poor teachers, are expected to receive more money with each year of experience. movement from M1 to M2–3 is quite simple. Each year, teachers are expected to select three objectives that they should achieve during the year. These are related to student outcomes, professional development and management of students or colleagues. A judgement is made by a leadership teacher on whether the person has been successful in this. The moves between M4, 5 and 6 must show increasing levels of accomplishment by the teacher. For example, lessons must be observed as consistently good and pupil progress must always be good. For a teacher to move from M6 to U1, there is a large change. Teachers must show that many aspects of teaching are graded as OUTSTANDING, large numbers of children must be seen to be making better than predicted progress and achieving very high examination grades. Teachers at U3 must be able to contribute to helping other teachers to become better. Teachers on the U scale must be considered as expert teachers. On reaching U3 (the ninth scale), there is no progression possible unless a teacher is able to take on a responsibility.

Teaching and learning responsibilities

Teaching and learning responsibilities are awarded on a sliding scale. Payment 3 is for a short-term duty with usually only a small responsibility. Payment 2 is for a permanent responsibility and is open to the governors and head teacher of the school to decide. Most schools will offer this money for duties such as being deputy head of a curriculum subject or for supporting responsibility for an age-group cohort of students in the school. Payment 1 is also open to the governors and head teacher to decide but it is often awarded for larger responsibilities, such as head of subject such as physical education or head of a year group.

Special-needs allowance is for those teachers who have skills which have regard to children who have a range of learning difficulties that are unique to that child and require special help to access learning.

Vignette (current curriculum leader for physical education)

I have been a teacher for 27 years. I have reached the top of my nine-point scale. I have also taken responsibility for a subject (physical education) in the school but the governors and head teacher do not consider this subject to be large enough to consider awarding me the maximum amount of £12,517. Instead, it is somewhere in between the minimum and maximum. Thus, my salary is the maximum U3 plus enough responsibility pay to take my overall salary to approximately £46,000. I can go no higher unless I take on a whole-school leadership responsibility. I am happy at where I am now and feel that any leadership duty is now likely to be awarded to someone younger than me.

BIBLIOGRAPHY

Almond, L. and Ezzeldin, K. (2013) 'Are Fundamental Movement Skills the Foundation of Physical Education?', *Physical Education Matters*, 8(3): 53–5.

Amateur Swimming Association (2013) *Learning the Lesson: The Future of Swimming. The 2013 School Swimming Census.* Loughborough: ASA. Available online at www.swimming.org/assets/uploads/library/School_Swimming_Census_2013.pdf (accessed 25 September 2014).

Amour, K. and Chen, H. (2012) 'Narrative Research Methods: Where the art of storytelling meets the science of research', in K. Amour and D. Macdonald (eds), *Research Methods in Physical Education and Youth Sport*, Abingdon: Routledge, 237–49.

Armour, K. and Jones, R. (1998) *Physical Education Teachers' Lives and Careers*, London: Falmer.

Armour, K. and Yelling, M. (2004) 'Continuing Professional Development for Experienced Physical Education Teachers: Towards Effective Provision', *Sport, Education and Society*, 9(1): 95–114.

Armour, K., Chambers, F. and Makopoulou, K. (2013) 'Conceptualising Teaching as Learning: The Challenge for Teacher Education' in S. Capel and M. Whitehead (eds), *Debates in Physical Education.* Abingdon: Routledge, 205–19.

Armour, K., Makopoulou, K., Chambers, F. and Duncombe, R. (2010) 'Career-long Professional Learning for the Professional Physical Education Teacher' in R. Bailey (ed.), *Physical Education for Learning: A Guide for Secondary Schools.* London: Continuum International, 37–53.

Association for Physical Education (2013) *Health Position Paper.* Worcester: AfPE. Available online at www.afpe.org.uk/advocacy-a-leadership/afpe-policy-statements/health (accessed 25 September 2014).

Bailey, R. and Kirk, D. (eds) (2010) *The Routledge Physical Education Reader.* Abingdon: Routledge.

Berg, P. and Lahelma, E. (2010) 'Gender Processes in the Field of Physical Education', *Gender and Education*, 22(1): 31–46.

Bloom, B. and Krathwohl, D. (1956). *Taxonomy of Educational Objectives: The Classification of Educational Goals, by a Committee of College and University Examiners. Handbook 1: Cognitive Domain.* New York: Longmans.

Boothroyd, G. (2004) *Are You A Proper Teacher Sir?* Cheltenham: SportBooks.

Brackenridge, C. (2001) *Spoilsports: Understanding and Preventing Sexual Exploitation in Sport*. London: Routledge.

Branson, C. (2014) 'Compulsory PE at all Four Key Stages: What Happens at Key Stage 5?', *Physical Education Matters*, 9(1): 71–3.

British Educational Research Association (2011) *Ethical Guidelines for Educational Research*. London: BERA. Available online www.bera.ac.uk/researchers-resources/publications/ethical-guidelines-for-educational-research-2011 (accessed 26 September 2014).

Brown, D. (2005) 'An Economy of Gendered Practices? Learning to Teach Physical Education from the Perspective of Pierre Bourdieu's Embodied Sociology', *Sport, Education and Society*, 10(1): 3–23.

Brown, D. (1999) 'Complicity and Reproduction in Teaching Physical Education', *Sport, Education and Society*, 4(2): 143–60.

Brown, D. and Evans, J. (2004) 'Reproducing Gender? Intergenerational Links and the Male PE Teacher as a Cultural Conduit in Teaching Physical Education', *Journal of Teaching in Physical Education*, 23: 48–70.

Brown, D. and Rich, E. (2002) 'Gender Positioning as a Pedagogical Practice in Teaching Physical Education' in D. Penney (ed.), *Gender and Physical Education: Contemporary Issues and Future Directions*. London: Routledge, 80–100.

Bunker, D. and Thorpe, R. (1982). 'A Model for the Teaching of Games in the Secondary School', *Bulletin of Physical Education*, 10: 9–16.

Burgess, R. (2013) 'Physical Education or Sport?', *Physical Education Matters*, 8(3): 19–21.

Cale, L. (2010) 'Becoming a Teacher' in R. Bailey (ed.), *Physical Education for Learning: A guide for secondary schools*. London: Continuum International, 3–14.

Cale, L. and Alfrey, L. (2013) 'Physical Education and Health: Moving Forwards or "Going Around in Circles"?', *Physical Education Matters*, 8(3): 70–4.

Capel, S. (2005) 'Teachers, Teaching and Pedagogy in Physical Education', in K. Green and K. Hardman (eds) (2005) *Essential Issues in Physical Education*. London: Sage, 111–27.

Capel, S. (2000) 'Re-reflecting on Priorities for Physical Education: Now and in the twenty-first century', in S. Capel and S. Piotrowski (eds), *Issues in Physical Education*. London: Routledge, 209–20.

Capel, S. and Whitehead, M. (eds) (2013) *Debates in Physical Education*. Abingdon: Routledge.

Capel, S. and Whitehead, M. (eds) (2010) *Learning to Teach Physical Education in the Secondary School* (3rd ed.), Abingdon: Routledge.

Chambers, F. (ed) (2015) *Mentoring in Physical Education and Sports Coaching*. London: Routledge.

Chappell, R. (2014) 'Gaining Success in School Sport: Comparing independent and state school experiences', *Research Matters*, 9(1): 54–8.

Chappell, R. (2013) 'The Way Forward? Independent Schools, State Schools, Physical Education, Sport and Ofsted', *Physical Education Matters*, 8(2): 37–41.

Charles, M., Marsh, A., Milne, A., Morris, C., Scott, E. and Shamsan, Y. (2008) *Secondary School Curriculum and Staffing Survey 2007*. Research Brief DCSF-RB026. London: Department for Children, Schools and Families.

Clarke, G. (2012) 'Challenging Heterosexism, Homophobia and Transphobia in Physical Education' in G. Stidder and S. Hayes (eds), *Equity and Inclusion in Physical Education and Sport* (2nd ed.), Abingdon: Routledge, 87–101.

Clarke, G. and Nutt, G. (1999) 'Physical Education' in D. Hill and M. Cole (eds), *Promoting Equality in Secondary Schools*. London: Cassell, 211–37.

Curtner-Smith, M. (2002) 'Methodological Issues in Research' in A. Laker (ed.) *The Sociology of Sport and Physical Education: An Introductory Reader*. London: Routledge, 36–57.

Curtner-Smith, M. (1999) 'The More Things Change The More They Stay the Same: Factors Influencing Teachers' Interpretations and Delivery of National Curriculum Physical Education', *Sport, Education and Society*, 4: 71–97.

Department for Children, Schools and Families (2009) *Gender and Education – Mythbusters. Addressing Gender and Achievement: Myths and Realities*. London: DCSF.

Department for Children, Schools and Families and Department for Media Culture and Sport (Sport England and Youth Sport Trust) (2009) *The PE and Sport Strategy for Young People – A guide to delivering the five hour offer*. London: DCSF, DCMS, Sport England and YST.

Department for Children, Schools and Families and the Qualifications Curriculum Authority (2007) *The National Curriculum: Statutory requirements for Key Stages 3 and 4*. London: DCSF and QCA.

Department for Education (2013a) *Statutory Guidance for the Induction of Newly Qualified Teachers (England): For appropriate bodies, headteachers, school staff and governing bodies*. DFE-00090-2013. London: DfE.

Department for Education (2013a) *Teachers' Standards: Guidance to school leaders, school staff and governing bodies. July 2011 (introduction updated June 2013)*. DFE-00066-2011. London: DfE.

Department for Education (2013b) *Evidence on Physical Education and Sport in Schools*. DFE-00093-2013. London: DfE.

Department for Education (2013c) *School Workforce in England: November 2012*. London: DfE.

Department for Education (2013d) *The National Curriculum in England: Framework for Key Stages 3 and 4*. London: DfE.

Department for Education (2010a) *The Importance of Teaching*. London: DfE.

Department for Education (2010b) *Physical Education and School Sport Survey 2009–2010*. London DfE.

Department for Education (1995) *Physical Education in the National Curriculum*. London: HMSO.

Department of Education and Science (1989) *Physical Education from 5 to 16*. HMI Series: Curriculum Matters No. 16. London: HMSO.

Department of Education and Science and Qualifications and Curriculum Authority (1999) *Physical Education: The National Curriculum for England*. London: HMSO.

Department of Education and Science and Welsh Office (1991) *National Curriculum Physical Education Working Group Interim Report*. London: HMSO.

Department for Education and Skills (2005) *Learning Behaviour: The Report of the Practitioners' Group on School Behaviour and Discipline*. Chair: Sir Alan Steer. London: DfES.

Department for Education and Skills (2002) *Learning Through Physical Education and Sport*. London: DfES.

Department for Education and Skills and Department for Culture Media and Sport (2002) *Learning through PE and Sport: A guide to the Physical Education, School Sport and Club Links Strategy*. Annesley, Notts: DfES publications.

Department for Education and Skills and Qualifications and Curriculum Authority (2004) *The National Curriculum: Handbook for Secondary Teachers in England*. London: DfES and QCA.

Department of National Heritage (1995) *Sport: Raising the Game*. London: HMSO.

Donovan, M. (1997) 'Role Overload and Role Conflict – Teacher or Coach', *British Journal of Physical Education*, 28: 17–20.

Donovan, M., Jones, G. and Hardman, K. (2006) 'Physical Education and Sport in England: Dualism, partnership and delivery provision', *International Journal of Fundamental and Applied Kinesiology*, 38(1): 16–27.

Dyson, B. and Casey, A. (eds) (2012) *Cooperative Learning in Physical Education: A Research-based Approach*. Abingdon: Routledge.

EACEA/Eurydice (2013) *Physical Education and Sport at School in Europe Eurydice Report.* Luxembourg: Publications Office of the European Union. Available online at http://eacea.ec.europa.eu/education/eurydice/documents/thematic_reports/150EN.pdf (accessed 25 September 2014).

Education Select Committee (2013) *School Sport Following London 2102: No More Political Football: Government Response to the Committee's Third Report of Session 2013–14.* Third Special Report. London: House of Commons. Available online at www.publications.parliament.uk/pa/cm201314/cmselect/cmeduc/723/72302.htm (accessed 25 September 2014).

Estyn (2012) *Physical Education in Secondary Schools.* HM Inspectorate for Education and Training in Wales.

Evans, J. (2014) 'Equity and Inclusion in PE (PLC)', *European Physical Education Review,* 20(3): 319–34.

Evans, J. (ed.) (1993) *Equality, Education and Physical Education.* London: Falmer.

Evans, J. (1990) 'Ability, Position and Privilege in School Physical Education' in D. Kirk and R. Tinning (eds), *Physical Education, Curriculum and Culture: Critical Issues in Contemporary Crisis* London: Falmer, 139–67.

Evans, J. (ed.) (1988) *Teachers, Teaching and Control in Physical Education.* London: Falmer.

Evans, J. (ed.) (1986) *Physical Education, Sport and Schooling: Studies in the Sociology of Physical Education.* London: Falmer.

Evans, J. and Bairner, A. (2012) 'Physical Education and Social Class' in G. Stidder and S. Hayes (eds), *Equity and Inclusion in Physical Education and Sport* (2nd ed.). Abingdon: Routledge, 141–58.

Evans, J. and Davies, B. (2002) 'Theoretical background' in A. Laker (ed.), *The Sociology of Sport and Physical Education: An introductory reader.* London: Routledge, 15–35.

Evans, J. and Penney, D. (2002) 'Introduction' in D. Penney (ed.) *Gender and Physical Education: Contemporary Issues and Future Directions.* London: Routledge, 3–12.

Evans, J., Davies, B. and Penney, D. (1996) 'Teachers, Teaching and the Social Construction of Gender Relations', *Sport, Education and Society,* (1)2: 165–83.

Fernandez-Balboa, J.-M. and Brubaker, N. (2012) 'Positioning Yourself as a Researcher: Four dimensions for self-reflection' in K. Amour and D. Macdonald (eds), *Research Methods in Physical Education and Youth Sport.* Abingdon: Routledge: 29–39.

Fernandez-Balboa, J.-M. (ed.) (1997) *Critical Postmodernism in Human Movement, Physical Education, and Sport.* Albany, NY: State University of New York Press.

Fisher, R. (2003) 'Physical Education in Europe: Policy into Practice' in K. Hardman (ed.) *Physical Education: Deconstruction and Reconstruction – Issues and Directions.* Schorndorf: Verlag Karl Hoffman, 137–52.

Fletcher, S. (1984) *Women First: The Female Tradition in Physical Education 1880–1980.* London: Athlone.

Flintoff, A. (1998) 'Sexism and Homophobia in Physical Education: The Challenge for Teacher Educators' in K. Green and K. Hardman (eds) *Physical Education: A Reader.* Aachen: Meyer and Meyer, 291–313.

Flintoff, A. and Scraton, S. (2005) 'Gender and Physical Education' in K Green, and K. Hardman (eds), *Physical Education: Essential Issues.* London: Sage, 159–79.

Flintoff, A. and Scraton, S. (2001) 'Stepping into Active Leisure? Women's Perceptions of Active Lifestyles and their Experiences of School Physical Education', *Sport, Education and Society,* 6(1): 5–21.

Flintoff, A., Chappell, A., Gower, C., Keyworth, S., Lawrence, J., Money, J., Squires, S. and Webb, L. (2008) *Black Minority Ethnic Trainees' Experiences of Physical Education Initial Teacher Training: Report to the Training and Development Agency.* Leeds: Carnegie Research

Institute, Leeds Metropolitan University.

Francis, B., Skelton, C., Carrington, B., Hutchins, M., Read, B. and Hall, I. (2006) 'A Perfect Match? Pupils' and Teachers' Views of the Impact of Matching Educators and Learners by Gender', Paper presented at The British Educational Research Association Annual Conference, University of Warwick, 6–9 September 2006.

Frapwell, A. (2014) 'National Curriculum 2014 and Assessing Without Levels', Physical Education Matters, 9(1): 18–19.

Frapwell, A. and Hawman, C. (2014) 'Game-Changing Physical Education', Research Matters, 9(1): 6.

Furlong, J. and Maynard, T. (1995) Mentoring Student Teachers: The growth of professional knowledge. London, Routledge.

Golder, G. (2010) '14–19 Accredited Qualifications' in S. Capel and M. Whitehead (eds), Learning to Teach Physical Education in the Secondary School: A companion to school experience. London, Routledge Falmer, 234–51.

Graydon, J. (1980) 'Dispelling the Myth of Female Fragility', British Journal of Physical Education, 11(4), 105–6.

Green, K. (2010) Key Issues in Youth Sport. Abingdon: Routledge.

Green, K. (2008) Understanding Physical Education. London: Sage.

Green, K. (2003) Physical Education Teachers on Physical Education. Chester: Chester Academic.

Green, K. (2000) 'Extra-Curricular Physical Education: A Sociological Perspective on a Sporting Bias', European Journal of Physical Education, 5(2): 179–208.

Green, K. and Scraton, S. (1998) 'Gender, Coeducation and Secondary Physical Education: A Brief Review', in K. Green and K. Hardman (eds), Physical Education: A Reader. Aachen: Meyer and Meyer, 272–89.

Green, N. (2013) 'Developing Qualities Through Physical Education: A Focus for the Future?, Physical Education Matters, 8(2): 55–7.

Griggs, G. (2008) '"Miss! This is way better than what we've done before": Exploring an alternative curriculum for girls' physical education', PE and Sport Today, October.

Griggs, G. (ed.) (2010) An Introduction to Primary Physical Education. Abingdon: Routledge.

Hardman, K. (2011) 'Physical Education Teacher Education: Harmonization and Curriculum Development' in K. Hardman and K. Green (eds), Contemporary Issues in Physical Education. Aachen: Meyer and Meyer, 175–93.

Hardman, K. (2007) Current Situation and Prospects for Physical Education in the European Union. IP/B/CULT/IC/2006_100. Brussels: European Parliament.

Hardman, K. and Green, K. (2011) Contemporary Issues in Physical Education: An International Dimension. Aachen: Meyer and Meyer.

Hardy, C. (1996) 'Trainees Concerns, Experiences and Needs: Implications for Mentoring in Physical Education' in M. Mawer (ed.), Mentoring in Physical Education: Issues and Insights. London: Falmer Press, 59–72.

Harris, J. (1993) 'Challenging Sexism and Gender Bias in Physical Education', Bulletin of Physical Education, (29)2, 29–37.

Harris, J. and Cale, L. (2006) 'A Review of Children's Fitness Testing', European Physical Education Review, 12(2): 201–25.

Hastie, P. and Hay, P. 'Qualitative Approaches' in Amour K and Macdonald D (eds) (2012) Research Methods in Physical Education and Youth Sport. Abingdon: Routledge, 79–84.

Hawman, C. (2013) 'No More Political Football', Physical Education Matters, 8(3): 10–13.

Hayes, L. Nikolic, V. and Cabaj, J. (2001) Am I Teaching Well? Self-evaluation Strategies for Effective Teachers. Exeter: Learning Matters.

Hayes, S. and Burdsey, D. (2012) 'Sticks and Stones May Break my Bones but Names Will Never Hurt Me: Challenging stereotypes in physical education and school sport' in G.

Stidder and S. Hayes (eds), *Equity and Inclusion in Physical Education and Sport* (2nd ed.). Abingdon: Routledge, 124–40.

Hayes, S. and Stidder, G. (eds) (2003) *Equity and Inclusion in Physical Education: Contemporary issues for teachers, trainees and practitioners*. London: Routledge.

Hines, B. *Kestrel for a Knave*. London: M Joseph.

Hirdman, Y. (1990) 'Genussystemet' in *Demokrati och Makt i Sverige*. Maktutredningen Huvudrapport SOU: 44. Göteborg: Graphic Systems, 73–116.

Hirdman, Y. (1988) 'Genussystemet – reflexioner kring kvinnors sociala underordning' [The gender system: Reflexions on the social subordination of women], *Kvinnovetenskaplig tidskrift*, 9(3): 49–63.

Hobson, . A, Malderez, A., Tracey, L., Homer, M., Mitchell, N., Biddulph, M., Giannakaki, M., Rose, A., Pell, R., Roper, T., Chambers, G. and Tomlinson, P. (2007) *Newly Qualified Teachers' Experiences of their First Year: Findings of Phase III of the Becoming a Teacher Project*. London: Department for Children, Schools and Families, Research Report DCSF- RR008.

Houlihan, B. (2002) 'Political Involvement in Sport, Physical Education and Recreation' in A. Laker (ed.) *The Sociology of Sport and Physical Education: An Introductory Reader*. London: Routledge, 190–210.

Houlihan, B. (2000) 'Sporting Excellence, Schools and Sports Development: The politics of crowded policy spaces', *European Physical Education Review*, 6(2): 171–94.

Houlihan, B. and Lindsey, I. (2013) *Sport Policy in Britain*. Abingdon: Routledge.

House of Lords Select Committee on Olympic and Paralympic Legacy (2013) *Keeping the Flame Alive: The Olympic and Paralympic Legacy. Report of Session 2013–14*. HL Paper 78. London: TSO.

Ives, H. and Kirk, D. (2013) 'What are the Public Perceptions of Physical Education? in S. Capel and M. Whitehead (eds), *Debates in Physical Education*. Abingdon: Routledge, 188–201.

Kay, P. (2006) *The Sound of Laughter*. London: Arrow Books.

Kay, W. (2014a) 'Why Bother with Physical Education?', *Research Matters*, 9(1): 11–14.

Kay, W. (2014b) 'Déjà vu or Here We Go Again', *Physical Education Matters*, 9(1): 20–3.

Keay, J. (2005) 'Developing the Physical Education Profession: New teachers learning within a subject-based community', *PE and Sport Pedagogy*, 10(2): 139–58.

Keech, M. (2012a) 'Youth Sport and London's 2012 Olympic Legacy' in J. Sugden and A. Tomlinson (eds), *Watching the Olympics: Politics, Power and Representation*. London: Routledge, 82–96.

Keech, M. (2012b) 'Sport Policy, Physical Education and Participation: Inclusive Issues for Schools', in G. Stidder and S. Hayes (eds), *Equity and Inclusion in Physical Education and Sport* (2nd ed.). Abingdon: Routledge, 176–89.

Keech, M. (2003) 'Sport Through Education? Issues for schools and sports development' in S. Hayes and G. Stidder (eds), *Equity and Inclusion in Physical education and Sport: Contemporary issues for teachers, trainers and practitioners*. London: Routledge, 211–31.

Kirk, D. (2013) 'What is the Future of Physical Education in the Twenty First Century?' in S. Capel and M. Whitehead (eds), *Debates in Physical Education*. Abingdon: Routledge, 220–31.

Kirk, D. (2010) 'The Practice of Physical Education and the Social Construction of Aims', in R. Bailey (ed.), *Physical Education for Learning: A guide for secondary schools*, 15–25.

Kirk, D. (2002) 'Physical Education: A gendered history' in D. Penney (ed.), *Gender and Physical Education – Contemporary Issues for Future Directions*. London: Routledge, 24–37.

Kirk, D. (1992) *Defining Physical Education: The Social Construction of a School Subject in Postwar Britain*. Studies in Curriculum History Series 18. London: Falmer.

Laker, A. (2002) 'Culture, Education and Sport' in A. Laker (ed.), *The Sociology of Sport and Physical Education: An introductory reader*. London: Routledge: 1–14.

Laker, A. (2000) *Beyond the Boundaries of Physical Education: Educating young people for citizenship and social responsibility*. London: Falmer.

Laker, A. Laker, J. and Lea, S. (2003) 'School Experience and the Issue of Gender', *Sport, Education and Society*, 8(1): 73–89.

Lamb, P. (2014) 'Ritual Associated with Participation in Physical Education: The power of excuse notes', *European Physical Education Review*, 20(1): 120–39.

Lavin, J. (ed.) (2008) *Creative Approaches to Physical Education*. London: Routledge.

Lawson, H. (1986) 'Occupational Socialization and the design of Teacher Education Programs', *Journal of Teaching Physical Education*, 5(1): 107–16.

Leaman, O. (1984), *Sit on the Sidelines and Watch the Boys Play: Sex Differentiation in Physical Education*. York: Longman for Schools Council.

Lloyd, C., Fry, A. and Wollny, I. (2014) *PE and Sport Premium: An investigation in primary schools*. Research Brief. London: Department for Education.

Luttenburg, J. and Bergen, T. (2008) 'Teacher Reflection: The development of a typology', *Teachers Teaching: Theory and Practice*, 14(5–6): 543–66.

Macdonald, D. (2002) 'Critical Pedagogy: What might it look like and why does it matter?' in A. Laker, A. (ed.), *The Sociology of Sport and Physical Education: An introductory reader*. London: RoutledgeFalmer, 167–89.

Mangan, J. (1981) *Athleticism in the Victorian and Edwardian Public School: The emergence and consolidation of an educational ideology*. Cambridge: Cambridge University Press.

Marchant, A. (2013) 'A Future for Physical Education and School Sport', *Education Matters*, 8 (2): 42–4.

Mawer, M. (ed.) (1996) *Mentoring in Physical Education: Issues and Insights*, London: Falmer.

McCullick, B., Belcher, D., Hardin, B. and Hardin, M. (2003) 'Butches, Bullies and Buffoons: Images of physical education teachers in the movies', *Sport, Education and Society*, 8(1): 3–16.

McPhail, A. (2010) 'Listening to Pupils' Voices' in R. Bailey (ed.) *Physical Education for Learning: A guide to secondary schools*. London: Continuum, 228–38.

Miller, A. (2002) *Tilting at Windmills. How I tried to Stop Worrying and Love Sport*. London: Viking.

Monaghan, L. (2014) 'Civilising Recalcitrant Boys' Bodies: Pursuing Social Fitness Through the Anti-Obesity Offensive', *Sport, Education and Society*, 19(6): 691–711.

Moon, J. (1999) *Learning Journals: A handbook for academics, students and professional development*. London: Kogan Page.

Mosston, M. and Ashworth, S. (1986) *Teaching Physical Education*. Columbus, OH: Merrill.

National Association for the Teaching of English (2014) *Surveying the Wreckage: The professional response to changes to initial teacher training in the UK*. Sheffield: NATE.

Nutt, G. and Clarke, G. (2002) 'The Hidden Curriculum and the Changing Nature of Teachers' Work', in A. Laker (ed.), *The Sociology of Sport and Physical Education: An introductory reader*, London: Routledge, 148–66.

Ofsted (2014) *Going the Extra Mile: Excellence in Competitive School Sport*. Manchester: Ofsted.

Ofsted (2013a) *Beyond 2102 – Outstanding Physical Education for All: Physical education in schools 2008–12*. Manchester: Ofsted.

Ofsted (2013b) *Promoting Improvement in Initial Teacher Education (ITE): Primary mathematics*. Ref. 20130016. Manchester: Ofsted.

Ofsted (2009) *Physical Education in School 2005/08: Working Towards 2012 and Beyond*. Manchester: Ofsted.

Olofsson, E. (2005) 'The Discursive Construction of Gender in Physical Education in Sweden, 1945–2003: Is meeting the learner's needs tantamount to meeting the market's needs', *European Physical Education Review*, 11(3): 219–38.

O'Sullivan, M., Bush, K. and Gehring, M. (2002) 'Gender Equity and Physical Education: a

USA perspective' in D. Penney (ed.) *Gender and Physical Education: Contemporary Issues and Future Directions*. London: Routledge, 163–89.

O'Sullivan, M., Tannehill, D. and Hinchion, C. (2010) 'Teaching as Professional Enquiry' in R. Bailey (ed.), *Physical Education for Learning: A guide to secondary schools*. London: Continuum, 54–66.

Parker, A. (1996) 'The Construction of Masculinity within Boys' Physical Education', *Gender and Education*, 8 (2): 147–57.

Penney, D. (2002) 'Equality, Equity and Inclusion in Physical Education and Sport' in A. Laker (ed.) *The Sociology of Sport and Physical Education*. London: RoutledgeFalmer, 110–28.

Penney, D. and Evans, J. (2013) 'Who is Physical Education for?' in S. Capel and M. Whitehead (eds), *Debates in Physical Education*. Abingdon: Routledge, 157–70.

Penney, D. and Evans, J. (2005) 'Policy, Power and Politics in Physical Education' in K. Green and K. Hardman (eds), *Physical Education Essential Issues*, London: Sage, 21–38.

Penney, D. and Evans, J. (1999) *Politics, Policy and Practice in Physical Education*. London: E & FN Spon.

Philpotts, L. (2012) 'An Analysis of the Policy Process for Physical Education and School Sport: The rise and demise of school sport partnerships' *International Journal of Sport Policy and Politics*, 5(2): 192–211.

Pollard, A. (2008) *The Reflective Teacher: Informed professional practice*. London: Continuum.

Pollard, A. and Tan, S. (1987) *Reflective Teaching in the Primary School: A handbook for the classroom*. Abingdon, David Fulton.

Quick, S., Dalziel, D. , Thornton, A. and Simon, A. (2009) *PE and School Sport Survey 2008/09*. London: Department for Children, Schools and Families.

Rees, R. (2012) 'Anyone can Teach Boys' Physical Education . . . Can't they?, *Physical Education Matters*, 7(2): 65–7.

Rich, E. (2001) 'Gender Positioning in Teacher Education in England: new rhetoric, old realities', *International Studies in Sociology of Education*, 11(2): 131–55.

Rossi, T. (1996) 'Pedagogical Content Knowledge and Critical Reflection in Physical Education' in M. Mawer (ed.) *Mentoring in Physical Education: Issues and Insights*. London: Falmer, 176–94.

Schempp, P. and Oliver, K. (2000). 'Issues of Equity and Understanding in Sport and Physical Education: A North American perspective' in R. Jones and K. Armour (eds), *Sport Sociology: An exercise in practicality*. Harlow: Longman, 145–52.

Schon, D. (1983) *The Reflective Practitioner: How professionals think in action*. Boston, MA: Arena.

Scraton, S. (1992) *Shaping up to Womanhood – Gender and Girls' Physical Education*. Oxford: Oxford University Press.

Sherlock, J. (1977) 'A Feminist View of Coeducational Physical Education', *Scottish Journal of Physical Education*, 5(2): 21–2.

Siedentop, D. (1994) *Quality Physical Education Through Positive Sport Education*. Champaign, IL: Human Kinetics.

Slezak, A., Ward, T. and Brooks, T. (2013) *The Physical EducatioN Revolution: A simple Approach for physical education teachers to stand out from the crowd, transform lives, solve the obesity crisis and awaken the sleeping giant in youth fitness*. Elizabethtown, KY: International Youth Conditioning Association.

Sport Scotland (2005) *Making Women and Girls More Active: A good practice guide*. Edinburgh: SportScotland.

Stidder, G. (2014) 'Training to Teach Physical Education in a Grammar School for Boys: Female narratives and mentor perspectives', *Sport, Education and Society*, 19(5): 552–68.

Stidder, G. (2012a) 'Training to Teach Physical Education in an Opposite-sex Secondary

School: A qualitative analysis of trainee teachers' experiences', *European Physical Education Review*, 18(3): 346–60.

Stidder, G. (2012b) 'The value of Reflexivity for Inclusive Practice in Physical Education', in G. Stidder and S. Hayes (eds), *Equity and Inclusion in Physical Education and Sport* (2nd ed.). Abingdon: Routledge, 17–33.

Stidder, G. (2009a) 'A comparative analysis of Secondary and High School Physical Education policy and practice for girls in the United Kingdom and the United States of America'. Unpublished PhD Thesis, Chelsea School Centre for Sport Research, University of Brighton.

Stidder, G. (2009b) 'Challenging Sex-role Stereotyping in Secondary Physical Education Initial Teacher Education: Amy's Story', *Physical Education Matters*, 4(4): 28–34.

Stidder, G. (2005) 'Trainee Teacher Perceptions of Job Advertisements in England with Regards to Gender and Physical Education', *European Physical Education Review*, 11(3): 309–33.

Stidder, G. (2002) 'The Recruitment of Secondary School Physical Education Teachers in England: A Gendered Perspective?', *European Physical Education Review*, 11(3): 249–69.

Stidder, G. (1998), 'Gender Grouping in Physical Education: An Investigation into Mixed and Single Sex Provision and the effects on Secondary School Aged Children', Unpublished Masters Thesis, University of Brighton, 1998.

Stidder, G. and Binney, J. (2011) 'Alternative Approaches to Teaching and Learning Physical Education in Secondary Schools', *Physical Education Matters*, 6(2): 27–32.

Stidder, G. and Griggs, G. (2012) 'Healthism and the Obesity Discourse: Approaches to inclusive health education through alternative physical education', in G. Stidder and S. Hayes (eds), *Equity and Inclusion in Physical Education and Sport* (2nd ed.). Abingdon: Routledge, 190–208.

Stidder, G. and Hayes, S. (2013) *Equity and Inclusion in Physical Education and Sport*. 2nd ed. Abingdon: Routledge.

Stidder, G. and Hayes, S. (2012) Physical Education and the Legacy of the London 2012 Olympic Games. *Physical Education Matters*, Autumn, (7)3: 8–10.

Stidder, G. and Hayes, S. (2010) 'Thematic Learning and Teaching Through Physical Education' in G. Stidder and S. Hayes (eds), *The Really Useful Physical Education Book. Learning and Teaching Across the 7–14 Age Range*. Abingdon: Routledge, 159–75.

Stidder, G. and Hayes, S. (2006) 'A Longitudinal Study of Physical Education Trainee Teachers' Experiences on School Placements in the South-East of England (1994–2004)', *European Physical Education Review*, 12(3): 317–38.

Stidder, G. and Hayes, S. (2003) *Equity and Inclusion in Physical Education and Sport*. Abingdon: Routledge.

Stidder, G. and Wallis, J. (2012) 'Inclusive Learning and Teaching Through Accredited Awards in Physical Education Within a 14–19 Curriculum Framework' in G. Stidder and S. Hayes (eds), *Equity and Inclusion in Physical Education and Sport* (2nd ed.). Abingdon: Routledge, 159–75.

Stidder, G. and Wallis, J. (2005) 'The Place of Physical Education within the Proposed 14–19 Curriculum: Insights and Implications for Future Practice (Part One)', *British Journal of Teaching Physical Education*, 36(4): 43–8.

Stidder, G. and Wallis, J. (2003) 'Accreditation in Physical Education? Meeting the Needs and Interests of Pupils at Key Stage Four' in S. Hayes and G. Stidder (eds), *Equity and Inclusion in Physical Education: Contemporary issues for teachers, trainees and practitioners*. London: Routledge, 185–209.

Stidder, G., Sugden, J. and Spacey, G. (2013) 'Football 4 Peace Ireland', *Physical Education Matters* 8 (4): 19–21.

Stroot, S. (2002) 'Socialisation and Participation in Sport' in A. Laker (ed.), *The Sociology of Sport and Physical Education: An introductory reader*. London: Routledge, 129–47.

Syed, M. (2010) *Bounce: How Champions are Made*. London: Harper Collins.

Tait, E. (1996) 'An Account of Laura's First Term on a School-based PGCE Course' in M. Mawer (ed.), *Mentoring in Physical Education: Issues and Insights*. London: Falmer, 73–88.

Talbot, M. (1993) 'Physical Education and the National Curriculum: Some Political Issues', in G. McFee and A. Tomlinson (eds,) *Education, Sport and Leisure: Connections and Controversies*. Eastbourne: Chelsea School Research Centre, University of Brighton, 34–64.

Taylor, C. (2013) 'Keynote Speech to the North of England Education Conference', 18 January. Available online at www.gov.uk/government/speeches/charlie-taylors-keynote-speech-to-the-north-of-england-education-conference. (accessed 1 October 2014).

Theodoulides, A. (2012) 'Personalised learning in Physical Education', in G. Stidder and S. Hayes (eds), *Equity and Inclusion in Physical Education and Sport* (2nd ed.). Abingdon: Routledge, 34–50.

Thornburn, M. and Horrell, A. (2014) 'Grand Designs! Analysing the conceptual tensions associated with new physical education and health and well-being curriculum', *Sport, Education and Society*, 19(5): 621–36.

Tindall, D. and Enright, E. (2013) 'Rethinking Teacher Knowledge in Physical Education: What do physical education teachers need to know? in S. Capel and M. Whitehead (eds), *Debates in Physical Education*. Abingdon: Routledge, 117–19.

Tinning, R. (1988). 'Student Teaching and the Pedagogy of Necessity', *Journal of Teaching in Physical Education*, 7(2): 82–9.

Tinning, R., Macdonald, D., Wright, J. and Hickey, C. (2001) *Becoming a Physical Education Teacher: Enduring and Contemporary Issues*. Frenchs Forest, NSW: Pearson Education Australia.

Tomlinson, A. and Allison, L. (2012) 'Foreword' in G. Stidder and S. Hayes (eds), *Equity and Inclusion in Physical Education and Sport* (2nd ed.). Abingdon: Routledge, xiv–xvi.

Tozer, M. (2013) 'One of the Worst Statistics in British Sport, and Wholly Unacceptable': The contribution of privately educated members of Team GB to the Summer Olympic Games, 2000–2012', *International Journal of the History of Sport*, 30(12): 1436–54.

Training and Development Agency for Schools (2010) *National Occupational Standards for Supporting Teaching and Learning*. London: TDA.

Training and Development Agency for Schools (2008) *Professional Standards for Qualified Teacher Status and Requirements for Initial Teacher Training*. London: TDA.

Trollope, J. (2013) *Sense and Sensibility*. London: HarperCollins.

Turvey, J. and Laws, C. (1988) 'Are Girls Losing Out? The Effects of Mixed-sex Grouping on Girls' Performance in Physical Education', *British Journal of Physical Education*, 19(6): 253–5.

Vickerman, P. and Hayes, S. (2012) 'Special Educational Needs and Disability in Physical Education', in G. Stidder and S. Hayes (eds), *Equity and Inclusion in Physical Education and Sport* (2nd ed.). Abingdon: Routledge, 51–65.

Ward, G. (2014) 'Learning Movement Culture: Mapping the landscape between physical education and sport', *Sport, Education and Society*, 19(5): 569–604.

Wheaton, B. (ed.) (2013) *The Consumption and Representation of Lifestyle Sports*. Abingdon: Routledge.

White, J. (2007) *You'll Win Nothing With Kids: Fathers, sons and football*. New York: Little Brown.

Whitehead, M. (2013) 'What is Physical Education?' in S. Capel and M. Whitehead (eds), *Debates in Physical Education*. Abingdon: Routledge, 22–36.

Whitehead, M. (2010) *Physical Literacy Throughout the Lifecourse*. Abingdon, Routledge.

Williams, A. and Bedward, J. (2001) 'Gender, Culture and the Generation Gap: Student and teacher perceptions of aspects of national curriculum physical education', *Sport, Education and Society*, 6(1): 53–66.

Youth Sport Trust (2014) *Getting Girls Active: Developing inspiring PE and sport through research and innovation*. Available online at www.youthsporttrust.org/how-we-can-help/girls-active.aspx (accessed 27 September 2014).

Zwodiak-Myers, P. (2013) 'Are Physical Education Teachers Reflective Practitioners?' in S. Capel and M. Whitehead (eds), *Debates in Physical Education*. Abingdon: Routledge, 140–54.

INDEX

Made in the USA
Lexington, KY
17 March 2017